THE SECRET HISTORY OF FLIGHT 149

THE SECRET HISTORY OF FLIGHT 149

THE MOST SHOCKING GOVERNMENT COVER-UP OF THE LAST THIRTY YEARS

STEPHEN DAVIS

First published in the UK by John Blake Publishing
an imprint of Bonnier Books UK
4th Floor, Victoria House
Bloomsbury Square,
London, WC1B 4DA
England

Owned by Bonnier Books
Sveavägen 56, Stockholm, Sweden

www.facebook.com/johnblakebooks
twitter.com/jblakebooks

First published in hardback in 2021
This paperback edition published in 2022

Paperback ISBN: 978-1-78946-536-5
Hardback: 978-1-78946-460-3
Trade paperback: 978-1-78946-461-0
eBook: 978-1-78946-532-7
Audio: 978-1-78946-460-3

British Library Cataloguing-in-Publication Data:

A catalogue record for this book is available from the British Library.

Design by www.envydesign.co.uk

Printed and bound in Great Britain by Clays Ltd, Elcograf S.p.A.

1 3 5 7 9 10 8 6 4 2

© Text copyright Stephen Davis 2021, 2022

The right of Stephen Davis to be identified as the author of this work has been asserted by
him in accordance with the Copyright, Designs and Patents Act 1988.

John Blake Publishing is an imprint of Bonnier Books UK
www.bonnierbooks.co.uk

I would like to dedicate this book to my mother Jocelyn,
who has always watched the news and bought a newspaper.
She set me on the path to a career in journalism.

CONTENTS

PROLOGUE

The shattered tail of a British Airways Boeing 747 sat in inglorious isolation on the runway of Kuwait airport in February 1991 amid the celebrations over the liberation of Kuwait by George H. W. Bush's Desert Storm.

The image went round the world, a reminder of the grim fate of many of those caught up in Saddam Hussein's invasion six months earlier.

In the wider shot, you can see the crumpled fuselage of Flight 149, which flew from Heathrow to Kuwait at the start of the invasion and never returned.

The picture was released with a story that quoted military sources. The 747, it said, was destroyed by the Iraqis as they fled in haste before the might of Stormin' Norman Schwarzkopf and his allied armour and air power.

No one seems to have asked why the Iraqis, who looted everything of value that they could get their hands on, down to light bulbs and bathroom faucets, would destroy such a valuable propaganda prize rather than simply fly it to Iraq.

The answer is that the Iraqis did not destroy the plane. The BA 747 was destroyed by American fighter planes at the request of the British.

Why, then, blame the destruction on the Iraqis when the sad image of the shattered wing of Flight 149 was shown round the world? Was it to hide the embarrassment of an 'own goal' or was it to cover up something else?

I was working on the news desk of the *Independent on Sunday* in London when the photo was released and I added it to my growing file on the mystery, a mystery that had begun with a simple phone call.

In August 1990, I had become interested in persistent rumours about Flight 149, after it landed in Kuwait as it was invaded by Iraqi troops.

All the passengers and crew had been taken hostage and were at the mercy of Saddam Hussein.

The British Foreign Office (FO) put out reassuring messages that the passengers were not in any danger. In fact, it was said, they were on a sort of unexpected holiday, drinking cocktails in the sunshine by the pool at luxury hotels.

My caller, a contact, begged to differ. There is something not right about all this, he said, you should investigate. So began a long search for the real story.

The world of 1990 was one in which it was easier to hide the truth. There were no mobile phones to photograph or live-stream events, no social media to contradict official statements. It was a world before Putin and Trump, in which it was still possible to believe that Western democracies would not go to war on the basis of misused intelligence, or that leaders would not lie every day to their citizens.

The investigation that led to this book involved over three hundred interviews in the United States, United Kingdom, France, Germany, Denmark, Canada, India, Malaysia, Australia, New Zealand, Iraq and Kuwait. I have had access to previously confidential documentation; the remarkable, unpublished diaries of American and British hostages; and talked to survivors and grieving relatives, lawyers and government officials, politicians and human rights campaigners, soldiers and spies.

Along the way, I have sat in a living room listening to a young woman describe how she repeatedly tried to take her life because she never recovered from her ordeal in captivity; heard a former flight attendant talk of his lifelong battle with crippling fear that ultimately ended his career; heard harrowing tales of rapes, assaults, mock executions and near-starvation conditions; engaged with CIA sources, who, out of conscience, helped me with classified documents; and interviewed soldiers at the heart of the most secret part of the British government who risked their livelihoods and their freedom to reveal the truth behind Flight 149.

CHAPTER 1

INVASION

The British Airways Boeing 747 was called *Coniston Water*. Maureen Chappell noticed the name as she stood in line to board the plane and it disturbed her. She was a frequent flier and she seldom bothered to notice the names of aircraft, but this one struck her as odd. She knew that Coniston Water was the lake in Cumbria where great British hero Donald Campbell, the holder of world speed records on land and water, was killed when his boat, *Bluebird*, flipped over during a 300-mph run. It was a story of disaster and death. *Strange name for a plane*, she thought. Her daughter Jennifer noticed the name, too, as the family entered the plane's front cabin. She was too young to remember Campbell but somehow the name stuck with her as she found her way to her seat. For some reason, it made her feel uncomfortable.

The Chappell family – husband John, wife Maureen and children John, fourteen, and Jennifer, twelve – were travelling in Business Class. John was returning with his wife to India where he was an electronics systems adviser to the Indian navy. The children were on vacation from boarding school. Jennifer was looking forward to a big party to celebrate her upcoming thirteenth birthday. All her friends in India had been invited. Apart from that, she and John Jr. felt the way they normally did on these long-haul trips: tired, hot and bored.

It was early evening at Heathrow, on Wednesday, 1 August 1990, and Flight BA149 was headed for Kuala Lumpur, Malaysia, via Kuwait and Madras. Departure had already been delayed for two hours. Apparently, a fault had been found in the auxiliary power unit, a small engine in the tail that provided air-conditioning. The delay seemed to put everyone – passengers and crew – on edge. The 747 they were waiting to board, registration number G-AWND, was one of the oldest in the British Airways (BA) fleet, having been built in Seattle some nineteen years earlier. It was also rumoured to have had a rather chequered history – an unhappy Jamaican, spurned by his lover, had apparently walked up to the plane as it sat on the tarmac and killed himself by jumping into one of the still-rotating jet engines.

*

Three thousand miles away in the desert just north of the Kuwait border, the Medina and Hammurabi armoured divisions of Iraq's spearhead Republican Guard were turning over the engines of their battle tanks, keeping them warm in the cool Arabian night. The divisions were equipped with Soviet-made, state-of-the-art T-72 tanks, as well as older T-54s and T-62s. They also had huge mobile 155mm howitzers that could fire seven shells a minute over a distance of nineteen miles.

The Republican Guard troops were the pride of Saddam Hussein's regime, and the men were confident as they went about their last-minute weapons checks. Recruited mainly from Tikrit, the power base of Saddam, they were the best-paid and best-fed troops in the Iraqi army. Now they were to be the cutting edge of Saddam's invasion of Kuwait, the dictator's way of settling a long-running dispute between the two countries over the lucrative oil fields that straddled their common border.

The Guards were well prepared: they had detailed maps of Kuwaiti positions and the movement of patrols around key buildings. They were briefed at 4 p.m. local time – five hours before Flight 149 finally took off. The Kuwaiti government was about to change, the officers told their men. Iraq was setting up a new government.

The Iraqi intentions had been clear for months. Back in March, in a speech at the Arab League summit, Saddam launched a savage attack on Kuwait, accusing it of waging economic war against his country and slanting its oil drills to steal oil from Iraqi fields in the border area. In the following months, the government-run Iraqi press made it clear that it would accept nothing less than total capitulation; no peace was possible unless Kuwait agreed that it had stolen oil worth US$2.4 billion. By mid-July, the Republican Guard, observed by American satellites, was undertaking large-scale military exercises. On 21 July, the Defense Intelligence Agency (DIA) – the Pentagon's spies – estimated that Iraq had enough tanks and troops at the border with Kuwait to order an attack at any moment. Four days later, CIA director William Webster briefed President George H. W. Bush, telling him the Iraqis were likely to invade. On the same day, the US ambassador to Iraq, April Glaspie, met with Saddam. Acting on instructions from Washington, she told Saddam that the United States regarded the dispute as an Arab matter and that they had no intention of intervening. Saddam took that as a signal to proceed.

His target, Kuwait, was a rich country, one that tended to

mind its own business and steer clear of the bloody disputes that preoccupied much of the rest of the Middle East. Most people in the West would have struggled to find it on a map.

Kuwait, nestled between Iran and Saudi Arabia with a coastline on the Persian Gulf, was a country of immigrants. Of its population of two million, only about eight hundred thousand were Kuwaitis. The rest were foreign workers, including four hundred thousand Palestinians and Jordanians and large numbers of Indians, Pakistanis, Bangladeshis and Filipinos. Only about 1.5 million of Kuwait's population of two million were in the country on 1 August. The rest had escaped the summer heat and were on holiday in cooler climes abroad. Those remaining included about fifteen thousand Westerners; for many of them, Kuwait was a paradise. The pay was good; Westerners could earn up to 50 per cent more than back home and it was tax free. The warmth of the weather on the golden beaches of the Gulf was matched by the warmth of the Kuwaitis, who were particularly friendly and tolerant towards their non-Muslim guests. The restrictions on things like alcohol were loosely enforced, if at all. The shopping was good – the latest fashions always available – and it was an easy place to get around, flat with excellent roads: an hour's drive in any direction got you right across the country. For families it was a particularly fine place to live. There were swimming pools, Western-style amusement rides, and waterskiing and windsurfing at the beach.

Between the Iraqi tanks and Kuwait was the Mutla Ridge, the only part of Kuwait that noticeably rises above the desert. Five miles from the border, its height masked the tanks from the prying eyes of Kuwaiti radar. But anyone who had paid attention to that morning's news, and who believed what they were hearing, knew that the Iraqis were out there somewhere in the desert night.

*

Clive Earthy, the cabin services director on the Flight 149, heard the news just after he left his home for the afternoon drive to the airport. Earthy had flown long-haul for more than twenty years and he was used to dealing with on-board dramas – passengers freaking out, drunkenness, fights, even sudden deaths. He had flown through some vicious storms and landed in places that he would not choose to visit for a holiday. He was widely thought to be the best senior purser in the fleet.

Though Earthy was known at the airline for his calm and cheerful disposition, the radio report filled him with a sense of foreboding as he sat in traffic on the M3 motorway. Iraqi troops were on the border with Kuwait, and some reports even had them across the border already. Peace talks to settle the bitter dispute between Iraq and Kuwait were not going well. The Foreign Office had issued a statement. The British Embassy in Kuwait was advising British nationals to keep their heads down. There was a contingency plan to evacuate them in the event of an emergency, the spokesman said, but it was not felt that the situation yet required the plan to be put into effect.

In Kuwait City, at the British Embassy, journalists were briefed that afternoon. John Raine, the information officer, told visiting journalists that even if the Iraqi army did cross the border, they would remain in the northern half of the country. Little fighting was expected and the city was not under threat. Several journalists decided there was no big story to be had so they booked flights home.

The embassy then closed for the Arab weekend, Thursday and Friday. But that night staffing levels were higher than usual. Ambassador Michael Weston was joined by his deputy and also a third man, Tony Paice, who was best known in Kuwait's diplomatic community as the station chief for the SIS, the Secret

Intelligence Service, Britain's overseas spy agency, more popularly known as MI6.

The US Embassy in Kuwait was also closed for the weekend, the staff having left in the afternoon, but there was a low-level state of alert. Senior diplomats were told not to go anywhere that they could not be reached by phone. US ambassador Nathaniel Howell had told the duty officer to inform him of any new developments but not to be too worried about reports of troop movements.

In Washington, analysts at the Defense Intelligence Agency pored over the latest satellite photographs. The most recent fly-by showed that Iraqi army camps, home to one hundred thousand troops just twenty-four hours earlier, were now empty. All that could be seen were hundreds of tank tracks in the sand, all heading in one direction – towards Kuwait. The DIA chiefs ordered the staff to go to Watchcon One, the highest alert level, for the first time in its history. It anticipated war.

*

At London airport, there were 367 passengers and 18 crew on board Flight 149 as it waited for clearance from the Heathrow control tower. They were American, British, French, Indian, Malaysian, Italian, Spanish, German and Australian, as well as one Canadian and two New Zealanders. Eleven of the passengers were children. Two of the passengers, Daphne and Henry Halkyard, were unhappy about being on the plane. The retired couple, in their sixties, were on their way back to New Zealand, to their home in the riverside town of Warkworth in North Island, after a holiday in Greece. Both were British born but they had lived in New Zealand for over thirty years and thus considered themselves real Kiwis. But they were dual passport-holders and for convenience they had decided to travel on their old British passports, passports that allowed visa-free access to more countries. Henry had served in the army in the Middle East. He had not enjoyed the experience and had no desire to return there. He was alarmed to discover that the flight was scheduled to land in Kuwait, for refuelling and a change of crew. The Halkyards also heard the news about Iraqi troop movements and they expressed their worries forcefully to the British Airways check-in staff and anyone else from the airline they could find. But no one seemed to be listening.

The Chappells also had questions when they checked in. John asked whether there would be any delay because of the Kuwait situation. He was stunned when the response was 'What situation? What's happening out there?' 'Surely, you read the newspapers?' asked John. 'I know nothing about any delay,' a British Airways staffer replied.

Gabriel Chardin, a thirty-five-year-old engineer employed by the French atomic energy authority, was en route first to Malaysia and then a connecting flight to Singapore, where he was to attend an official party to celebrate the twenty-fifth birthday of that nation-state. When Chardin arrived at Heathrow, he received two unwelcome surprises: the flight had been delayed, and it still was going to land in Kuwait City. Chardin went to the BA desk and was reassured. He should not worry – if there was any problem the plane would be diverted to the United Arab Emirates, the plane had enough fuel for any extra distance, there was nothing to worry about.

As Chardin sat in the Departures lounge, he thought about his ticket. He had paid for it himself. It was expensive. His luggage was already on the plane. He talked to an American passenger nearby who was also wondering whether or not to board the flight. The American had also asked questions at the BA desk, and he, too, had been reassured. *After all, it is British Airways... they know what they are doing... we should not be worried*, Chardin thought to himself. He and his fellow passenger decided they would fly. As the flight waited for take-off, Clive Earthy, the senior purser, talked to the pilot, Captain Richard Brunyate, about the landing in Kuwait. Brunyate, forty-two, was one of the airline's top pilots, with twenty years' experience, and had become a 747 captain a year earlier. He had a real understanding of, and feeling for, the Middle East, and not just because he had flown there frequently. He spent eight years of his childhood living in Baghdad, where his father Jack was a businessman, and Richard himself had later worked for a company run by Palestinians in Lebanon.

Brunyate told Earthy that he had been having a heated discussion with BA's management at Heathrow. When he had arrived at the airport, having also heard the news of Iraqi troops on the border, he had asked BA management for a special security briefing. Told there wasn't one, he insisted on more information. Heathrow management said they had also taken soundings at the Foreign Office and that the flight could safely proceed.

Aware that some of the passengers were anxious about what they had heard on the news, Earthy made an announcement over the plane's PA system. 'We have been assured that it is safe to fly to Kuwait,' he told them. That was the government advice but 'if there are any problems, the plane will be diverted'. Up and down the aisles, the passengers breathed sighs of relief. Some even clapped. They were grateful for the reassurance and eager now to get on with their journeys.

Just before the plane's doors closed there were two sets of late arrivals. First was a high-ranking member of the Kuwaiti royal family, Brigadier Sheikh Fahad al-Ahmad al-Sabah, who arrived with his bodyguards and settled into First Class. He fulfilled two important roles. As minister of sport, he looked after the country's football team, a job that made him one of the most popular figures in the royal family. He was also a key figure in Kuwait's intelligence service. He had just returned from a meeting in Washington with the CIA, a meeting in which he had outlined the threat to his country from Iraq and also discussed the likely American response if Saddam invaded.

A number of passengers noted the second group of late arrivals. Paul Merlet – a wealthy French anaesthetist travelling to Malaysia with his wife, Monique, and children Philippe, twenty, and Karine, seventeen, for a family holiday – was sitting halfway down the plane. He saw nine or ten muscular, clean-cut young men walk past him and take seats at the rear of the aircraft. None of them spoke. He first thought they were oil workers. Edward Hammett from Essex, who occupied a window seat near the back of the plane, was one of three engineers from a contract company travelling to India to work on an offshore oil rig. Hammett planned to sleep for most of the flight. He had to start work as soon as he reached India. As he made himself comfortable just before takeoff, in his preferred window seat, he saw the group of young men coming down the aisle. They had crew cuts and looked extremely fit. Hammett thought they had a military bearing.

Flight 149 finally took off at 7:04 p.m. UK time, 9:04 p.m. in Kuwait. Everything proceeded smoothly. Captain Brunyate phoned down to Clive Earthy several times to update him on the news from Kuwait. He was reassuring. He was keeping in touch with London via high frequency radio, with the line kept open so that any new information could be sent through to the 747 immediately.

In the cabin, the passengers started to relax after Earthy's announcement. The cabin crew moved around the plane, taking drink orders. Gabriel Chardin thought they seemed to be more generous with the alcohol than usual.

Jan Bhatt, an Indian-born American engineer, was happy to be on board. He was looking forward to the flight because at the end of it would be India and a reunion with his family. Bhatt was not a particularly healthy man – he suffered from both high blood pressure and diabetes, but he had brought all his medicines with him. They were in his bag in the hold of the plane.

Earthy went through the cabin handing out landing cards for Kuwait. When he reached the group of young men, the late arrivals, he was surprised that they appeared to be uninterested in the cards. 'We don't have time for them,' one said. 'But you will need them when you land,' Earthy insisted. The men casually took the cards, giving no indication they would have any use for them.

*

Meanwhile, back on the border, the Republican Guard was on the move. The Hammurabi division headed down the well-paved Abdaly highway towards Kuwait. Further west, the Medina division churned through the sands towards the Rumaila oil field. Iraqi Special Forces in helicopters headed over the Arabian Gulf bound for Kuwait City. A large Iraqi naval force, including Soviet-built Osa fast-attack craft armed with anti-ship missiles and machine guns, had left the Umm Qasr naval base near the Kuwait border and was making 20 knots in calm seas towards the three main ports on the Kuwait mainland.

Near the border between Kuwait and Iraq, American technicians manning a radar observation post noticed something unusual. (The men were civilians, under contract to the Kuwaiti government, and they worked for USLOK, the US military's Liaison Office Kuwait.) Their mission was to keep an eye on anything that happened in the border region, and their presence was a gesture of support from Washington to Kuwait. They were sitting in an air-conditioned control van just south of the Mutla Ridge. Several hundred feet above them, attached to the van by cable, flew a small blimp carrying a Westinghouse APG-66 radar, which could see for thirty miles in any direction. On the monitoring screens something had appeared that looked like a giant iron pipe, several kilometres long and wide.

In fact, it was Iraqi armaments, cresting the Mutla Ridge – tanks and support vehicles as far as the eye could see, completely filling the screens.

The technicians sent a flash report to headquarters and the duty officer phoned his boss, Colonel John Mooneyham, the chief of USLOK, at his apartment in Kuwait City. 'Are you sure they are tanks?' Mooneyham asked. The response was 'yes' accompanied by a lot of choice Anglo-Saxon words. Mooneyham quickly agreed to raise the alarm. He ordered the men to cut their blimp loose, abandon their post, and race back down the highway to Kuwait City.

Back in the city, at 1:45 a.m. local time, what was to be the last aircraft to leave Kuwait took off, a Swissair flight to Geneva. On board were the wife and young son of BA's Kuwait manager, Laurie O'Toole. Somewhat surprisingly, O'Toole was sending his family back to Geneva just two days after they had returned to Kuwait from a holiday.

Meanwhile, as Captain Brunyate flew across the Mediterranean, he passed Flight BA148 going in the opposite direction. Everything at Kuwait airport was normal, was the message from pilot to pilot.

But hundreds of miles to the east, in Middle East airspace, other Kuwait-bound flights were being turned away, warned that Kuwait airport was closed 'for security reasons'.

The Kuwaiti armed forces, however, were not on full alert. They had been stood down for weeks to avoid provoking the Iraqis during the peace talks. There was no increase in patrolling or security to match the latest Iraqi troop movements. Many senior officers had in fact just taken their annual holidays abroad.

Jamail Sultan Saleem was part of just a small overnight guard at the main Kuwaiti naval base at al-Jilaya. Saleem was half-British and had done his military training in England. Three Iraqi gunboats carrying marines entered the base in the early hours of 2 August, after slipping through the channel between Bubiyan Island and the mainland. Saleem and his guards spotted the intruders in the harbour and opened fire with heavy machine guns, destroying two of the Iraqi craft at the waterline. But the Iraqis managed to land men on the beach, about two hundred in all, and they brought heavy mortars. For two hours Saleem and his small group held the much larger force at bay. Defying odds of more than twenty to one, they kept the Iraqis pinned down, and the deadly mortars out of range. Finally, the Iraqi marines managed to establish firing positions on the beach, and they launched a barrage of high explosives in the direction of the Kuwaiti positions. Saleem died along with his men, blown apart as the shells landed.

At the Dasman Palace, Kuwait's royal family was told that an invasion had started. Emir Sheikh Jaber al-Ahmad al-Sabah, the country's ruler, had an escape plan prepared. He and his extended family, which comprised most of the country's key officials, piled into a convoy of Mercedes and Range Rovers and headed south for the border, and the safe haven of Saudi Arabia.

In their hurried departure, they neglected to issue any orders for the defence of their country, so there was no official alert to the Kuwaiti armed forces that an invasion was under way. The Iraqi forces met little resistance as they smashed across the border and headed rapidly south. One Kuwaiti unit, the 35th Armored Brigade, using old British-made Chieftain tanks, made a heroic stand on the road to Kuwait City, defending the access to the capital and its airport. Outnumbered, outgunned and surrounded, they held the Hammurabi division at bay for several hours until their ammunition ran out. They were all captured or killed.

British Prime Minister Margaret Thatcher was in Aspen, the exclusive ski resort in Colorado, in the American Rockies. She had left Heathrow on the morning of 1 August and was due to meet President George Bush for talks at the Aspen Institute Conference, a high-powered think tank. The president was due to open the three-day conference, Mrs Thatcher to close it. She had gone to the United States despite intelligence reports that Iraq had sent troops to the border.

At 3 a.m. Kuwait time, early evening in Colorado, her foreign policy adviser, Charles Powell, phoned to tell her the Iraqis had invaded. Thatcher immediately ordered two warships from Mombasa, in Kenya, and Penang, in Malaysia, to head for the Gulf, about a week's sailing time away. The one British ship already in the Gulf, HMS *York* in Dubai, was alerted. A dialogue then began between London and Washington, which was already digesting urgent advisories from the CIA and the Pentagon that an invasion had begun.

Earlier, some Pentagon analysts had suggested that if the Iraqis did invade it might just be a limited attack to reclaim the disputed border region. Others predicted that the Iraqis' real interest was Kuwait's northern oil fields, possession of which would leave Saddam in control of one quarter of the world's oil supply. Yet others had argued that Saddam was just bluffing. But satellite photos now unmistakably showed the Republican Guard's Hammurabi Division heading straight down the main highway to Kuwait City.

*

Aboard Flight 149, Paul Merlet, the French anaesthetist, watched Sky News, which was broadcasting pictures of Iraqi troops on the border with Kuwait. Merlet pointed this out to the cabin crew, who told him not to worry. Flight 149 flew on, only an hour away now from its first refuel, at Kuwait International Airport.

At 4:13 a.m. local time, on 2 August, BA Flight 149 touched down in Kuwait City for the planned refuelling stop and crew changeover before heading on to Madras. Passengers looked out the windows as the plane landed to the south of the capital and could see nothing in the darkness but the lights of the city. Moments after, the plane came to a standstill.

When the door was opened Clive Earthy was greeted by a man in an officer's uniform who told him he had come to collect some of the passengers.[1] The man was clearly in a hurry – *You are late, we need to get them off quickly*, he told Earthy. Earthy assumed he was talking about the Kuwaiti VIP and his guards but, no, the officer wanted the group of young military-looking men who had boarded the plane just before it departed. They were summoned from the back of the aircraft and left as quickly and quietly as they had arrived. After they left the airport, the rest of the passengers would never see any of them again.

Most of the remaining travellers chose not to disembark and dozed as the cleaners boarded the plane. But the Kuwaiti intelligence chief and his four bodyguards did leave. So, too, did George Saloom, an American banker from San Diego travelling with his wife, Deborah, and son, Preston. He was due to take up a new job with a local bank and start a new life for his family. His youngest son, Nathan, had remained behind in the United

---

1   Much later, Clive would try and fail to recall more details about the mystery officer, but he had been too busy dealing with multiple crises and then captivity to pay much attention. He is sure of one thing though – the officer was European, not a Kuwaiti.

States for medical treatment. The Salooms had found their flight a little nerve-racking. They were in First Class and had noticed the intelligence chief and what seemed to be his bodyguards. The man spent much of the flight pacing about, smoking and receiving updates on the flight from the cockpit.

When the plane landed, the clearly agitated Kuwaiti VIP and his colleagues were first off. The Salooms followed. They cleared immigration, which seemed quicker and quieter than usual. The immigration official had just one question: 'What are you doing here?'

Outside the terminal, a driver waited for the family. As they left the airport and headed north towards the city they heard a loud noise. It sounded like thunder – or an explosion. They asked the driver what it was. He didn't speak much English but he shrugged his shoulders and said not to worry. The radio was on, broadcasting nonstop news in Arabic. The driver seemed nervous but he kept saying to the Salooms in broken English, 'Don't worry, don't worry.' The route to the hotel seemed circuitous; they passed several intersections where soldiers were sitting in trucks or jeeps. There was another loud bang in the distance, this time even more like an explosion. A few minutes later as they drove up to their hotel, the Meridien, they heard two loud explosions. As they hurried through to the check-in desk inside the lobby, a burst of automatic fire sprayed the street outside the hotel's front door. They turned around to see armed troops surrounding them.

*

The Kuwaiti cleaners who were supposed to be preparing the flight for the next leg of its journey seemed nervous and were irritating India-bound engineer Edward Hammett. At the back of the 747, Hammett noticed that they were not really getting on with their job. He wanted to sleep; instead he was annoyed to see the cleaners racing up and down the aisles, every so often stopping and talking among themselves in small groups, muttering in low voices so that the passengers could not hear.

Up in Business Class, John Chappell, Jr. noticed the cleaners behaving strangely. 'These guys did not want to be on the plane. They weren't doing the job properly and couldn't do it fast enough. I thought, *This is all a bit odd*... And as they were making their way off the plane, that's when Jenny nudged me to look out of the window.'

As twelve-year-old Jennifer Chappell stared out at the darkened airport from her window seat, three fighter planes had suddenly come into view, flying very fast and very low. Jennifer then saw something drop from the bottom of one of them. For a brief second, she thought she might be witnessing a midair collision. Then there was a loud bang. The whole 231-foot length of the British Airways 747 shook violently. Chaos ensued. People jumped up from their seats, jostled each other, tried to run, shouted. *Get out! Get out! Get out, out of the aisle, move! Get out of the plane!*

Edward Hammett was dozing at the back of the plane when he heard the shouts. 'The next thing I knew, some of the cabin crew were rushing down the aisle yelling, "*Get off get off get off get off.*"' He could see flashes outside, and then someone announced over the plane's PA that the airport was under attack and the passengers needed to make an emergency evacuation. In the rush, Hammett's shoes and books got knocked under a seat and he had to leave the plane in his socks.

Inside the terminal, where he had gone to stretch his legs, Gabriel Chardin, the French engineer, was told by a visibly nervous fellow passenger, 'War must have been declared but they don't want to tell us.' As she spoke, a two-hour delay in their onward flight was announced over the airport PA system.

Almost immediately the airport manager came running into the terminal, shouting loudly that the airport was now closed. With that he turned on his heel and sprinted straight out of the terminal building. The bewildered passengers had no time to figure out what was happening. Seconds later, bombs started to fall.

Chardin saw two MiG jets fly past the windows, a high-speed blur, but so close that he could clearly make out the markings on the wings. 'There was a very bright white light: the planes were shooting at the control tower. Bombs were falling and exploding.' Quickly, he crouched down in case the terminal windows blew out.

On board Flight 149, one of the stewardesses yelled at people to leave their personal possessions and just get off the plane, but people were still pulling their bags out of the overhead lockers. She swore at them, 'Move, for fuck's sake, leave your gear!' But she herself was standing in the middle of the aisle and no one could get past. She completely blocked the exit for business-class passengers. John Chappell tapped her on the shoulder and told her in no uncertain terms to get out of the way. His children, John and Jennifer, just grabbed what they could and ran. They raced down the air bridge and into the terminal and didn't stop until they found someone in a British Airways uniform, steward George Parris. They stood next to him as they waited for their parents. It was a while before Jennifer realised that she had left her asthma inhalers on the plane.

As the other passengers struggled to get off, the plane shook violently, its long wings flexing as explosions went off around the airport, knocking people off their feet. The 747 had just been filled with aviation fuel – fifty-seven thousand gallons of it. The plane was a sitting duck as the Iraqis strafed the runway, and one hit could turn it into a giant bomb.

Maureen Chappell smelled a whiff of cordite as she got off the plane. When she found her daughter, Jennifer said desperately, 'Mum... Oh, my God! They are bombing the plane, Mum!' Maureen tried to calm her daughter down. 'It's going to be all right,' she soothed Jennifer, 'don't worry.'

Seconds later, another passenger burst in, hysterical, sobbing, saying over and over again, 'We are all going to be killed. They are bombing the runway.'

Maureen turned to the woman and spoke sharply. 'I would rather you didn't say that in front of my daughter. I am trying to calm her down. We don't know what is going to happen.'

But Jennifer said, 'It's okay, Mum, I saw it happen. I know what's going on.'

Inside the terminal, passengers and crew mingled in confusion. John Chappell, who had served in the military, told his children to stay away from its enormous glass windows and to get under chairs if there was an explosion. To calm their nerves, and his, he produced a pack of playing cards and the family played several rounds of Snap.

The dull thud of bombs exploding close by mixed with the sounds of jet aircraft swooping overhead. In the distance, tanks and infantry could be seen moving around the airfield. The spearhead of the Iraqi forces, the Hammurabi Division, was surrounding the airport, moving in from the seventh ring road around the city. MiG jets had just attacked the nearby Kuwaiti Air Force headquarters. The passengers were stranded on a battlefield.

The passengers from Flight 149 – and the relief crew who were to fly the plane on to Madras – watched helplessly as the Iraqis took control. Young John Chappell didn't think they would be leaving soon at all. He had noticed something strange about the Kuwaiti guards still in the terminal: all their gun holsters were empty. They had been disarmed.

According to the Departures board, all flights were cancelled. Flight 149 was the sole arrival.

Normally the terminal would have been heaving with passengers and staff during this stopover, but apart from those who had come off the flight, and those waiting to board it, there was no one else in sight. A rumour started that there had been a coup and that the Kuwaiti government had been overthrown. There was no mention of a hostile invasion. Someone even suggested there might be a transfer to the nearby Airport Hotel to await the next departure 'as soon as possible'.

The evacuation from the plane itself was rapid but mostly orderly. It had taken about three minutes. The first attack had been aimed at the other side of the airport, the military side, where Iraqi jets had cratered the runways and taxiways to prevent the Kuwaiti Air Force from taking off. But then the sounds of war grew closer to the main Departure area. The thud of mortars and artillery shells and the rattle of small-arms fire drowned out conversation. Edward Hammett told the British Airways staff that it was crazy for everyone to stand so near the windows. 'This is daft. All these passengers and all these kids. If anyone drops a bomb outside there are going to be hundreds and hundreds of casualties because there are huge sheets of glass right in front of us.'

He felt the BA staff were more concerned about themselves than the passengers. The lack of organisation made him angry. People were gathering in small groups, but no one was taking charge. Various people were trying to take head counts but Hammett thought to himself, *No one really knows who is here.* The ground staff at the airport seemed not to grasp the gravity of the situation. The passenger list had been left on the plane, one staff member said.

*

The British consul in Kuwait City, Larry Banks, had been called at home and ordered to return to the embassy. As he drove along he could hear jet aircraft overhead. Suddenly, a Kuwaiti police car blocked his path. The officers refused to let him through. At the end of the road, he could see a gun battle going on – intense crossfire as some Iraqi infiltrators exchanged fire with the guards at the Dasman Palace. Banks tried to go around another way but he was stopped again, this time by a soldier who ordered him out of his car at gunpoint. The diplomat didn't know at the time whether the soldier was Kuwaiti or Iraqi, but he had an automatic weapon and he seemed ready to use it. Banks was manhandled as he was hustled down towards the beach outside the embassy to join several hundred other civilians who had also been caught on their way to work.

There was intense gunfire. The Iraqis were shooting at cars that refused to stop and at boats in the bay. Rounds zipped over Banks's head and he saw his car, still up on the road, disintegrating as it was hit by a volley of bullets. The British consul raced around the beach, picking up rocks and building a wall to shelter behind. He dug deep into the sand with his hands, crouched behind the makeshift barrier, and waited.

Brigadier Sheikh Fahad al-Ahmad al-Sabah and his bodyguards had left the flight just after it landed and arrived at the Dasman Palace gate just after the emir's departure. Seconds later, he was dead. Killed defending the palace, pistol in hand, according to some; hit in the head by a stray bullet while sitting in his car went another story. All over the city, and in the desert to the north, hundreds of his countrymen were also dying.

Boston-born dentist Robert Morris had been at a US Embassy drinks reception. The embassy staff and marines present appeared to have no idea about the imminent invasion. Bored by the diplomats, Morris left early and returned to his apartment only to be rudely awakened just before dawn by a blast that rocked the apartment block: a shell had exploded just across the road. Later that morning, Morris's eighth-floor apartment became a gathering point for friends and acquaintances of all nationalities from elsewhere in the block trying to get a better look at the fighting. It was a perfect location for viewing: it offered an elevated, central perspective. Some of the spectators identified the soldiers in the streets below as Iraqi.

There was some discussion about leaving quickly across the southern border into Saudi Arabia. Some people called their families but Morris called the *Boston Globe*, his hometown paper, first and gave a running commentary on an airstrike on a palace on the Gulf Road. Then he got through to his wife, Jill, and explained what was happening.

Morris and the others tried phoning the US Embassy to find out what the recommended course of action was, but the line was dead. The Americans were angry that they had had no warning of the invasion, yet the emir, and possibly others, had clearly known about it. Within four hours of the explosion, Iraqi troops entered the apartment block and inspected everyone's ID cards. It was terrifying. The neighbours had spent the morning wondering if they were going to be shot at or bombed, and now they were face-to-face with Iraqi soldiers. A Muslim occupant of the block was chastised for associating with foreign infidels. The 'infidels' awaited their fate.

*

Cliff Lindley was woken in the early morning at his villa in the suburb of Mushrif by the sound of jet aircraft overhead. He was not pleased. He lay in bed until his alarm went off at 5 a.m. Then he ate his cornflakes and read the English-language *Arab Times*, whose headlines all concerned the breakdown of the peace talks between Iraq and Kuwait.

Lindley, from the British Midlands, had been in Kuwait for three years as a development engineer for Kuwait Airways. His workplace was a block of offices inside the international airport. As he drove to work he noticed there were few cars on the road. But it was early morning and the start of the Arab weekend so he was not alarmed. There also seemed to be a lot of desert sand swirling in the air, which struck him as strange since there was no wind. When he entered the airport car park, he found it empty. He walked into the suite of offices and they were empty, too. Not one of his colleagues had turned up for work. As he sat at his desk wondering what on earth had happened, his phone rang. It was an old Kuwaiti friend. 'The Iraqis are here, the runway has been bombed, you had better get out of there,' his friend said, speaking rapidly. 'They came about midnight. They are all over the place.'

Lindley thanked his friend, hung up, and went to the window and looked out towards the airfield, where he could see machine-gun emplacements and armoured vehicles. He thought the soldiers were Kuwaiti. They could easily keep the Iraqis at bay for a while, he told himself; there was plenty of time. He was not unduly worried. He planned to get some money, stock up on water, and return to his villa to wait it out. His wife, Wendy, was on holiday back in the UK with their two sons, but his twenty-one-year-old daughter, Jane, was still in Kuwait, where she worked.

As he headed home he discovered that most of the cash-dispensing machines at the banks were shut. He finally found an active one close to the city centre but he had to wait in line. There was a queue at the petrol station, too. Lindley began to feel anxious and decided to make his way to the local co-op to stock up on food. Hundreds of people were already lining up there, but with their usual hospitality the Kuwaitis let the Westerner through to the front.

As Lindley resumed his homeward journey he could see soldiers everywhere. He waved and cheered. 'Go get the bastards,' he shouted, giving them a V-for-victory salute with his fingers. But as he drove past, he realised to his horror that he was yelling at the Iraqi army. He kept going, not daring to turn around.

At the US Embassy, it was clear the invasion force had reached the city. A gun battle was raging outside the compound walls. The embassy staff were frantically phoning American nationals to tell them to keep their heads down. They also began to destroy classified material on computer disks and hard drives. With no time to shred all the paper documents, they built a fire in the embassy yard to burn them. They even burned all the money from the safe, and they burned the evacuation plan.

Reports came through that the Kuwaitis were being defeated and that some British army officers had been picked up and were being beaten and tortured. Some US Embassy personnel who had wives and children wanted to make a run for the border. But Ambassador Howell ordered them to stay. There were no calls from the British Embassy to its citizens living in Kuwait.

At the airport the Iraqis had taken charge. They decided to load everyone onto buses and to take them from the terminal to the Airport Hotel, a ten-minute-ride away. There was no water or food at the terminal. The buses were driven by British Airways staff but escorted by the Iraqis, with a jeep in front of the convoy and a truck full of troops behind. The mood was quiet, subdued. The Iraqis were polite. None of the passengers were hassled.

When the first buses arrived at the hotel and the passengers got out, they noticed the Iraqi army was already there: armed soldiers in desert camouflage and black berets. Some officers wore the red beret of the Republican Guard. Through the dining room windows others could be seen enjoying a leisurely breakfast. It looked as if they were on holiday rather than in the process of invading another country. The passengers and crew had to wait until the meal was finished.

Young John and Jennifer Chappell, who were both hungry by now, pressed their faces up against the windows and watched as the Iraqis ate. One group of senior officers appeared to be having a strategy session at the breakfast table. They were moving salt and pepper shakers around the table, back and forth, and studying each move. They noticed the children watching them but they didn't seem to mind. They looked confident and relaxed.

Inside the hotel there was some jostling as over four hundred people lined up to find a room. Many were unlucky but John Chappell managed to flash his British passport and was allocated two rooms, one for him and Maureen and one for the children.

The children were in awe of the hotel lobby. It was like an Aladdin's cave, full of shiny glass cases displaying gold Rolex watches and state-of-the-art televisions and stereos. For a moment, Jennifer hoped that a bomb would go off and break the cases, so that they could help themselves to some of the treasures. She fancied a nice watch; her brother had his eye on a new Nintendo game.

John Chappell was allowed to send a telex to his boss in Glasgow, but he was told to be very careful about what he said. He kept it brief: 'Stuck in Kuwait. Unable to proceed due to local dispute.'

Edward Hammett had no luck in finding a room. Instead he claimed a space in the lobby, on a padded bench. Others set themselves up in the billiard room, either on the floor or on the billiard tables themselves. Hammett talked to the Iraqi soldiers. They told him there would be no problems if everyone stayed indoors. But the French passengers were very unhappy and constantly demanded to be let out. Mrs Merlet kept on shouting at the soldiers. She wanted to go where *she* wanted to go. The soldiers seemed close to shooting her, they were so frustrated. Each time she went to the hotel entrance and demanded to leave they said no. Finally, she accepted that she was not going anywhere. She, and the rest of the passengers, were hostages.

The Iraqis questioned the British Airways staff closely, demanding to know exactly what was on the plane. Negotiations followed. A deal was cut. The BA staff could return to the plane to pick up their own belongings and the passengers' hand luggage. In return the Iraqis could have all the booze and cigarettes carried on the flight.

The crew managed to get to the plane and collected most of the hand luggage, including baby food for the infants on the flight. In the luggage hold they found a distressing sight. Two dogs had been on board. The larger one was still alive, just, but the smaller one had died in the heat. The stench was awful.

Captain Peter Clark, the pilot due to fly Flight 149 on the next leg of its journey, was allowed to start up the plane's engines and the air-conditioning and move the plane to keep its big tyres in working order. The crew still held out hope they would be allowed to fly out soon, and they wanted to be ready.

At the Airport Hotel, the Iraqis were still having problems with the French – and so were the British Airways crew. A meal was served, but the portions were small. The hotel was already rationing its food. One French woman refused her portion and angrily remonstrated with the BA steward serving it, slapping him hard across the face. John Chappell watched in horror.

At the Regency Palace Hotel, where Flight 149's London–Kuwait crew had spent the night, Clive Earthy woke and looked out of his window. He saw an invading army on the beach.

Earthy talked to the crew in the other rooms. Stewardess Nikki

Love knocked on the door of her colleague, Jacqui Hunter. Love opened the curtains and spotted more soldiers. Hunter thought they must be Kuwaitis, but when the soldiers saw the women looking they made an aggressive gesture, a hanging-by-the-throat motion. They quickly closed the curtains again. Iraqis, then.

*

Outside the Airport Hotel, there was a battle going on. From the window of her room, Jennifer Chappell looked down on the car park. She saw Iraqi tanks drive straight through it, rolling over cars, crushing them. She saw people in the cars trying to get out. She called her brother over to take a look.

John hadn't heard gunfire before but when he heard what sounded to him like a loud electric drill or, more accurately, a series of drills, he told his sister to get down, pushing her into a crouching position beneath the level of the window. As he watched a Kuwaiti tank in the distance, something else caught his eye. It was a Kuwaiti soldier, silhouetted against the buildings as he ran across the back of the car park. Suddenly two Iraqi soldiers appeared and pointed their automatic weapons at the running man. They fired, emptying their magazines. It took just a couple of seconds. The Kuwaiti soldier spun, then turned as his chest exploded, and then he fell to the ground, dead. There was very little left of him. A stretcher arrived from somewhere to pick up the remains. John ducked down again beneath the window with his sister. It wasn't an adventure any more. Real guns were killing real people. *We can't stay here*, he thought. *We've got to get right away from here. We've got to get out.*

CHAPTER 1

TRAPPED

The invasion was swift and brutal. Iraqi armour had no trouble slicing across the border and getting to the capital. Hundreds of Kuwaitis died in the first twelve hours. But it was not a completely successful mission. Lead units of the Republican Guard got lost on the ring roads around the city. Most of the Kuwaiti army and air force escaped to Saudi Arabia, fifty miles to the south, while Kuwait Airways flew many of its jetliners out of the country or managed to divert them. The long convoy of Mercedes and Range Rovers carrying the Kuwaiti royals successfully crossed the border in the dead of night.

In the city, residents awoke to life in a war zone. Hundreds of other Westerners were living and working in a Kuwait now under occupation.

The loud rumble of traffic had disturbed British Airways' Kuwait manager, Laurie O'Toole. It was 4 a.m. in Kuwait City and O'Toole had been asleep for just forty-five minutes, having returned from the airport where he had overseen preparations for the arrival of

Flight 149. *Why is there so much traffic and what is that clanging sound?* wondered O'Toole.

He looked out his bedroom window and saw the road jam-packed with military vehicles, a long line all heading in one direction, down the road from Basra and towards Kuwait's city centre. Jeeps, soldiers on foot, and tanks were the source of the noise. O'Toole went up to his roof for a better view and saw helicopters overhead. He ran back down to his flat and phoned the airport. No answer. Then he tried the British Embassy. All lines were engaged. A few minutes later he heard the sound of gunfire. From back on his rooftop perch he could see Iraqi tanks blasting away at Kuwaiti army headquarters.

O'Toole was alone. His family was en route to Geneva and his deputy in Kuwait's BA office, Amanda Ball, had also left that morning for London, to attend a wedding. O'Toole kept trying to call the airport and the embassy.

*

At his apartment on the fourth ring road in Kuwait City, Colonel John Mooneyham, the head of the American military liaison team that ran the observation post that had originally raised the alarm, took the news of the invasion calmly. Mooneyham was ex-Special Forces, a Vietnam veteran, and cool under fire. As his early warning team headed south to stay ahead of the Republican Guard tanks, he showered and dressed. A call from the US Embassy confirmed the invasion was on and all roads were closed. The message: Stay put until we see what happens.

Mooneyham had known about the troops massing on the border; he received regular intelligence from the Westinghouse balloon, but he too thought Saddam was bluffing. Now Mooneyham called all the people working for him and told them to stay put. All were Americans, and all were potential hostages.

The Mooneyhams – John, wife Ellen and eleven-year-old Nathan – shared a duplex with the embassy's economics officer. They lived next door to the emir's elderly sister. The colonel went to the rooftop and saw several helicopters flying past, about a hundred feet away. They looked like US CH-47 troop carriers but these had Iraqi markings. The economics officer called to say that he was going to make for the Japanese Embassy, three blocks west of the apartment, and that he would take Ellen and Nathan. It was assumed the US Embassy was surrounded.

Alone in his apartment, the colonel made a contingency plan. He needed an E and E – what the military calls escape and evasion – route out if the Iraqis came to take him hostage. He began loading canned goods and a suitcase of clothes into his blue Chevy Impala, one of the cars given to the American unit by the emir.

*

President George Bush appeared on television within hours of the invasion to answer questions from reporters on the White House lawn.

> *Associated Press*: Do you contemplate intervention as
> one of your options?
> *Bush*: We're not discussing intervention.
> *Associated Press*: You are not contemplating any
> intervention or sending troops?
> *Bush*: I'm not contemplating such action.

Stewart Griffiths was not watching the news. He was on the road north to Jahra, on the modern freeway that links Kuwait and Iraq. Griffiths, an oil engineer, worked on an installation close to the border. He had lived in Kuwait with his wife, Barbara, for five years, but the couple were thinking of returning to the UK. This was meant to be his last contract.

As he drove north, he saw plumes of smoke in the distance. When he reached Jahra he was diverted away from the city centre through backstreets until he emerged on the other side. None of the police told him the reason for the diversion, nor did he ask.

Griffiths started up the long road to the top of the Mutla Ridge. He was flagged down by what he thought was a group of Kuwaiti soldiers, who had set up a roadblock. They asked who he was and where he was going. 'I am English,' Stewart replied. 'I am going to work at Abdaly, on the pipeline.' The soldiers waved him through, but a few hundred yards farther another group of soldiers stopped him, and an officer told him to turn off his engine. Armed soldiers surrounded the car and Griffiths was ordered to get out, at the point of an AK-47.

'What is happening?' Stewart asked the officer.

'You have been captured,' was the reply. 'You are a prisoner of the Iraqi army. The Iraqi army led by the great Saddam Hussein has freed the Kuwaiti people from oppression.'

Griffiths was herded into a group with three Indian workers who had also been heading to the refinery. They watched as huge columns of trucks and tanks went past, all heading south. The four men were ordered back into their cars and told to keep driving north, towards Iraq. A mile later, they were again ordered out of their cars. But this time they were forced off the road and into the desert sand, where they were made to kneel down. The soldiers watched them, their fingers on the triggers of their AK-47s.

For an hour and a half the men knelt in the heat, the sound of continuous gunfire in the distance. More men were brought to join them and made to kneel. They seemed to be Kuwaitis. Griffiths and the Indians were given a banana and some dirty water to share between them. A minibus pulled up and a bleeding Iraqi soldier was carried from it. He had been shot in the stomach.

An Iraqi officer appeared and ordered Griffiths back into his car. The officer climbed in beside him and told him to drive him down the road from the ridge. After a couple of miles they stopped at what appeared to be a command post. Soldiers with radios milled about everywhere, most of them smiling and looking relaxed.

A sound made Griffiths look up. He saw a squadron of Iraqi helicopters overhead, heading for the city. Seconds later, two of them disintegrated in midair, hit by missiles from a Kuwaiti fighter plane that had appeared from the west. The whole command post seemed to open up with small-arms fire shooting into the sky. Everyone seemed to be shouting and running. Griffiths was ordered to hide behind a petrol tanker. He refused, realising it would turn into a fireball if it were hit. For a second, he seemed to be alone. He began to run into the desert, running for his life, away from the madness behind him, the burning helicopters and the dying men.

Two shots rang out, the bullets whizzing over his head. He stopped running and put his hands up. The Iraqi officer caught up with him and dragged him roughly back towards the post, ordering him to lie under a troop truck until the battle was over. Griffiths lay there, his eyes closed, trembling with fear. He felt close to death. He wondered what was happening to his wife Barbara back in the city.

*

Life-and-death decisions were being made all over Kuwait. Among the two thousand or so trapped Westerners was a group of British army engineers. The men were from REME (Royal Electrical and Mechanical Engineers) and they were on secondment to the Kuwaiti army, with a contract to maintain the Chieftain tanks the British had sold the emir.

'Secondment' was a strange posting. The REME men became Kuwaiti officers: they wore Kuwaiti uniforms rather than British, were paid by the Kuwaiti government, and had to obey Kuwaiti rules. Most of them enjoyed their time in Kuwait: it was sunny and stable and a good place for families to live.

Jerry Blears, a REME expert in optical systems and thermal imaging, knew he would miss the city when he returned to the UK with his wife, Jackie, and their children, Colin and Rachel. The family had planned to drive back to Britain at the end of September and had even bought a new car in which to make their once-in-a-lifetime road trip.

At 5 a.m., Jerry was awakened by Senior Warrant Officer Mick Haynes and ordered to wake the men and round them up to meet in the mess at 6:30 a.m. Haynes then informed them of the Iraqi invasion. Haynes had a second, more far-reaching, announcement. The government in London had revoked their secondment, which meant that once again they were British military personnel. Under these new orders, they were reminded, they were subject to British military jurisdiction, as were their families. They were ordered to stay put in Kuwait. No one was to attempt to escape on his own. This was a direct order from Colonel Bruce Duncan, the commander of the REME detachment and the most senior British military officer in Kuwait.

Jerry was not worried. The REME group had a detailed evacuation plan in place, and the history of Middle East conflicts suggested that ex-pats and other foreigners were usually allowed to go home. They did not feel there was any need to rush. The men got started on phase one of their evacuation plan: load up cars with supplies and get ready to leave.

International phone lines were cut in the REME camp early on 3 August, severing the soldiers' links with the UK. A foot patrol of Iraqi soldiers passed through on the way to the neighbouring refinery. They wanted to get to the surface-to-air missile site that was located there. Mick Haynes spoke to the patrol and urged them to leave. Within hours they were back and this time they locked the gates of the camp, which was surrounded by tall fencing topped with barbed wire. The soldiers were trapped and realised they were no longer in control of their situation.

A larger force of Iraqis arrived at the compound and rounded up all the men. Jerry was cleaning dishes when an Iraqi came into his house and dragged him outside at gunpoint, as his horrified wife and daughter looked on. The women and girls in the camp were forced to stay inside while the men stood outside in a group. The Iraqis also rounded up the teenage boys. Jerry pleaded with them to release the younger boys, who had been in Kuwait for the school holidays. They are just here for a visit, he told the soldiers, they are just children. Eventually, the boys were allowed to go inside with the women and girls. The men were forced into a minibus and were driven out of the camp. The women in the compound heard bursts of machine-gun fire shortly after the bus left. It sounded like an execution. Rumours of random executions and rapes began to spread throughout the city.

*

People congregated in Bostonian Robert Morris's apartment, waiting for news and perhaps hoping for safety in numbers. Most people brought along some food to share, but at this point it was thought the invasion would last only a few days. Morris was more worried that people were running up his phone bill by calling their friends and families abroad. After a couple of days, it was no longer an issue: the Iraqis blocked international calls. From their vantage point above the street, the group could see drivers being stopped and forced to abandon their vehicles, then taken prisoner. Meanwhile, soldiers were looting the stores and loading the stolen goods into the abandoned cars, which they then drove away. Their gold cards are AK-47s, Morris observed. So many soldiers were trying to carry off their loot that cars became gridlocked as they got stuck behind abandoned vehicles. The stolen cars drove up onto the pavement to get around the blockages.

The bottom three floors of Morris's apartment block housed a mall containing more than 130 shops and boutiques, with thirteen floors of apartments above. The looting of the mall like 'it was an open store' made the residents very uneasy. As well as their personal safety, they were concerned about their cars in the building's car park; some people went down to check on them. Many of the cars had been broken into or stolen, and were now being loaded up with stolen VCRs, televisions, and other expensive goods from the mall. Reports came from other people in the building that some women on the lower floors of the apartment complex were being repeatedly raped by Iraqi soldiers. Their husbands were beaten and taken away or forced to watch. One of the Western women who had been hiding in Morris's flat was too scared to walk back to her apartment alone, because the Iraqi soldiers she had encountered in the hallways made lewd comments about her and had frequently hammered on her door.

Paul Kennedy, an Irishman married to a Thai woman, was held at gunpoint while Iraqi soldiers attempted to rape two female friends of his wife who were staying in his apartment. The women, one of whom was forced to strip naked at gunpoint, managed to evade the soldiers and lock themselves in the bathroom. Their tormentors then had a chat and a cigarette but eventually left. The Thai women were very distressed by their ordeal, so Morris offered them and

Kennedy refuge in his apartment. He gave up his room for them and shared with his nephew.

The group learned that the Iraqi secret police were taking up residence in the Plaza Hotel, part of the same complex, and that all of the hotel's former foreign guests had disappeared. They realised the Iraqis would be looking for foreign hostages to barter with, and this made them very anxious to avoid being seen and, if possible, escape the country.

Morris and his Australian neighbour, John Levins, decided to venture out of the apartment to reach a local church, where it was rumoured that the minister, Pastor Maurice, and his wife had been attacked. As they reached the church an Iraqi soldier with an AK-47 jumped down out of a tree and arrested them, directing them at gunpoint to a police station near the Sheraton hotel. Morris was kicking himself that he and his companion hadn't been more cautious in their first foray from the apartment in three days.

After a few hours at the police station, they were taken to the Sheraton, where the Iraqi army had set up their temporary headquarters. Morris and Levins were held in the grand ballroom with around seventy other hostages of different nationalities. They recognised some of their fellow captives. Several hostages complained that as diplomats, they should not be held. After some hours, several of them, and an aircrew from Air India, were released.

An Iraqi major asked if there were any more diplomats in the room and John Levins raised his hand. Morris and two others followed suit. Morris was taking a chance, as the only proof of his 'diplomatic status' was an expired UN passport in his apartment from his time working for the UN Development Programme. One of the others was in the US Air Force. The four men were taken to another room for questioning and the Iraqi major asked each who he worked for. All pretended to have links to the UN or the Kuwaiti government. The airman said he represented the US government and was there to assist the Iraqis. He was retained as a hostage, but the three others were allowed to go to get their documents.

The soldiers were in evening prayer at this point, so the men managed to slip out the front door unnoticed and disappeared into the crowd. Morris and Levins returned to the apartment and informed the group that hostages were being taken. They called their embassies to tell them what had happened.

They decided that the Al Muthanna area had become too dangerous for Westerners. They would flee the country. Morris had a friend from the US Embassy who said they could stay at his villa on the other side of town, which might be safer in the short term. Morris and members of his group headed there, and over the next few days they assessed possible escape plans and loaded up their cars with clothing and treasured possessions. The first attempt was over quickly – they were stopped at a checkpoint just outside the city and turned back.

They then learned that a meeting had taken place at one of the hotels to plan an escape across the border to Saudi Arabia. Maps of the route were faxed back by French nationals who had already got out this way and were now safe. Fortunately, the Iraqis had not yet cut the phone lines between Kuwait and Saudi. The next day, Morris and his group headed south in two vehicles, Morris's BMW 635 and a small Honda with two other members of the group. They failed again and were turned back. Morris and his nephew then sped north, finally finding a turn-off where they saw hundreds of vehicles crossing the desert. Morris was not sure that his two-wheel drive vehicle could make it, but they were so desperate to escape he risked it. Three times they became bogged down in the sand and had to dig themselves out in the searing heat. Morris felt 'light-headed and sick to the stomach' from a combination of colitis (for which he had run out of painkillers), heat, and anxiety about their situation. The final time the car got stuck, others, both Egyptian and Kuwaiti, tried to help them move but the car wouldn't budge. They had little water and felt that walking across the desert at the hottest time of the day was suicidal, so they abandoned the car, with Morris's family's most valuable possessions in it, and walked back to the highway to hitch a lift back to the city. After a few hours, they were back in their villa.

*

Thirty-eight-year-old Apostos 'Paul' Eliopoulos, an American computer specialist, had lived in Kuwait for three years. After he received a call from the marine guard at the US Embassy telling him there had been an invasion, he hid for two days alone at home near the airport in the south of the city. (His wife, Angela, and children Alex and Nichole were on holiday.) On August 4, running short of supplies, he went out by car with two friends to get gas and food. They were stopped at a checkpoint near the port of Shuwaikh and ordered out at gunpoint. The soldiers spoke to them in Arabic, which none of them understood, and poked them with their weapons, forcing them under a highway overpass.

Suddenly, there was firing all around and Eliopoulos found himself in the middle of a gun battle. He crouched low behind a pillar to avoid being hit. A few feet away, a Kuwaiti soldier was being held prisoner. Another burst of fire came and one of the Iraqi soldiers was hit; it looked bad. The other Iraqis became very agitated. One of them walked up to the Kuwaiti prisoner, pointed his AK-47 at the man, and in cold blood shot him in the head.

Eliopoulos and the others were then herded into a truck and taken to the Kuwaiti Ministry of Defense headquarters, which had been commandeered. The men were taken into a small room in what appeared to be a makeshift interrogation centre, which filled rapidly with Westerners and Kuwaiti POWs. Soon more than a dozen people were crowded into the hot and sweaty room, with no space to stretch out.

Soldiers kept coming in and pulling men out of the room for questioning. Eliopoulos could hear screaming coming from a nearby room – the sounds of torture. The door opened again and another man was pulled out, often to replace someone who had been badly beaten. One man's face was completely disfigured and covered in blood, his clothes torn. The air was filled with moans, and the smell of urine and excrement. *We are next*, Eliopoulos thought.

But when it was his turn to be taken from the room it was to meet an officer who spoke good English and who merely questioned him for fifteen minutes. There was shouting but the officer did not touch him. Eliopoulos told the officer he worked with computers, for the Ministry of Defense and Kuwait Airways. He returned to the small room, where the comings and goings continued for hours. Eliopoulos spent the night huddled in fear, crouched on the blood-and urine-soaked floor, sleeping fitfully as the interrogations went on and on, all night long.

In the morning some soldiers came into the room and pointed at Eliopoulos and some of the other Westerners. 'You, you, and you... out.' He was put into a truck outside with an armed guard and they travelled around the city making stops to pick up other hostages. Eliopoulos did not really focus on where they might be going; he thought he was on his way to be executed. The ride took several hours.

Three Iraqi soldiers rode in the back of the truck with Eliopoulos and the others, and he noticed one of them gazing at him. He also noticed the soldier had an erection as the man came over, gun in hand, and began fondling his face. Others in the truck inched away from Eliopoulos. The American thought he was about to be raped. He decided there and then that he would rather die than be raped. He was preparing to shove the man aside and jump out of the truck when it stopped to let more people on, guarded by more soldiers. His tormentor stopped touching him and moved down the truck, smiling and leering, but he left Eliopoulos alone after that.

The truck headed north towards the Iraqi border and arrived at what looked like a customs area. The hostages kept asking for an officer so they could tell him they were civilians and should be freed. They wanted to avoid being taken into Iraq at all costs. The men would ask and the soldiers would poke them with their guns in reply. The men kept their hands up to show they didn't want a fight, that they were not troublemakers – they just wanted to talk to an officer. Suddenly one of the soldiers poked Eliopoulos in the ribs with his gun and then swung it around without warning and smashed the butt into the American's face, knocking him to the ground. The blow broke his glasses and bloodied his nose. There would be no conversation with an officer.

The group was held in a pen until early afternoon, when they were taken out and lined up against a wall with some Kuwaiti POWs, facing the soldiers with guns, execution-style. But there were no shots. The soldiers had had their fun and the group then bundled into a minivan.

The van was crowded with about a half-dozen Westerners and as many captured Kuwaiti soldiers. The vehicle headed across the border and then stopped. The soldiers pulled one of the badly beaten Kuwaitis out of the van. The man kept saying, '*La, la*' ('No, no' in Arabic) over and over again. An officer cocked his gun on top of the man's head and the two soldiers stepped away so they would not be splashed by the blood. A woman in the minivan next to Eliopoulos started yelling at the soldiers. They moved her out of sight. Seconds later Eliopoulos heard a shot, and as the van drove off again he saw a woman's body lying by the side of the road.

Welcome to Iraq, Eliopoulos thought.

*

Back in the city, at the Airport Hotel, John Chappell considered his limited options. As a former military man, he knew the airport was a strategic target for any counterattack. John wanted to get his children as far away as possible. Apart from anything else, young John and Jennifer had just witnessed their first deaths. So the Chappells used their business-class status to talk their way onto a bus carrying some of the passengers further into the city, to the luxurious Regency Palace Hotel.

The bus left under guard. The Iraqis made the men sit on the floor, hands on heads, with the women and children on the seats. As they left, the convoy came under fire. It took four anxious hours to cover the fifteen miles to the Regency Palace.

Other passengers and crew were moved to various hotels in the city. Flight 149 steward Neil Dyer and his wife, Denise, a stewardess, were on the same bus. It was a gruesome journey, punctuated by the sounds of artillery. They passed cattle trucks stacked with bodies. They could see the soles of the feet of dead men under the covers of the trucks. At one checkpoint, one of the Iraqis on board put his hand up Denise's skirt. She tried to move away but the soldier kept feeling up her leg. Neil was sitting in front of her, oblivious to what was happening. Denise silently prayed that he would not turn around, afraid of what he might do. Eventually some of the other men on the bus saw what was happening and moved towards the soldier. He pulled away and disappeared.

One bus was met by Iraqi conscripts. After the passengers got off, a stewardess got back on the bus to check under the seats for belongings left on board. She sensed movement behind her and turned to see a smiling Iraqi soldier, an AK-47 over his shoulder, offering her a cigarette. She could see her colleagues had disappeared into the hotel, just twenty feet away, and there was no one else in sight. She shook her head no and tried to walk past the soldier but he blocked her way, grabbed her, and tore at her clothes. At first, no one heard her screams as he raped her. The stewardess tried to fight him off but the soldier was too strong. One of the stewards, Tahel Daher, was walking back to the bus when he heard the sounds of a struggle. He ran forward and shouted at the soldier to stop. The soldier had the woman by the hair, a machine gun at his side, and he kept going. Daher saw the gun and dared not get too close. But he shouted at other soldiers nearby: 'Please stop him. You can't let him rape a girl like this!'

'He is just having fun,' one of the soldiers replied.

'*Fun? This is fun? Raping a girl?*' Daher yelled at the man. Eventually the soldiers intervened. The distraught stewardess was led away and the soldier disappeared.

The woman was comforted by Denise Dyer, who decided to keep the ugly news to herself to prevent a panic. But other BA staff told Clive Earthy, who had also arrived at the hotel by this time. He demanded to speak to the senior Iraqi officer. When the officer arrived, he turned out to speak good English. He was furious when Earthy told him what had happened. He snapped out a series of orders. Soon, twelve Iraqi soldiers were lined up in the hotel lobby.

The stewardess, still sobbing, was brought to the lobby along with Daher. 'Can you identify the man?' the officer asked. The girl pointed to a man in the line-up. The steward pointed to the same man.

The officer pulled the man out of the line and unholstered his pistol. He offered the gun to the steward. Would he like to shoot him? Daher said he couldn't. If he'd had a gun in his hand at the time of the rape, he would have, but he couldn't now, not in cold blood. No, Daher told the officer, you deal with him.

The man was taken away. For the rest of the day, he was kept outside in the baking sun, hands tied behind his back, head bowed, in full view of many of the passengers and crew now holed up in their rooms. Shortly before dusk, the man was hauled away, towards the beach. Minutes later, shots rang out. The BA staff was informed that the soldier had been executed.

CHAPTER 3

'DON'T TRY TO ESCAPE'

Most of the Flight 149 captives spent the first days of their captivity in the Regency Palace. Initially there was enough food – Danish pastries for breakfast, salad with cheese and ham for lunch, and stew for dinner – and the Iraqi soldiers were polite and kept their distance. But as the food and service deteriorated, along with people's tempers and tolerance, meal times became increasingly fraught. At times, it was like a stampede, with people pushing each other to get to the buffet. The hotel staff did their best to serve their guests and look after them, even after it was no longer clear whether they would be paid or whether any of the guests would be settling their bills. 'Give it to British Airways' was the usual response of passengers when asked about a bill. Eventually the hotel management stopped asking.

Soon after John and Maureen had checked into their room, there came a knock on the door. It was Captain Brunyate. He was apologetic: 'Look, I am really sorry about this. If I had known about it I would never have landed.' He told them he had put extra personnel on the flight deck as the plane came in to land, to look for signs of trouble and to monitor the local radio communications. Nothing untoward had been reported to him.

British Airways staff set up a help desk in the hotel lobby, manned by stewardesses. They wore their uniforms, a sign that the airline was still taking its responsibilities seriously. To the passengers, it seemed as if the airline would sort things out, eventually. After all, it was one of the world's major carriers, with a long history of travelling to the Middle East and contacts at the highest level of government. The passengers and crew were getting news and updates from Captain Brunyate and also Laurie O'Toole (BA's manager in Kuwait), who had been part of the warden system set up by Western residents in the city during a previous invasion scare. As a warden, O'Toole was allowed by the Iraqis to travel around to the embassies and to the four hotels where the passengers were being held.

O'Toole told the BA staff and the passengers to stay where they were: it was their safest option, he said, and no one was to attempt to flee the city. The advice from the British Embassy was the same: don't try to escape.

O'Toole gave everyone an impression of calmness, and it seemed that the airline's senior staff were all singing from the same hymn sheet. But privately, Captain Brunyate worried. He began to keep a diary. When he first heard of the invasion, he wrote, 'I had a chilling feeling that I had experienced before in both Beirut and Baghdad, a sort of "here we go again".' Then, as he tried to work out what might happen next, his worries increased. 'I fear for the future when the Iraqis get organised,' he continued. 'It seems as though there is a lot of confusion in the Iraqi camp as to what to do with us. Try not to let my anxiety show but am experiencing a certain amount of panic.'

At this point, the Iraqis were still not in full control of the city and were keeping only a loose rein on their 'guests'. In the early days, the guards at the hotel could easily be avoided. Another Brunyate diary entry reads: 'We went for a long walk outside the hotel and found several concerned Kuwaitis who offered help. They say it is very dangerous to stay at the hotels.'

At the hotel, everyone watched Margaret Thatcher on CNN. Her stance was tough and uncompromising towards the Iraqis. The trapped passengers heard her use the dreaded word 'hostage' for the first time. Some of them, like BA steward Charles Napier Kristiansson, began to loathe the Prime Minister. Clive Earthy, the purser, felt she was almost daring Saddam to take hostages by confronting him.

Life at the Regency Palace for Jennifer Chappell had become a real-life adventure. 'It was almost like what you see in war films where the British prisoners in the prisoner of war camps almost turn it into a little Britain. Everyone sort of gets on with it and you pool everything together and have as much fun as you can. We had a little community within the hotel.'

On 5 August, Jennifer celebrated her thirteenth birthday. It was far from the grand Indian party the family had planned, but the hotel staff and crew did their best. The hotel manager organised a party in one of the suites, with a disco and some snacks. That night a big chocolate cake appeared from the kitchen and the British Airways crew made a card for her. It had aircraft, a TriStar and a 747, on the front and they had all signed it. From the Regency Palace she got a framed picture signed by the owner and managers. A Malaysian gave her the solid silver ring he'd had made for his daughter, a daughter he wondered if he would ever see again. The kids and the crew all had a dance on the disco floor, Madonna's 'Hanky Panky' being a popular track. At midnight everyone sang

'Happy Birthday' at the top of their voices, in celebration and defiance, and the sound echoed around the hotel corridors.

On Monday, 6 August, at 7 a.m., the phone rang in the Chappells' room. The hotel receptionist told them to assemble in the lobby with their few remaining possessions. When everyone had arrived downstairs, the hotel manager announced that they would be taken to Baghdad by bus, provided that they made their own arrangements for food and water and somewhere to stay when they got there.

This offer made John Chappell and the others uneasy. They didn't want to go to Iraq; they still held out the hope of leaving Kuwait the way they had arrived. After several hours waiting in the lobby, the guests were told that the 'offer' had been withdrawn and the trip cancelled. They could go back to their rooms.

Most people spent the rest of the day feeling uneasy. Around 6 p.m. heavy gun and mortar fire could be heard just outside the hotel. Seconds later, a group of Iraqi soldiers burst into the dining room, just as the guests were starting dinner. They were ordered to stay where they were while all their rooms were searched. This took several hours; finally, at about 9 p.m., they were allowed back into their rooms.

When the Malaysian and Indian passengers were later let go on Saddam's orders, the Americans, British, and others realised they were definitely no longer 'guests'. There was now a guard on every floor and at the doors, and antiaircraft guns on the roof. Edward Hammett, the oil engineer who had lost his shoes as he fled the plane, was determined to escape barefoot if necessary. 'We were thinking we would have to get organised because we might need to get away. We started looking for vehicles.'

After the rape of the stewardess and other incidents, Hammett's group also became minders for the women, some of whom were being stalked by the Iraqis. The Iraqi officers tried to keep their soldiers in line. One who stole a watch from one of the rooms was pistol-whipped right in front of Hammett, in the corridor outside the room where he was caught.

For the most part, the Iraqi soldiers milled around, scavenging for food and water, and seemed to be generally at a loss as to what to do next. Often, they looted and stole bedding items for their hastily constructed fighting positions, complete with beach umbrellas for overhead protection from the searing summer sun. They seemed to have reached the end of their supplies and were having to live off the land. They took food and water from the locals and siphoned fuel for their tanks and trucks from the rich Kuwaiti refineries.

Hammett's group kept busy working out the best escape routes from the hotel. They ventured out into the city and found an abandoned Toyota to use as an escape vehicle. Hammett, a former auto-electrician, hot-wired it, and they drove it back to the hotel basement, hiding it in a corner by surrounding it with large packing crates.

As stewardess Jacqui Hunter recalled, in the gilded cage of the Regency Palace, in the lobby and the salons, an air of normality still prevailed – at least on the surface. 'It was like a strange kind of kibbutz community with everyone helping out, cleaning rooms and sorting things out and thinking of activities to stop people being bored. It was very strange. And that would be interspersed with watching CNN news bulletins. People's emotions were like this – you'd find yourself laughing really hysterically about something and then you'd go to your room and get very low and very afraid.'

There was really only one main topic of conversation for everyone: stay or go? Some people wanted to make a run for it before the Iraqis sealed the border. Others argued just as forcefully that they should all stay put in the hope that they would be freed. The most persuasive voice was still that of Laurie O'Toole. His job was to keep track of those who had been on the flight, a job made more difficult by the discovery that the only copy of the passenger list had definitely been left on the plane.

O'Toole walked around the hotel every day, telling all who would listen that they should stay there. His advice from the embassy was that it was still too dangerous to travel. Still, six of the men decided to ignore his pleas. They slipped away at night, in two convoys of stolen cars, and headed across the flat expanse of desert to the south, towards the Saudi border. Two of them, including a German from Flight 149, got away, but the other four were caught by Iraqi patrols and brought back to the hotel at gunpoint. The angry debates went on. Each side used the fate of the convoy as evidence that they were right.

More sobering news was to follow. Forty-nine-year-old Douglas Croskery was a confident man. A long-term British resident of Kuwait, he had decided to make a run for it: he knew the country well, spoke Arabic, and, most importantly, did not have to worry about his wife, Thelma, who was on holiday when the invasion started. His three children were out of the country, too. He left the city at midnight with a twenty-strong party of Kuwaitis, travelling in a convoy of six vehicles. Croskery was at the rear, driving a Daihatsu Rocky. They managed to avoid all the Iraqi patrols, but eight kilometres from the border one of the vehicles got stuck in the sand. It was abandoned and its passengers distributed among the other five cars.

Croskery had a local Kuwaiti teenager named Fahad al-Muteb next to him, and a father and his two young children in the back. As the convoy neared the border, it approached a fork in the road. The leader took the right fork, thinking it was the way to the border post. But this road led to an oil installation and a dead end. Realising their mistake, the vehicles turned around. Too late. A group of Iraqi soldiers who had been looting cars near the border spotted the fugitives as they were completing their U-turn. The soldiers shouted at them to stop. Croskery's car was the last in line. No one will ever know if he did not hear the shouting, or tried to drive on regardless. An Iraqi soldier fired at the car, a long burst from his AK-47. The rounds missed the father and his children in the back, but hit the Briton in the back of the head, killing him instantly. The other occupants screamed as his skull was splattered over the windshield.

Fahad jumped out of the car, yelling, '*You've killed him! You've killed him!*' The two Iraqi soldiers levelled their guns at the terrified boy. 'I will kill you next if you don't get into the car and start driving,' said one. The soldiers pulled Croskery's body out of the car, and the shaking teenager got into the car and raced away. The last view he had of Croskery was in the rear-view mirror, his body lying face down in the sand.

Despite the tragedy, other desert escape attempts continued. A German rally driver, Ottmar Lange, successfully led three groups to safety through sweltering days and sub-zero nights down a route known as the Pipeline because it followed an oil pipeline and power pylons to the border. But that route had to be abandoned when Lange was shot at by an Iraqi patrol. Failed attempts added weight to the 'let's stay and see what happens' camp. People carried on as best they could, trying to keep busy while waiting for help to arrive.

'Stay put' was the message for BA crew and passengers, too. Flight 149 was going nowhere until there was a political settlement. One day, Jennifer Chappell came across Laurie O'Toole and other senior staff having a whispered conversation in the hotel barber shop. They ignored her as she lingered nearby. She strained to hear their words. They were talking about an escape plan. Dates and times, numbers, exit routes. An excited Jennifer ran to find her parents. 'They are going to escape,' she said. 'The BA people are going to escape.' John and Maureen shook their heads. 'Don't worry,' said Maureen, 'they won't desert us. They are not going to try to escape without us.'

Chief purser Clive Earthy was definitely prepared to wait it out. Life in the hotel had settled down into a routine. But as time went on, he did worry more. The most obvious way out, the abandoned plane, sat outside at the airport, untouched and unmaintained. He started to wonder if the plane would ever fly again. Earthy manned the information desk in the hotel lobby, where passengers and crew could visit each day to get the latest news. He would ring Laurie O'Toole and Michael Weston, the British ambassador, for updates.

Earthy and others were not impressed with Her Majesty's representative in Kuwait. In the first week of the invasion the purser had gone with Brunyate to see Weston at the British Embassy, and the pair told him there were lots of abandoned vehicles in the hotel basement, enough to form a convoy. Could he arrange for Foreign Office representatives to meet them at the Saudi border if they made it that far? Weston refused, telling them such convoys were forbidden and that anyway, the crisis would be over 'in a day or two.'

The very next day, the Iraqis closed the borders and people were turned back. *The ambassador is an arsehole*, Earthy thought when he heard the news. Many of the hostages felt that Weston had ruined their chance to get out in the first week, when the Saudi border was still open.

Reports on CNN convinced Earthy that Saddam would not

leave Kuwait in a hurry, so he and his crew went into crisis planning mode. They prepared the basements of the hotels where passengers and crew were being held so that they could be turned into makeshift hospitals. They stuck the hotel's entire stock of sticky labels along the floors to show the way to the emergency exits. This took two days.

Earthy and Brunyate discussed the merits of trying to escape. Brunyate was particularly keen: he seemed to be really anxious to avoid capture by the Iraqis. He was also the one who somehow had managed to find contacts for safe houses.

Richard Brunyate was indeed a worried man. He spent his days reassuring the passengers, but at night he could not sleep. He dreaded being captured by the Iraqis. When living in his beloved Baghdad, his father, Jack, had mixed in senior political and social circles and had fallen foul of a fast-rising politician from Tikrit: Saddam Hussein. Perhaps it was this history that made Brunyate walk 'out of the hotel one day past the guards. I was in shirtsleeves and flip-flops and told them I was going for a stroll. I just knocked on a lot of doors until I found a contact.'

Of course you could not, in a terrified city under occupation, simply go and knock on a few doors and discover a resistance contact. Brunyate, it was clear, knew where he was going and who he needed to talk to.[2] It was only much later that his crew found out why.

The Kuwaiti resistance had warned Brunyate that the Iraqis would soon begin rounding up all Westerners in the city's hotels, and they urged him to try to escape. Brunyate was torn between his duty as BA captain and his fear of what would happen to him if the

---

2   In the course of several interviews I did with Brunyate, he was very sketchy on these details. He said he'd knocked on doors looking for empty buildings and ended up meeting a Shia man who was the leader of a resistance cell.

Iraqis got tough. Eventually, he called a secret meeting of his crew. Stewardess Maxine Woods was present:

> Dick called a meeting of his crew, seventeen of us. He said that while he had been out stealing cars he had bumped into a member of the Kuwaiti resistance who had offered him a safe house to accommodate twenty odd people. And he felt that obviously he had to offer it to his crew as a priority, which he did. We had five minutes to make a decision, whether we wanted to stay in the hotel or leave with him. I made the decision to leave because things were not that good at the hotel, soldiers were living on the fourth floor and it seemed very uncomfortable. You had to be realistic that things weren't going to last for ever and, if things really go pear-shaped, I wanted to be with people I knew as a group. Safety in numbers.

Brunyate told them he had personal and military reasons for trying to escape, that there was no way he could be under the Iraqis' control. Later, his crew understood the full significance of his words. According to Hunter, Brunyate explained that the newly discovered safe house could not hold all sixty cabin crew members:

> I am hoping that it will be a safe place for us but I know I have to go as I cannot be rounded up. I will take you guys with me on the understanding that nobody asks the Kuwaitis any questions, nobody does. Everyone does what they ask us to do and what I ask you to do. These people are laying their lives on the line for us until the situation can be resolved. It could be that we will go into hiding and the rest

of the cabin crew will then be released. That could happen – I just don't know.

Or it could be that if we remain in hiding and we are found, maybe we will be punished. I am letting you know all these possible scenarios but what I do want you to know is that I am definitely going, with my engineer and my first officer. I am inviting you to come too but you must not tell anyone else out of the cabin crew.

Brunyate said they had only a few moments to think about their decision. If they joined him they could bring only the smallest of bags. He reiterated the need to do exactly as they were told, or they would put themselves and the people looking after them in serious jeopardy. The crew had to make a very tough decision. They could escape, but they couldn't tell their BA colleagues. There were three crews at the hotel – Brunyate's the crew due to take over Flight 149 and fly it on to Madras; and a third crew on a layover. Among those listening to the escape plan was stewardess Nikki Love, who had begun a romance with steward Michael Cooper. But Cooper was in another crew and she was ordered not to tell him about the escape. Ultimately, she decided to stay behind with him.

Hunter and Woods were packing in their room, waiting for the call, when a sudden thought struck them. They were due to see Laurie O'Toole later that morning as they were supposed to be doing some work for him, but he wasn't there – unusual for the BA manager who was a key source of information and assurance to most passengers.

Eventually, there was a knock on the door. Mike Cooper, Nikki Love's new boyfriend, came in. He had learned of the escape plan. Cooper was an ex-Royal Marine. He was trained to keep calm in a

53

crisis, and he was known at the airline for his steady demeanour. But now he was angry about the plan to escape.

Jacqui Hunter was scared. 'I was very afraid because that was the bubble being well and truly broken. I really didn't know how to respond at that point. I remember one of the girls asking can I take a hairdryer? It was really, really strange. You felt that you were running out on your colleagues, betraying them by not telling them something and you felt you might also be putting yourself at unnecessary risk'.

'I was packing this skinny little bag thinking I don't know, I just don't know. Cooper was saying this is crazy, we should just stay together. It was dreadful, the feeling of leaving and betrayal and going into the unknown, putting your faith into something that you really didn't understand or know much about.'

Then Brunyate called on the phone.

Maxine Woods recalled: 'He said the shit has hit the fan, we need to get out now. He told us to meet him in the car park under the hotel. He told us to try not to make it look obvious that we were leaving. I took my passport and bag and left everything else in the hotel room.'

Jacqui Hunter: 'We said goodbye and Nikki was in floods of tears, and Michael [Cooper] was shaking his head in disbelief at what was happening. We just walked away, and it was terrible. These were people that we'd shared tears and laughter with and others that we couldn't say anything to as we walked by them. Maxine and I talked to each other as if we were going to the gym.'

Woods and Hunter were told to pretend that they were going to the sports complex, but instead they went through the hotel kitchens to the fire escape. They climbed down and entered the underground car park. Brunyate was waiting in a car with his first officer Gordon Gault, engineer Brian Wildman, and purser

Malcolm Butcher. The stewardesses lay on the car floor and they drove out of the car park, avoiding the checkpoints until they reached the safe house. Brunyate sent Gault and Wildman back to the hotel with the intention of bringing more of the crew, but they ran into a new checkpoint and found themselves staring down the barrel of an AK-47. They were ordered out of their vehicle at gunpoint and informed they were under arrest. Coolly, they asked the Iraqis if they could park their car first. The soldiers agreed so they drove it around a corner, abandoned it, and walked as quickly as they dared back to the safe house. It would be their home for the next three weeks.

Others were not so lucky. Stewardesses Helen Curtin and Claire Palmer were making their way down into the basement when they heard a security guard. In a panic, they dived into a closet and hid there until the man passed. Then they crept out, only to have to run into the Ladies' toilet when they heard footsteps again. They sat quietly, but finally decided to leave when they heard the guard starting to padlock the toilets. They returned to their room.

Earthy and some others were ready to leave in a second car and were about to head out of the side entrance when an Iraqi lorry pulled into the car park, ruining their chances. They were trapped. Earthy was left to face the wrath of those left behind when they discovered the plan. He felt it was every man for himself but most of the passengers took a different view. Edward Hammett discovered that the escape vehicle he had so carefully hidden away had been taken. He was furious. Yet there was no sign of Laurie O'Toole to complain to; he was also gone. He had left the hotel on his own and gone into hiding.

The departures of Brunyate and O'Toole left many of the passengers feeling alone, especially when, within hours of the escape, new troops arrived at the hotel and ordered everyone to pack up and prepare to leave: destination unknown.

CHAPTER 4

THE MISSION

Saddam Hussein's Revolutionary Command Council announced that Kuwait was to become the nineteenth province of Iraq and that Kuwait City was to be renamed Kazimah. The Iraqis said they were returning the country to its historical roots. License plates were to be changed to read 'Kuwait: Province of Iraq'. The Kuwaiti flag and pictures of the emir were banned. Saddam gave a triumphant victory speech, a grim reminder, according to Western commentators, of the many intelligence warnings ignored by the West over the previous months.

But while the talk in public was of diplomacy, in London and Washington action plans had been prepared in anticipation of an invasion. A hand-picked group of men had received special 'warning orders' from the British government. Some of the team were military, others were employed by the government in slightly more unofficial roles. The group was briefed individually and told to prepare for a high-risk mission, one that had been approved at the highest levels of government.

A group of soldiers, spies, technicians, and government officials assembled in London. Those who attended worked at the secret heart of the UK government. They were there for a final mission briefing and final orders. Among those present was a representative from the Joint Intelligence Committee (JIC), which advises the government on intelligence matters and is responsible for assessing and giving early warning of external developments and threats likely to affect British interests. JIC members traditionally include the heads of the three security and intelligence agencies – MI5, Britain's domestic intelligence service; MI6, the UK's spies overseas; and GCHQ, the agency that monitors communications – plus representatives of the Foreign and Commonwealth Office, the Ministry of Defence (MOD), the Department of Trade and Industry (DTI), the Home Office (HO), and Her Majesty's Treasury. The room was packed with about twenty-five people, both uniformed and civilian. Also on hand to lend their expertise were communications experts from the Signals Regiment.

The briefing was blunt and detailed. New intelligence suggested that Saddam Hussein intended to invade Kuwait. It was too late to stop him, but it was necessary to ensure that the invasion did not succeed. The team was to get into Kuwait before the invasion started and set themselves up to provide human intelligence: the best kind of intelligence, better at that time than any satellite photo or communications intercept. It was also, of course, the most dangerous kind to acquire.

The team would link up with assets already in Kuwait to provide reliable 'eyes on the ground', mainly in the capital, Kuwait City, in preparation for the invasion, and report back all troop movements, their morale and capability, whether they were Republican Guard or conscripts, and their locations. After locating units, fuel supply dumps, and military storage depots, they could direct air strikes to destroy them. They would also liaise with a resistance network being set up in Kuwait to orchestrate 'a workable and coherent network that could strike Iraqi targets when called upon'.

Most important of all, they had to help predict the intentions of the invading force. Would Iraqi troops go on to threaten the oil fields of Saudi Arabia, so vital to the world's economies? Would the Iraqis take up defensive positions or an aggressive stance with deployment along the Saudi border, thus threatening the kingdom and the oil supply to the West? Saddam Hussein in control of northern Saudi Arabia would alter the balance of power in the Middle East.

On this intelligence rested decisions that could move armies and change the future of nations. If, that is, the team could get in and get the intelligence out.

So great was the fear of Saddam in Saudi Arabia, the team learned, that if the threat materialised, Prime Minister Margaret Thatcher was prepared to contemplate the unthinkable. There would be no time to assemble sufficient assets on the ground to deter an invasion of Saudi Arabia, so Thatcher would, in that event, authorise the use of a tactical nuclear weapon on the battlefield.[3]

The team were shocked by the suggestion – the use of even a small nuclear weapon in southern Kuwait would kill thousands, civilians as well as soldiers, and render parts of the country uninhabitable. It also could pollute the very oil fields in northern Saudi that they were trying to protect.

---

3   In an interview in 2020 for the TV series accompanying this book, Charles Powell denied Thatcher had been prepared to use the nuclear option, but senior sources who attended the meeting told me her threat was clearly outlined. The team being inserted into Kuwait were required to know that it was an option.

Thatcher herself in an oral history of the Gulf War discussed her preparedness to use WMDs (weapons of mass destruction) against Saddam if he used it on Allied troops. She was an enthusiastic advocate for nuclear weapons throughout her career, and at one stage was reported to have been prepared to use them against Argentina in the Falklands War.

There was much gallows humour as the soldiers discussed the prospect. How far away would they have to be before they sent the intelligence that would trigger such an attack? Would the Prime Minister really go that far?

The briefings made clear that at some point Saddam would invade Kuwait – it was just a matter of knowing when. They had intelligence from the Americans via the CIA and NSA (National Security Agency), and even more detailed reports from MI6, reports based on human intelligence, that Saddam's troops were on a war footing, ready to roll. The team viewed up-to-date satellite photographs of Iraqi bases and troops massing on the Kuwaiti border and fuel dumps being erected next to them, ready for a major refuel before the roll into Kuwait.

The briefers said they expected the Kuwaitis to resist the Iraqi invaders for between twenty-four and seventy-two hours, plenty of time for the operatives to deploy.

The intelligence analysts were divided about Saddam's ultimate intentions. Some predicted he would threaten Saudi Arabia as a bluff in the hopes of negotiating a deal with the West that would let him keep Kuwait.

One thing that was definite, though: the logistics of the mission. Detailed discussions had taken place about the best way to get the team into Kuwait. It had to be fast and reliable, and avoid awkward border crossings and checkpoints. The men had to be able to carry their surveillance gear with them without being too conspicuous. It was decided the simplest method was to fly direct to Kuwait. There were some reservations about the potential dangers of this in the lead-up to the briefing, but by the time the briefing began it was already the preferred method of infiltration. The choice was British Airways commercial Flight 149.

Yes, there was a risk to using a civilian aircraft, but on balance it was considered an acceptable risk. After all, given how long the Kuwaitis were expected to fight to defend their country, the plane would have landed, the team deployed, the plane refuelled and crew changed over, and 149 would be long gone by the time Iraqi units reached Kuwait City.

A briefer later recalled, 'It was keep it simple, as they say. It became obvious from HUMINT [human intelligence] coming in via Iraqi, NSA and CIA sources that Saddam was going to invade Kuwait. Flight 149 was viewed as the most expedient way of getting in, one that would arouse the least suspicion. It struck us all as the best method and by far the safest and most secure route in. Made sense to us all.'

The briefing ended and the team left to make final preparations for the trip to Kuwait.

CHAPTER 5

THE INCREMENT

The four two-man teams and an intelligence officer were mostly drawn from a group known as the Increment. The existence of the Inc was, and still is, one of the UK government's best-kept secrets, although it has operated under various names over the years.[4] It is a group designed for so-called black ops, where soldiers and spies are sent on missions of which the government can deny all knowledge.

The Kuwait mission was the latest in a long line of deniable operations involving Special Forces working with spies. The use of soldiers and spies in teams goes back to Northern Ireland and the secret war with the IRA, and the targeting of key Irish terrorists. It was a model later copied by the CIA's paramilitary teams. Civilian transport was often used to ferry these undercover teams around, even if there was a risk to other passengers. In one instance in

---

4   The equivalent group was recently known as E Squadron and took part in an operation to destabilise Colonel Gaddafi in Libya, an operation that backfired when six of the group were discovered, arrested by rebels, and only released after secret negotiations.

1980, a British Airways flight was diverted to Tehran to pick up a team that had been stranded. The plane was sent in despite the fact that the Islamic revolution against the shah was in full swing and Westerners in the city feared for their lives. After the storming of the Iranian Embassy in London in 1980, covered live on TV, brought the SAS (Special Air Service) worldwide publicity, the need to set up another, more secretive, group became apparent.

The Inc is drawn from the SAS and the SBS (the Special Boat Service), the spies of MI5 and MI6, the Intelligence Corps, and the Signals Corps. It includes both men and women. All its members resign their existing Ministry of Defence and government jobs and formally join the private sector. Others who have left their units for one reason or another – sometimes because of injuries – are recycled into the Inc. This last group are known in the business as Dunlops (as in tyres – retreads).The use of the Inc was designed to provide ministers with perfect deniability. Members of the Inc are paid from secret, overseas bank accounts, and, crucially, they are promised immunity from prosecution for 'crimes' committed while overseas. Most of the Inc's missions are run by MI6.

Although the core activity of MI6 is spying – using its own agents and others recruited overseas – its charter, known as the Order Book, requires it to maintain a capability to plan and mount military-style special operations. MI6 officers set the objectives of the operation and obtain clearance for it from the Foreign Secretary. Thereafter, the operations are executed by the Inc, often with the backing of other officers and men from the three branches of the armed forces.

The Inc was perfect for the Kuwait job. The group all had something in common: they were all experienced undercover operatives and their average age was mid-thirties.

The ninth man was an MI6 officer who was supposed to

continue his journey on Flight 149 to Madras after confirming that the team had all successfully got away. He carried a forged Iraqi passport, which could cause him a major problem if he got trapped on the ground in Kuwait after an invasion. But that was not considered likely – Flight 149 would be long gone when the invasion started.

*

The team travelled separately to Heathrow. Their bags contained the team's main radio and surveillance gear, disguised as professional camera and geophysical surveillance equipment to tally with their cover story, which was that they were going to Kuwait to do engineering work. It was assumed that the plane would land, refuel, disembark some of the passengers, and then continue on to its next destination, Madras, before the invasion started. None of the civilians on board would be any the wiser.

No weapons were taken on board. Staff in Kuwait had concealed weapons and rations in various storage places hidden around the city so that they could be collected later. They had also arranged for a couple of locals to work as baggage handlers at the airport to help the team get their gear out of the plane quickly without too many questions being asked. Transport had been organised, too, the vehicles to be collected from a local car dealer just minutes from the international airport.

Despite the team's careful preparations, their last-minute arrival had attracted the interest of some of their fellow passengers and their one-way tickets caused raised eyebrows among the crew. One stewardess in particular was very curious on the journey to Kuwait and started questioning some of the men.

A member of the team recalled:

Both X [his other team member] and I were quite heavily tanned and I was asked by one stewardess if I lived in Kuwait. I replied that I didn't but I had just returned from a survey job in Africa and was now on my way to another in Kuwait. Some cabin crew asked if I was travelling with anyone else and just happened to ask X the same question and two others from our lot even though we all sat well apart on the plane. One stewardess kept pushing the issue, asking if I was a soldier really, which was pretty bizarre to ask midflight. One even openly flirted with X. X joked it off saying he would love to oblige and be her James Bond, but then bluffed that sadly he was just a humble engineer. In retrospect this was a bad idea as it only reinforced his connection with me, having the same job.

The rest of the flight was uneventful. The team believed they would have enough time after landing to get their operation under way.

*

The first the team knew of the invasion was when they left the aircraft. The team could see the evidence with their own eyes – lots of vehicles fleeing the airport, fires seen in the distance, and soon the sound of gunfire. Only minutes later the Iraqi forces arrived.

The British Embassy in Kuwait had gone into crisis mode: it was the middle of the night, the embassy was undermanned, and all the careful planning was now in jeopardy. Meanwhile the mission teams were trying to offload their gear from the aircraft and get out of the airport.

They had disembarked into the transit lounge and were eager to get out as it was obvious fighting was closing in towards the airport terminals. Several passengers commented on how they were allowed to leave already, to which some man and a stewardess replied that they must be 'spy types'. The teams collected their baggage ahead of the other passengers, which caused more chatter.

By the time they got away, they could clearly see large smoke plumes rising and gunfire getting louder and nearer. There was panic everywhere. The men were lucky not to be stopped by hordes of marauding Iraqi troops flooding into the city. They saw several checkpoints where Kuwaitis were dragged from their vehicles and shot on the spot. At one point, an Iraqi helicopter flew parallel to two of the men and their driver before moving away.

One team reached their initial destination, a backstreet warehouse, from which they observed looting, shooting, and beatings.

Eventually an Iraqi patrol turned up. The two men nearly died of heart failure when they saw an armoured personnel carrier slowly crawling down the street towards them with a full troop of Iraqis.

The patrol carried on past them and stopped outside another building several hundred yards down the road. The troops stormed in and a few minutes later emerged with a group of men and two women. They dragged their captives to the patrol vehicle, pulling them by the hair and beating them with their rifle butts. The prisoners were screaming and crying but the soldiers just threw them into the back of the wagon. There was nothing the team could do. They had a job to do, which was to stay in hiding. They were relieved when the patrol drove off.

The men sat it out for four long days. They were becoming dehydrated and their rations were running low. On the fourth day, they heard a noise outside. In walked a Kuwaiti teenager, followed by an even younger boy. They had bread and water. The boys looked up as if expecting to see someone. For fifteen minutes the two men waited, not moving, not making a sound. When they were sure the coast was clear they made themselves known to the boys, who told them they had been sent to help. In addition to the much needed food and water, they brought good news: their father would come the following day with a tractor and trailer to pick the men up and take them to their objective, the town on the Saudi border. The boys' father was a farmer. He had permission by the Iraqis to travel around the southern part of Kuwait to collect pipes to assist the invaders with their water supplies.

One of the team later recalled: 'How the man was contacted I still don't know to this day but the opportunity presented itself so we had to take it. The two young lads left fast and scuttled away. We were tired, hungry, and the longer things dragged on, the worse we began to feel, lying on the hard wooden floor.'

Early the following day the farmer duly arrived with his tractor and busied himself loading the pipes. He did not look in the direction of their hiding place, nor attempt to contact them. The team watched and waited; minutes later, they saw why the farmer was ignoring them. A jeep with two Iraqi soldiers on board had followed him to the warehouse.

'It was tense, as the farmer opened the double doors below us and we heard him talking to the two Iraqi soldiers. The farmer started to hitch up a large double trailer and then to place large irrigation pipes one by one onto it. The Iraqis were not helping. God, they must have been there a couple of hours and we are thinking fuck off, they are only pipes, what are you waiting for?'

Fear mixed with admiration as the two men watched the wiry farmer lift the heavy pipes onto the trailer, an awesome feat of strength. The Iraqis just kept watching. Eventually they left, and they gathered their gear and went down to meet the Kuwaiti.

'I walked into the open warehouse and the farmer simply smiled, no hesitation or fear at all. He was old. He smiled so I knew he was our man. We soon established that he had been issued with a paper and pass permit that would allow him to drive nearly all the way to the Saudi border, despite the long distance, with these pipes to be delivered to an Iraqi unit digging in. It was going to be a long and arduous and uncomfortable journey, but we had no other option really, and as he had shown up in the first place, it all seemed to be following a plan, of a sort.'

The plan involved the two men climbing into a wooden box in the middle of the double trailer. The box was then to be covered with pipes. Each of the two men had the same thought: the box looked exactly like a coffin. It was a hot and hellish journey. Once the two men were in the box and the pipes were placed over them, the farmer drove off, slowly and steadily heading south, mile after mile. In the box they were jammed close together. The tractor stopped frequently at vehicle checkpoints, each time filling them with dread. Each time the farmer produced his transit papers and was waved through. But there was no break for the two men hiding in their box.

My nerves were fit for fraying. You have just got to suffer in silence and survive the best way you can because that is the name of the game, basically. You push out your parameters. When you think you have gone to the limit, you push them out even further.

Eventually, after eight hours' travelling, we stopped two miles short of a small village. Very quickly the old man removed the pipes and we got out of our mobile coffin. We offered to help him restack the load but he ushered us away fast as we were in almost open desert ground. He indicated the direction of a small, mainly disused factory and warehouse stowage container park about a mile from us. With that we headed off, stiff as hell and still bloody hungry.

The village that they walked into was small, with one huge old hangar made from corrugated steel. Fenced-off areas, which appeared to be full of containers stacked high, surrounded the town. It was a storage location and transit dump for containers, with a small petrol station that refuelled trucks passing through.

A main road ran from north to south directly through the middle of the village and headed off towards the Saudi border. Another road intersected it in the village. This formed a crossroads that headed east and west towards major towns on either side. The place was almost deserted apart from two Iraqi trucks and a small detachment of about twenty Iraqi soldiers manning the fuel station. The village was a perfect spot from which to observe Iraqi troop movements across southern Kuwait and up to the Saudi border.

Under cover of darkness they made their way to one of the old container storage areas on the farthest eastern side of town. Several open-sided, hangar-type warehouses stood with a jumble of containers stored within them, sheltered from the heat but still open on all sides. The two men climbed into one of the containers, which was stacked on top of two others. They were able to look directly south, towards the Saudi border, and in the far distance they could see the first border signs. From their hideaway it was about five hundred meters to the main road. They had a perfect view of the long convoys of vehicles moving up and down the road.

Here the troops were Republican Guard with Russian-built T-54 and T-72 tanks. The two men had found their target, Saddam's elite troops, and they quickly sent this information back to the UK commanders. Later, they were able to observe the Iraqi troops digging in to defensive rather than offensive positions, indicating that for the moment they were not planning to encroach across the border into Saudi Arabia. This was human intelligence of the most valuable kind, the kind that even the best satellite surveillance could not provide – 'it was gold, it was platinum, it was the crown jewels'.

The two men were close enough to the Iraqi forces to identify individual units – and close enough to be caught if they were careless. They had to keep still, and keep quiet, for hours on end. Once, they were alarmed when they attracted the attention of a friendly dog. It started hanging around the containers, sitting directly in front of their hideaway, looking up at them. If the Iraqis down the road spotted the dog, they might wonder what was attracting its attention and walk over to check it out. One of the men made an improvised catapult of some rubber bands and fired an old rusty bolt at the dog. It ran off. But it returned an hour later just as the sun was coming up so he repeated the exercise and this time hit the dog right on the nose. The dog yelped in pain, so loudly that for a moment the soldiers thought the Iraqi patrol nearby must have heard. But nothing happened. The dog never returned and they settled down to wait out the day.

The container was unbelievably hot and they were sweating and dehydrating fast with their very limited supply of water. During the day they counted eleven major convoys of Iraqi troops, four of which were transporters moving T-54s and the more modern T-72s to forward positions. They managed to get away another signal. By nightfall, the two men were completely exhausted – hungry, thirsty, and cramping up. Worse, one of them had become ill and was losing strength rapidly. He had severe food poisoning. Unless he got help, and soon, the two men were not going to be leaving Kuwait.

CHAPTER 6

A LONG WALK HOME

The planners of the mission had some of the world's finest troops at their disposal, the latest communications equipment, satellite coverage, the best intelligence assets in the Middle East, and the resources of MI5, MI6 and the CIA, plus the Pentagon's Defense Intelligence Agency. It was an operation of the highest importance, personally approved by Prime Minister Margaret Thatcher with the backing of the Bush administration in Washington.

And what sort of rations were left for the men to pick up to sustain them on this top secret, highest-priority mission? Expired ration packs. This food included tins of processed cheese.

Both men were hungry. One of them didn't like processed cheese. The other tucked in – it was only after he had eaten more than half the tin that the men noticed its use-by date. He also ate some of the remnants of the bread they had received from the young Kuwaiti lad before their trip south in the tractor trailer. The men were not too worried though; they had both eaten food well past its date on other missions, without any ill effects.

Within an hour X started getting stomach cramps, which they initially attributed to the onset of dehydration. His comrade crawled out of the container and climbed down to the ground to see if he could find any extra water, but there were Iraqi troops nearby and he was forced to return empty-handed.

By this time, X was getting increasingly sick. Within two hours he was retching but bringing up only bile. His condition deteriorated rapidly, due to a combination of the sickness, tiredness, and now cold, as well as the lack of proper food and drinking water. His colleague gave his companion sips from their last remaining water bottle, putting it to X's mouth at intervals until he was able to swallow it and keep the fluid down.

But it was clear their mission could not go forward. 'I sent a report and request that we needed immediate exfil [exfiltration] as in dire situation. We received confirmation that a US CH-53 helicopter would be on route from a US ship. It would land nearly twelve miles away to our northeast, away from the Iraqi concentration of forces. It would land within a low depression of a dried-up wadi delta. Problem was we had to get there by 0400 or CSAR would have to abort as it would be flying out in sunrise time.'

The proposed rescue point was not the closest safe haven: that was just down the road they were watching, which led to the border with Saudi Arabia and friendly troops. But the area between their hide-out and the border was crawling with Iraqi patrols. The wadi was in the opposite direction, the less obvious route, and it was in the middle of an empty desert. They were twelve miles from a potential rescue, twelve miles that two supremely fit men could easily cover at a run. But they were no longer two supremely fit soldiers. They were both tired, hungry, thirsty, and suffering from cramps, but X was much worse – he was seriously ill and at times incoherent. It was clear that he could not walk twelve miles, let alone run. He could hardly stand. 'We have got to go,' his colleague told him. 'We have got to get to the rendezvous.'

X replied that he could not move. *Leave me and make a run for it yourself*, he told his mate, who refused point-blank to leave his fellow soldier behind:

It was a case of do-or-die really so we ditched the majority of our gear, just carrying our weapons, the remainder of our food, ammo, and radio set. We buried the rest by hand, under a container. We had to make the pickup point or we would be in serious shit, and X would in no way make it back to a road and the option of surrendering.

I sent our last sit-rep [situation report], saying we were on our way but also stated that if we missed the deadline we would stay holed up at the wadi until the following night. Our batteries were almost dead and that turned out to be the last signal I sent. I knew staying an extra day was not much of an option. A day out in the full sun if we missed the CSAR would be fatal in our present dehydrated condition.

The two men crouched low as they left the container complex. They headed off to the northeast into the open desert, which was completely flat as far as the eye could see. X was in agony as he kept cramping up and still occasionally trying to vomit. The night was cold. X was running a high temperature but he was longer sweating, as he was dehydrated, and was getting worse. His speech became slurred and his vision blurred.

After less than a mile and a superhuman effort, X collapsed completely. He was just a dead weight. His mate had no option then but to hoist the sick man over his shoulder in a fireman's carry, to try to ignore his own pain and concentrate on putting one foot in front of the other. He visualised the CSAR helicopter and the moment when the two men would be on it, and safe.

A mile further on, both of his legs cramped up and he fell to the ground in agony. X slipped off his shoulder and lost consciousness.

'All the training you have done... you feel you have pushed all your parameters as a human being. Now another big ask is being thrown at you and you know to survive, you have just got to keep pushing yourself.'

He lay still for a few minutes, gathering the last vestiges of his physical and mental tenacity. He forced himself to his feet and grabbed the water bottle. He realised that he had no choice but to drink the last of their water, a few sips, something to keep him going. He picked X up again and moved on, saying a silent prayer that the ground was flat. He could not possibly have walked up a hill.

He moved on doggedly through the desert night, stopping every so often to read his map and compass and get his bearings, as well as to listen out for the sounds of vehicles that would signal an Iraqi patrol. But he heard nothing. To keep himself going he would pick a point on the horizon, a rock or a bump, then head for that, measuring his paces, trying to keep to a straight line although his strides were all over.

My arms cramped up at one point as well as a muscle down my neck, which was so painful it brought tears to my eyes. But I dared not stop and put X down as I knew I would not be able to start again.

You know you are on your own, you are on reserves you never knew existed, but you know that you can't stop, because to stop is death. So you mentally cut away the pain barrier, you strip away all the human points of your senses, and you are going along that sand feeling like you are six feet off the ground because you are no longer feeling anything, it is all in your head. You are in that wadi, that's where you are, your brain is saying *the wadi, the wadi, the wadi* and nothing else.

When he stopped to take a reading, the reality of the pain and the place they were in hit home: 'I knew that if I had stopped and made a hide for the following day and then tried to make the pick-up point the following night, I was fucked. It was the most exhausted I have ever felt in my life, before or since. And thirsty, fuck, I wanted to drink and drink and drink.'

They walked for hours, as he concentrated on putting one foot in front of the other. He stopped for another reading. When he looked up he could see a change in the desert ahead of him. The ground seemed to drop away. It was the sign of a wadi. He checked his map and compass again. It looked like the right location. About a mile away. He drove himself forward, afraid that they would miss the pickup time. They were so close now, so close to safety, so close to the chance to lie down and have a drink of water.

They reached the wadi. He put X down and double-checked the map. They were in the right place. They had made it, with twelve minutes to spare. Soon he heard the sound of a helicopter flying fast and low across the desert, the sound coming closer. He pulled out a strobe and flashed the recognition sign. He was afraid the helicopter would miss them and fly straight overhead but the pilot spotted them from two miles away.

Two men jumped out with a stretcher and carried X on board, then inserted a saline drip into his arm. 'All I wanted to do was just lie down in that helicopter. That's all I wanted to do. As soon as I hit that chopper I was gone. Get me out of here.'

The CH-53 took off and headed out under cover of darkness

across southern Kuwait to a cruiser, the USS *Antietam*, waiting in the Gulf. As he slipped into a deep sleep – 'more like a coma' – he wondered what had happened to the rest of the mission. Where were the other teams?

CHAPTER 7
CAPTIVITY

As the Iraqi forces tightened their control over Kuwait, and the hostages awaited their fate, in Washington and London there was feverish debate about the best response to Saddam's actions. Negotiations? Remove him by force? An embargo? At the White House, there was division; President George H. W. Bush seemed uncertain about whether to commit American troops. Margaret Thatcher favoured an uncompromising reaction: she was on the phone every day urging the president to draw a line in the sand and put together a military coalition to drive the Iraqis out of Kuwait.

The hostages were a major problem in any military planning. The allies set up a rescue-planning team, but the task was daunting. Several thousand Westerners were scattered all over Kuwait and Iraq.

In the UK, relatives of the passengers were told that everything possible was being done to bring them home. Journalists who asked why the plane had been allowed to land in Kuwait were told in off-the-record briefings that Flight 149 had landed well before the invasion had started. It was just 'bad luck' that it had been caught on the ground. Lord King, then the British Airways chairman, visited Downing Street to demand an explanation. Thatcher reportedly told him that the best advice had been that Saddam would not invade, that he was just 'sabre-rattling'. Everyone was caught by surprise when the tanks crossed the border, she said.

The Americans were worried about their embassy staff, now surrounded by Iraqi troops and tanks and with limited food and water supplies. Pentagon planners began drawing up a rescue plan. They called it Operation Pacific Wind and it was typically complicated; it involved F-15E Strike Eagle fighters, attack helicopters, F-117 stealth attack fighters, AWACS radar planes, and a Delta Force team in helicopters. Two stealth fighters were to attack Kuwait City's power plants, knocking out all the city lights, while two others would focus on the antiaircraft guns on the hotel across the road, and its officers' quarters. In the diversion thus created, helicopters carrying troops would swoop in and land in the embassy compound and fly out with the rescued staff. Delta Force began practicing at Fort Bragg and in the Nevada desert, using mock-ups of the embassy.

*

In Kuwait City, two of the Inc teams had reached their rendezvous points without detection and linked up with a resistance network. Soon, they were preparing to carry out their intelligence-gathering tasks. But the third team had disappeared. No messages were being sent back to its UK commanders.

In fact, these two men had been picked up at the airport by friendly Kuwaitis and provided with weapons and rations. They had then been driven to what was to be their observation point close to the airport, an area now swarming with Iraqi troops. But they walked straight into a building that was already occupied by a heavily armed Iraqi platoon. Outnumbered and seriously outgunned, they had had no choice but to surrender. They were taken away for questioning and their gear was examined.

The men told their captors that they were engineers, a cover story reinforced by their one-way tickets to Kuwait City. When asked about their guns, they replied that they had bought them for protection because the city was dangerous. Bizarrely, the Iraqis believed their story, perhaps because the weapons had been acquired locally and were not of the standard usually carried by Special Forces. Had the men been exposed as spies or Special Forces, they would have been tortured. Despite some hours of questioning, the engineering cover story held up and the men were added to the general population of human shields. They were taken to one of the hotels, ending up alongside some of the other passengers from the flight, who were of course none the wiser.

*

One of the first tasks of the mission teams had been to report on the Iraqi army's positions, telling Washington and London whether the invasion of Kuwait was the end game or whether an attack on Saudi Arabia and the seizure of its oil fields was the ultimate objective, which would give Saddam a stranglehold over the West's economies.

The teams saw clear evidence that the Iraqi forces were digging in and adopting a defensive rather than an aggressive posture. At the front line, they were digging huge tank berms, sand traps designed to repel a tank attack. The observers quickly passed messages back to London and Washington, to say that it did not look as though Saddam was preparing to attack Saudi Arabia.

The Saudis themselves did not believe they were about to be

invaded. They had sent scout teams across the border the day after the invasion and these reported that there were no Iraqi troops in sight. An American offer to send a fighter squadron to assist them was turned down.

Soon afterward, the Saudis received another, more unusual offer of help. A member of a wealthy family met with King Fahd's brother, Prince Sultan bin Abdul Aziz, the defence secretary, to propose a jihad against the Iraqis. The man, who had fought with the mujahideen in Afghanistan, told Prince Sultan he could raise an army of one hundred thousand holy warriors to drive the Iraqis out. He said they had to do the job themselves and that American troops must be prevented from being stationed on Saudi soil at all costs.

Prince Sultan promised to pass on the offer but said it was likely to be declined. The wealthy Saudi and potential jihad leader, a man named Osama and one of twenty heirs to the bin Laden fortune, stormed out of the meeting. Osama bin Laden warned that American troops on sacred Saudi soil would be an insult to all of his faith.

US Defense Secretary Dick Cheney together with General Norman Schwarzkopf arrived in Riyadh, the Saudi capital, for a meeting with King Fahd. They came with the words of President H. W. Bush: both publicly and privately, he was saying the invasion 'will not stand'.

Despite the intelligence from the Inc teams in Kuwait, Cheney and Schwarzkopf told the king that Iraq might move against Saudi Arabia. They showed him satellite photographs of the Iraqi positions and outlined their plans to bring in two hundred thousand allied troops. Richard A. Clarke, who sat in on the meeting as a member of the State Department (he later became head of counterterrorism for the United States between 1998 and 2003), described the meeting:

Cheney asked General Schwarzkopf to brief the king on what the Iraqis *could* do with the large military force they had just inserted into Kuwait. With large maps and photos, the general showed that the Iraqi tanks *could* be in Dhahran, the Saudi oil city, in a matter of hours. Cheney then played his card, an offer from President George H. W. Bush to deploy thousands of US forces to defend the kingdom. The US forces would leave when the Iraqi crisis passed or at any time the king wanted them to go; we sought no permanent military presence, Cheney assured Fahd.

The king turned to his brothers and solicited their reaction. They were unanimously opposed to an American intervention, to US forces being on the soil of the land of the two holy mosques. There had been much internal criticism of the decision to bring French forces in eleven years earlier to retake the Holy Mosque of Mecca from religious fanatic terrorists. It sounded to us from the brothers' discussion that the king would reject the American offer.

Fahd talked at length about how hard he and his family had worked to build a modern country from a backward desert collection of tribes. I wondered where he was going with the monologue when he finally stopped, took a breath, and then said, 'Tell President Bush to send the forces. Send them all. Send them quickly. I accept his word that the forces will leave when this is over.' The decision and its clarity surprised us. King Fahd thought about it for a moment, then said, simply, 'Yes.' The US delegation was stunned; they had the go-ahead to set up bases with troops and weapons in one of the world's most devout Muslim nations.

General Schwarzkopf said later he 'almost fell off his chair' when the king gave his approval.

The Americans moved quickly. Two squadrons of F-15 fighters were deployed from Diego Garcia and Guam were to Saudi Arabia. The 82nd Airborne Division, two thousand men with Sheridan tanks and anti-tank weapons, arrived in Dhahran. They were to be the 'trip wire' – if Saddam's army attacked Saudi Arabia, the 82nd's job was to slow them down until help arrived. Help *was* on the way – four US aircraft carriers, the *Eisenhower*, *Independence*, *Saratoga* and *John F. Kennedy*. This was the beginning of what was to be called Operation Desert Shield.

When Osama bin Laden discovered that the US offer had been accepted in preference to his 'holy warriors' and American troops were going to arrive on holy soil, he vowed revenge. He proved to be a man of his word.

This was truly a moment when history changed gears.

Clarke himself later wrote:

The rise of Al-Qaeda in the 1990s, the US invasion of Afghanistan, the second US war with Iraq, the rise of ISIS, all followed that August 1990 decision to deploy large US forces to the Gulf. There were many social and political pressures that contributed to the upheaval in the Arab and Islamic world, but the continued US military presence in the region and the way those US forces were used were major contributors. This chain of events also contributed to the Arab Spring and the creation of failed states in Iraq, Yemen, Libya, and Syria. Taken together, these events caused the deaths of hundreds of thousands, turned millions of people into refugees, and cost trillions of dollars.

It was a momentous decision made as the Iraqis were taking up *defensive* positions in Kuwait, a misuse of intelligence with consequences that have lasted decades.

There is in fact almost no evidence that Saddam intended to invade Saudi Arabia in the lead-up to the now famous (or infamous) meeting in Riyadh, or that the US and UK governments had any intelligence to contradict the reporting on the ground.[5]

Jean Heller, a journalist with Florida's *St. Petersburg Times* (now *Tampa Bay Times*), obtained satellite photos of Kuwait that did not support Bush's claim of an imminent Iraqi invasion. In fact, the photos showed no sign of a massive Iraqi troop build-up in Kuwait: 'The troops that were said to be massing on the Saudi border and that constituted the possible threat to Saudi Arabia that justified the US sending of troops do not show up in these photographs. And when the US Department of Defense (DOD) was asked to provide evidence that would contradict our satellite evidence, it refused to do it.'

The pictures, taken by a Soviet satellite on 11 and 13 September 1990, were analyzed by two satellite image specialists: Peter Zimmerman, a nuclear physicist, and a former image specialist for the Defense Intelligence Agency who wished to remain anonymous.

As the paper reported, the specialists saw few Iraqi troops or

---

5   Analyst Robert Farley, writing in *The National Interest* magazine (April 9, 2015), said, 'Could the Iraqi Army have sustained an advance into Saudi Arabia? Into the northern border areas, perhaps. Into the interior, probably not. The Iraqi Army had little experience with long range logistics over forbidding terrain (most of the fighting in the Iran-Iraq War had taken place along a relatively small region of the border), and managing a heavily armored force with huge fuel and ammunition requirements is no small task. American, and even Saudi, airstrikes would have greatly complicated the already overwhelming task facing Iraqi logisticians.

The Iran-Iraq War also demonstrated that the Iraqis had little flair for improvising operations on the fly. The successful offensives of the last year of the war, as with the invasion of Kuwait, depended on extremely careful, detailed planning with constant rehearsal and good intelligence. Thus, there was little chance that Iraqi forces could have successfully undertaken an offensive into Saudi Arabia without prior planning. Hussein and his senior commanders almost certainly understood this, which is one reason they apparently gave little consideration to a full invasion of Saudi Arabia.'

weapons in Kuwait. They said the roads showed no evidence of a massive tank invasion, there were no tent cities or troop concentrations, and the main Kuwaiti air base appeared deserted. Both analysts agreed there were several possible explanations for their inability to spot Iraqi forces: the troops could have been well camouflaged, or they could have been widely dispersed, or the Soviets deliberately or accidentally produced a photo taken before the Iraqi invasion. But the latter explanation was not considered likely and, given the reported massive deployment, the specialists found it 'really hard to believe' they could miss them even if they were well camouflaged and/or widely dispersed.

An Iraqi general later claimed that Saddam had issued preparatory orders to go into Saudi, but crucially, the orders came only *after* King Fahd had invited American troops in and after they started to arrive.

As Osama brooded on the rejection of his plan, the Iraqis moved to tighten their control of Kuwait. Iraqi television announced on 15 August that all Americans, Western Europeans and Australians were to report to hotels in Kuwait City or face 'unspecified difficulties'.

The BBC World Service broadcast the following, approved by the Foreign Office, and it was heard all over Kuwait and Iraq:

In a very grave and sinister development, the Iraqi authorities have advised that the British community should assemble at a single point in Kuwait. The United States community has received a similar instruction. The Iraqi authorities have advised that, in order to better protect the British community... that British citizens should move to the Regency Palace Hotel on 16 August. The Iraqis have stated that, if the British community does not move voluntarily, it will face unspecified difficulties. The embassy takes this to mean that the Iraqis will take measures to ensure that British citizens are moved to one location.

If you choose to move, please take all food from your residence with you to give to the hotel management to help with their food stocks. We suggest that you take no more than one suitcase per person with you to the hotel.

The border with Saudi Arabia is officially closed. The Iraqis have said that foreigners may travel to Baghdad but are not permitted to leave Iraq. As for those citizens in Baghdad, the British Embassy is doing all that it can to assist them. Items such as toiletries, books, and games are being provided by the embassy... a doctor is on duty and medicines are being provided as required.

This announcement led to several agonising days for the Westerners hiding out in Kuwait. Should they turn themselves in, or stay where they were and hope for the best?

For those already at the Regency Palace Hotel, though, there was no choice. They were already prisoners. The calm and unity that had sustained the passengers and crew from Flight 149 was shattered by the escape of Brunyate, O'Toole, and the others.

Maureen Chappell recalled the aftermath of their escape: 'We were given the impression that if anyone was going, we were all going, as a group. We thought everything was being worked out together, as a whole group. It was either all or nothing. And when we found that they'd gone, the mood changed and we thought well, are we being looked after by them or aren't we? And I think some people thought then that you were on your own, really. We started to wonder what would happen now.'

John Chappell felt that Brunyate especially had been put in a tough position. He could understand why he had gone. The captain had let it be known that he had a military background and there were good reasons why he could not fall into the hands of the Iraqis.

O'Toole's departure was a different matter. With him gone, the Chappells felt the passengers and remaining crew had lost their link to the outside world through the embassy.

Maureen Chappell said, 'O'Toole would come in and give daily reports and he would be saying, we're negotiating, we're going to get a plane, you're going to be flown out – and then when he left we felt quite devastated and let down.'

Most passengers decided it was now every man for himself. But the bitterness among the passengers paled in comparison with that of the BA crew, like Charles Kristiansson, who felt that both the captain and the airline's manager had left them in an impossible situation, not only still captive but also dealing with the passengers alone.

The situation quickly worsened for those left behind. Angry Iraqi soldiers arrived within hours of the escape, racing through the hotel corridors and blowing whistles and banging on doors. Then sudden spot searches were made of the rooms, with everyone forced to assemble in the dining room while this was done. Everyone went to bed that night wondering what terrors the next day held.

The night after the escape, they were woken in the middle of the night and told to gather their belongings and report to the lobby. The hotel manager addressed them. 'You are either going to be taken by bus to Basra and flown to Baghdad, or taken to Kuwait airport and flown to Baghdad,' he announced. He spoke pleadingly to the group but his face said something different: he was sceptical of the Iraqi plan. It was 1 a.m. The passengers were divided into family groups and assigned to different buses. Crew members joined together as 'family' for mutual protection. Air stewards Mike Cooper and Nikki Love decided to travel together as a couple. The Chappells joined a line to pick their passports out of a pile and identify themselves to the Iraqi soldiers. They were told that the family groups would be going to Basra by road and then by air from Basra to Baghdad. As the Chappells boarded the coach, the hotel manager was handing out bottles of water. 'You're not going to Basra,' he whispered to John and Maureen. 'I know where you're going. It's not Basra.'

The manager did not have time to tell them their real destination. Finally the coach, a minibus carrying eighteen people, headed towards the airport with an armed escort. Hours went by. Several turns and changes of direction later, even experienced locals on the coach did not know where they were. It was clear they were not on the way to the airport, or to Basra. Finally the bus stopped in the desert, in the middle of nowhere, in the pitch black night. It was very cold, and very quiet. They were a long way from any traffic, or town, or military outpost. They could glimpse some Iraqi soldiers waiting in vehicles nearby. *It's a rest stop*, said one optimist from the back of the bus, slightly too loudly.

John was frightened. When he looked at the faces of the Iraqi escort they looked nervous, too. *We have been taken out to the desert to be shot and disposed of*, thought John. *This is it*, thought Maureen, *they are going to shoot us now.*

The Iraqis got out of the coach and more soldiers pulled up in a jeep and trucks. Some of the people on the coach became hysterical. People who had claimed at the hotel that they had run out of cigarettes suddenly produced them and started smoking. The last cigarette of the condemned.

The Chappells tried to reassure their children but young John and Jennifer could sense the fear. Jennifer Chappell remembered,

We were driven for a while round and round Kuwait, here there and everywhere. They were either trying to avoid hotspot areas or just confuse people as to where they were taking us. We eventually pulled up – I think it was an oil refinery. And there was a little tin shack that they pulled up in front of, I mean very small, the kind that looks like the outdoor toilet in an Australian outback film. Just a tiny little tin shack. At that point I thought that that was it, they were going to take us all of the bus, stuff us all in there, and just shoot us.

I remember thinking I wasn't bothered about myself or my brother or even my Mum to be honest, for some reason all I was bothered about was my Dad. I was just worried about losing him. I just thought they were going to kill us all and leave us piled up in that shack.

More of the passengers began to cry. Nikki Love sobbed and said repeatedly that they were going to die. Mike Cooper kept telling her that things were going to be all right. The fear was fed by the obvious nervousness of the guards, who stood around with their weapons. They seemed to be waiting for orders. The group sat on the buses and waited to learn their fate.

CHAPTER 8

SURVIVAL

The Iraqi soldiers paced about in the desert night, trying to keep warm. Inside the coaches, the hostages waited. Some prayed silently, others talked quietly. There were sobs and the occasional swear word. But no one moved, or got up, or tried to run. They just sat there as the hours ticked by – waiting to die, most of them thought. Except it wasn't hours, it just felt like it. No more than thirty minutes had elapsed when those who still had the courage to look out of the window saw the Iraqi troops climb back inside their trucks. Seconds later, the buses' engines started up and the convoy moved slowly down the road. There were no cheers or claps or sighs of relief. Most of the passengers were just glad to be alive. Besides, they did not know what was going to happen next: only that their 'execution' seemed to have been postponed, at least for the moment. (The passengers never did find out the reason for the long wait in the desert. One theory was that one of vehicles had got stuck in the sand and the soldiers looked scared because they did not want to be sitting ducks out there, open to attack by the resistance fighters.) The passengers were none the wiser after their next stop, either.

The convoy headed off again and arrived at their destination just as the sun rose. The IBI camp, named after the contractor that built it, had until recently been the home of the British forces liaison team (BLT) in Kuwait, people like Jerry Blears of REME and his family. The BLT soldiers had all gone – they were 'guests' of the Iraqis elsewhere – but their families remained and were now surrounded by Iraqi troops.

The busloads of hostages were lined up in the blazing sun and allocated accommodation. One of them, a long-term resident of Kuwait, suggested to the guards that it would be quicker if everyone got out of the heat and the hostages sorted things out between themselves. Inevitably this resulted in a free-for-all. Little did the others know that this man had previously lived at the camp, and he went straight to a house where he knew there was a freezer full of food. Others ended up with nothing. This was the first of many disputes over food.

The Chappells found accommodation next door to the family of Stuart Lockwood, whose father was a warrant officer with the liaison team. Their new home was Bungalow Number 8, IBI Camp, Kuwait. But home wasn't a word they wanted to use.

The house had been ransacked. Personal effects, discarded rubbish, clothes, and furniture were piled up inside; indeed they had to push hard against the door even to get in. The whole place was filthy. The bathroom was so disgusting that John refused to let Maureen and the children in. The toilet had been used repeatedly without being flushed and there was excrement on the walls and the floor. John did the clean-up job of his life.

The kitchen wasn't much better – there was food all over the floor, and the fridge and freezer doors had been left open so all the contents were putrid. It took two days to clean up the mess. The Iraqis came knocking on the door, asking, 'Have you got children?' The families with children got a case of Carnation milk, and their parents got cigarettes. Later a pickup truck arrived with other provisions. John thought that everyone would go out and queue up and the food would be shared. Instead, it was like a day at the sales, another free-for-all that left some families with lots of food and others with hardly any at all. The Chappells got very little.

That night there were stern words at a camp meeting. It was finally decided that all the food deliveries would be placed in the bungalow of BA steward George Parris and rationed from there. It quickly emerged that some people were 'luckier' than others, finding untouched and still edible food supplies in their bungalows. One family was having bacon and eggs every morning for breakfast while the Chappells subsisted on bits of cornflakes and Carnation milk. Later their diet expanded – to pasta, rice, and more of the dreaded Carnation milk. One meal was put together from a packet of cornflakes, which had been found spilled all over the dusty floor. After the children had gone to bed, John and Maureen picked the cornflakes off the floor, one by one, and cleaned the dust off them before putting them in a container. They were served with Carnation milk the next day. The adults were always hungry; their children got most of the food but they were still hungry, too. According to Maureen, life at the camp was 'a guaranteed three-stone weight loss'. They started calling the camp the Health Farm.

John Chappell went out scavenging daily, looking through the abandoned homes for anything edible. If he did find anything, he hid it on a bed in the villa, which he made up to look as if someone was sleeping in it, to deter thieves. Jennifer and her brother went searching, too. Jennifer recalled:

93

Always hungry, I was, always hungry. I did find some ice lollies though, some ice lollies and some sweets. There was a clubhouse and at the back of the clubhouse was the children's play area and we were exploring in there. We found some stilts and things like that and some games. And there was a freezer in there and being children you're nosey, and I opened the freezer and was quite shocked to find that the freezer actually did still work and there were the ice lollies and sweets. And I think that's where where the 'look after after yourself' kind of thing comes in, because we decided that we weren't going to tell the other children what we'd found and we sat there and just stuffed ourselves.

There may have been only a limited supply of ice lollies, but alcohol was a different matter. The warrant officer and sergeants' mess of the IBI camp had plentiful supplies, untouched by the marauding Iraqis. There was a kit to brew beer and a local spirit called 'flash'. Flash was an acquired taste, a bit like vodka according to the optimists, but it had to be cut with two-thirds water to make it drinkable. Otherwise it was like 'nitro-glycerine, handle with care', went the camp joke. One night three of the French lads, passengers from Flight 149, drank some unadulterated flash and they weren't seen for three days – they were practically comatose.

There were forty-eight people in camp, eight from Flight 149 and the rest seized locally. A high barbed wire fence and big gates completely enclosed the camp. Initially the Iraqis wanted to put soldiers inside the camp, but the hostages persuaded them it would be better if they stayed outside. They promised there would be no trouble and no escape attempts.

One day the Chappells were visited by three Iraqi officers who marched into their bungalow, the family's passports in their hands. The Chappells had to line up in front of them while the officers sat down and interrogated them. 'Why do you go to India so often?' the senior officer asked.

'I work for the GE company. My company manufactures light fittings and General Electric appliances. I am one of the managers of the factory in Madras,' John replied. This was a total fabrication. He did not want the Iraqis to know that he worked for a major defence contractor, Marconi Avionics.

'Are you a chief engineer?' the Iraqi asked.

'As you can see, I'm only a small engineer,' John replied. The Iraqis laughed and then left.

*

Flight 149's passengers and crew were by now scattered all over Kuwait. Edward Hammett was taken to Kuwait University. In a lecture hall, his group came face-to-face with the Mukhabarat, the secret police.

Iraqi troops separated the passengers into random groups while an officer from the Mukhabarat used a bullhorn to tell them they were being taken to different locations 'for your own protection and safety and for the protection and safety of the Iraqi army'. The secret police would take everyone's names, he said, once they had been divided up.

There were some tearful farewells in the lecture hall. Some of the stewardesses cried because they had been separated from their friends. 'We got the feeling that they couldn't survive without each other,' Hammett remembers. The various groups organised some discreet swapping of people between the groups while the Iraqi soldiers' backs were turned and before the secret police collected the names.

Hammett's group was taken to a villa, where twenty men and eight women were held in three bedrooms. As there were just two beds, most slept on the floor. Through the two windows they had a view of what looked like the gardens of the emir's palace. The day room had a television where the group gathered to watch Margaret Thatcher talk about the invasion. The flight had landed before the start of the invasion, she said. *Why is she lying?* the passengers asked themselves. Some of them wondered what had happened to the young men who had boarded the plane at the last minute.

Hammett's group was mostly British. Other hostages included David Fort, who had been travelling with Hammett, and Canadian Willard Nernberg, on Flight 149. They all worked for the same company.

The captives lived cheek-by-jowl with the Iraqi military; the villa had been turned into a brigade headquarters and communications centre, with senior officers living upstairs. It very quickly became clear that the Westerners were human shields, designed to deter allied air raids. Their proximity to the officers meant food was not really a problem as they shared the same cooks. Sometimes they even got breakfast – eggs and cereal.

Hammett recalled one morning meal:

Those poor old Iraqi cooks were pretty hard done by. They used to get slapped around. Not only were they looking after all of us but thirty to forty officers upstairs, and there were only two of them in a tiny little domestic kitchen.

I came down for breakfast one day and the cook had made scrambled eggs with toast and he put those in front of me. The Iraqi officer saw them and went ape as he hadn't got his. He saw the cook serving me and he went slap, slap, six or seven times on the man's face. The cook just stood there and took it, he didn't say anything, he didn't change his expression. He had his eyes closed. And then the officer walked off.

A normal day consisted of watching television and playing cards, although eventually they were allowed to take some exercise. They could all walk around the courtyard, all apart from Edward Hammett, that is, who had lost his shoes in the hurried evacuation of Flight 149 and who was still without any footwear. The ground was too hot for bare feet or socks.

Hammett was usually the first to rise, at 6:30 a.m. There was a better chance of getting breakfast that way. He was still in his original outfit, a T-shirt and trousers he had worn on the plane, but a spare pair of boxer shorts allowed him to have fresh underwear every day. There was a rotation to use the bathrooms and to wash.

David Fort was losing weight rapidly due to a combination of poor diet and stress. By the end of his ordeal he lost about fifty pounds. In his weakened state, and in the heat, he moved more slowly. One day he was trying to get downstairs. A young soldier, probably a conscript, was behind him, trying to hurry him up. The soldier had a Kalashnikov. Impatient, he pushed Fort, who tumbled down the stairs, badly twisting his knee. He was in constant pain for the rest of his captivity.

*

Eventually, the hostages moved again. They were told to pack their bags and were taken down the road, walking about a thousand yards. Their belongings were put in a truck. For the first time in days, they could see the outside world. It was a nice day, a pleasant walk. They were taken to the flats where the palace servants had lived, a spot near the American Embassy, which they could see during their walk. They waved to the embassy staff as they walked past. Their new home was right in the middle of the headquarters of an engineering brigade.

Hammett:

> We all began to realise that we were our own salvation and began to look at ways and means of getting out of the rattrap that we would be in if the invasion by coalition forces took place. We clambered onto the roof one day to see what was happening and discovered that the Iraqis had stored explosives, small-arms ammunition, and mortar shells in all the garages that they had excavated in front of the building.
>
> There were bunkers dug in front and ammunition stored underneath us. We were sitting on top of a load of explosives. We were human shields, we were protecting that ammo. The Iraqis also put a military hospital next to us.

Ammunition vehicles came and went all the time. At first the ammunition was mortar shells and small arms, but later large artillery shells arrived, as well. What Hammett and his group did not know was that their new home had already been selected by Pentagon planners as a bombing target; as part of the plan to rescue those trapped in the American Embassy nearby, bombing their building would be part of the diversion. *But the Americans did not know the hostages were there.*

The Mukhabarat, the secret police, paid regular visits to the hostages, who quickly realised that these were the people who could get things done. 'They are the power behind the throne. If you complained and they thought that it was a decent complaint you got what you wanted real quick,' said one. Thus those sleeping on the floor got beds; the secret police obviously considered that to be an unnecessary hardship.

To start with, the hostages had no cooking facilities at their new home and were given disgusting, often rotting food from the Iraqi kitchens. But just four hours after the hostages asked for one, a bottled gas cooker was delivered. Ten minutes later, parcels and parcels of food arrived – they even got fresh fish that day.

Conditions improved slightly. Now they could visit the hospital (mainly for aspirin) by going up to the roof and walking across the other roofs to get to it. The guards did not seem to mind. Every day at 2 p.m. they were allowed exercise, which consisted of walking up and down outside the ammo bunkers. They could see everything that was going on and began to make notes of what they saw. They thought the information might be of use one day to any invading allied forces. Every day on the news there were reports of troops gathering in the Gulf, reports that both encouraged and depressed them.

As Edward Hammett remembered, 'You stop thinking after a while, it's just a waste of time. You stop wondering about what will happen to you. News grabs you for two or three days while you digest it, then you have to think about something else.'

One thing Hammett thought about all the time was escape. His windows and the windows in the next room opened out onto gardens behind the building. 'We thought if they come to kill us, will they come storming up the beaches? At least we'd have a bit of a chance by going out of the window into the garden. The windows had a wooden frame screwed into the wall. We loosened all the screws so you'd just have to pull it.'

An Iraqi major who began visiting the hostage sites in Kuwait told them they were guests, not prisoners. But he also said it was unsafe to leave and he warned against escape attempts. Everyone knew by now that Douglas Croskery was dead. But in the best British tradition, the hostages nevertheless decided to set up an escape committee.

Back in Britain, Foreign Office attempts to downplay the hostage crisis had been largely successful. But a small and determined group of relatives and MPs were starting to push hard for news of what was really going on. One of them was Thelma Croskery.

On the day of her husband's death, Thelma had been invited to a neighbour's wedding, but she was so worried about her husband trapped in Kuwait she decided not to go. Her children, David and Jackie, went to the wedding; her other daughter, Leslie, was on holiday in France. That night Thelma got a call from the Foreign Office.

The person at the end of the phone said, 'We've had a sighting that Dougie has been shot. That is all we've heard, we don't know anything else.' They didn't have any more information for me; they didn't even ask if I had anyone with me to look after me.

I wrote down on the notepad by the phone, 'Dougie has been shot,' just like it was a normal phone message. I stared at the pad until the kids came home. As soon as they saw my face they knew something was wrong. I led the kids into the kitchen and told them that their dad had been shot but we didn't know anything else. Jackie let out a sound that I had never heard before, like a wounded animal. David went outside and started kicking the wall, hurting his foot in the process.

That night was strange. I even managed to sleep. I just wouldn't believe he had been hurt. We didn't hear anything from the Foreign Office in the morning so in desperation I rang a friend of Dougie's in Kuwait. Unbeknownst to me, he was one of the ones that had been in the convoy with him. 'Is Dougie all right?' I asked. 'I wish I could give you good news, but I can't,' came the reply. That's when it sank in.

Croskery was the first British casualty. As time went on, relatives and friends of all the others became more and more anxious. But still the message from the UK government remained the same: don't worry, they are being looked after, most of them are living in luxury hotels.

*

The Bush administration was also busy downplaying the crisis. Meanwhile, in Kuwait City, life became increasingly grim, a daily battle for survival. The Iraqis put a price on the head of Westerners in hiding.

American dentist Robert Morris, a Vietnam combat veteran, was still in hiding with a group of Westerners in his apartment block in the city when he heard the news. 'It was a cash reward for handing in Westerners. We were hearing that Kuwaitis who hid Westerners were strung up and castrated in front of their own families. Some Arabs offered refuge to foreigners and then suddenly turned them in to the police.'

Morris's group became obsessed with their security. 'Our phones were still working. We worked out systems for calling each other, three rings, hang up, then three more rings. The person calling never spoke first. To take our telephones into more soundproof rooms, we extended phone lines with lamp wire. Sometimes we sneaked up and down the corridors to meet each other. On the hall floor outside my apartment, I positioned a piece of broken mirror against the wall so the entire length of the corridor was visible from my partly open door.'

Knocks on the door were in code. Everyone learned to detect the footsteps of group members. The group constantly decreased and increased in size, as people left or were captured, or others joined. Together they bought food, medicine, and other essential items, and Morris and the others spent hours thinking of ways to make the apartment more secure. They used a Lotus spreadsheet on Morris's PC to keep track of their supplies. Between them they had stockpiled enough food to last them nine months should supplies dry up. Morris had a low-blood-sugar condition, so maintaining a decent food supply was crucial to his health.

They hid the food, along with important documents and valuable possessions, in false ceilings, in the air-conditioning ducts, and behind bookcases. The supplies were to be shared equally, so if someone was caught, the rest would still have enough to live on.

The air-conditioning was still functioning, which protected them from the 120-degree heat outside, but they were worried that the electricity and water supplies to the building might be cut off by the Iraqis. To prepare for this they stored water everywhere: old grape juice bottles, bathtubs, and even the bidets. They ate only fresh food, storing all canned foods and legumes so that they could still feed themselves if the power was cut off. They started breaking into abandoned apartments in the complex in search of more food and medical supplies. It was very important that they didn't get sick – anyone going to hospital was being taken captive.

Morris's group was helped by a man named Imad who lived in the apartments. He was a Syrian who had studied in the United States at George Washington University. He was very pro-Western and took it upon himself to protect the group. He became their guardian angel.

Imad organised watches within the building by people living in the Al Muthanna complex, but always assigned himself to watch the area where the Westerners were hiding. To deter soldiers and looters who might be searching the building, he knocked out all the lifts except one and stole a key for that one from the main office, so he could shut it down at will. He went to Basra and got a welding torch and welded several security doors shut. The group took the doorknobs off the remaining security doors so they could not be opened. Imad also organised the purchasing of food and brought it in late at night. He warned the others if he heard that Iraqi soldiers were planning to enter the building. When Imad went to reregister his car one day following a demand from the Iraqi army, he was questioned by the secret police with a gun held to his head. They ordered him to give up any Americans he was protecting. He denied all knowledge of any Americans and was allowed to go. For such loyalty and for all the help he gave them, Morris saw Imad as a 'saint'. 'He never wavered. Despite being of another culture and religion, he was willing to risk his life for us Christians.'

The mere process of staying alive was tiring. Sometimes the group felt morose and hopeless, as they had no idea when they would be free again. Morale was often low. They constantly felt scared and 'hunted': they knew Iraqi snatch squads were looking for Westerners. Said Robert Morris: 'We were never free from the fear of capture, torture, and execution.' He began to suffer flashbacks to events in Vietnam, incidents that had lain submerged in his subconsciousness for over two decades.

As the Iraqi forces tightened their control over the city, and incidents of brutality grew, the trapped residents became ever more obsessed with their security. They fastened new locks and bolts to the doors and fashioned tiny peepholes to check on visitors. Some

103

replaced the nameplates by their door with those of Arabs who had already fled. Noise was kept to a minimum. They took showers at 3 a.m. to avoid the sound of running water during the day. The heavily tinted windows were kept shut and the blinds closed with the lights turned off to avoid being spotted from outside. Rolled-up towels were placed at the bottom of their doors to block out light and noise. The only light at night was from the television, with the sound muted. Telephone calls were kept to a maximum length of one minute so they couldn't be traced.

Unknown to the others, a member of the group was jeopardising everyone else's security by keeping a list of people in the building on his computer and leaving notes under apartment doors advising people to contact him. Then Paul Kennedy (the Irishman who, with his Thai wife, had taken refuge in Morris's flat) found a list with all their names on it in the apartment of an elderly couple. The apartment was the scene of one of their periodic security meetings, and it appeared someone made the list at the meeting and then just left it lying around. This caused a huge row within the group when it was discovered. The man was accused of risking everyone's lives. Paul Kennedy was particularly outraged and threatened to assault the other man: such a reaction was an inevitable consequence of the strain they were all living under.

Morris himself had a narrow escape when he accidentally broke one of his own rules. His phone rang, and without thinking he answered, 'Hello, Dr Morris.' A female voice asked in Arabic if he was still living in Apartment 826. Then a male voice, which he recognised as the Palestinian employee of the Ministry of Housing, who had originally found Morris the apartment, came on the line and asked the same question. The dentist was extremely shaken and put the phone straight down. Now someone knew who he was, and where he was. He moved in with Paul Kennedy for ten days and swapped door numbers with a neighbour, so his apartment was now numbered 824. No one seemed to come looking for him so he moved back into his own apartment. He was safe for the moment, but Morris later found out that his name was on a list of Westerners given to the Iraqi secret police by the Ministry of Housing. 'That son-of-a-bitch was probably trying to ingratiate himself with the Iraqis by giving them an American hostage,' Morris surmised.

Almost constant gunfire could be heard from the streets surrounding the building where the group was hiding. Whenever they peered out of the window they could see Iraqi soldiers and armoured vehicles in the streets below. The confinement led to feelings of isolation, paranoia, and claustrophobia. Some attempted to alleviate this by crawling up to the roof to sunbathe.

The paranoia was justified. Despite all the precautions, people were still being caught. An elderly British couple, Ken and Magda Hoyle, had a poodle, Samson, and they insisted on walking him on the roof in full view of the Iraqi secret police in the adjacent Plaza Hotel. One day when they returned to their apartment from walking Samson, they found the secret police waiting. They were taken to the Regency Hotel and questioned. They managed to call the others, using the pre-arranged code, to tell them what was happening. They were being taken to Baghdad.

CHAPTER 9

SIEGE: PART I
THE DIARY OF GEORGE SALOOM, FLIGHT 149 PASSENGER

The round-up of Westerners in Kuwait began with one obvious target: Americans. They were regarded as the prize hostages and if an American was a soldier in Commander-in-Chief Bush's army as well, so much the better. US citizens trapped in Kuwait included businessmen and bankers, oil workers and engineers, embassy staff and military personnel, including those serving in Colonel Mooneyham's military liaison team.

The Americans were only too aware of their propaganda value to Saddam. The dictator had vowed to 'pluck out the eyes' of anyone who helped the 'Western imperialist powers' retake Kuwait. Ambassador Nathaniel Howell decided that all the military personnel in hiding throughout the city should relocate to the embassy compound, a diplomatic safe haven, albeit one surrounded by Iraqi troops.

Howell had been ambassador in Kuwait since 1987. He was coming to the end of his tour but the Senate had not yet named a replacement. His wife, Margie, had returned home to Virginia before the invasion, and his two grown sons were also back in the States. He had known that troops were massing on the border in southern Iraq, but originally thought his countrymen were safe where they were, as he did not expect the Iraqi forces to invade the city.

Some people ignored the instructions to come to the embassy compound. They reckoned that the Iraqis knew where the embassy was but would have a lot harder job finding individuals in their own homes. American civilians trapped in the city's luxury hotels were more vulnerable. These included George Saloom, who had been a passenger on Flight 149 with wife Deborah and son Preston, all of whom were now at the Meridien Hotel, which was surrounded by Iraqis. Saloom kept a diary, a now visceral depiction of the hostage experience.

August 5, 1990, Kuwait City, Kuwait
All telephone communications outside the hotel are down!
Fair amount of activity, troop movement outside but no
real indication that troops are withdrawing… We are
feeling fairly helpless! Not much, if anything, we can do.
Have no idea when we will get out of Kuwait and what
I will be doing with respect to employment. I am a *little*
upset that the British Airways plane (BA 149) was allowed
to land last Thursday morning.

August 7, 1990, Kuwait City, Kuwait
Today a very special day, today is Deb's and my nineteenth
wedding anniversary. Of course, there are extenuating
circumstances; being in Kuwait, under a 'war time'
environment. I pray that something will develop over the

next several days. I just need to learn more patience and understanding. Most everything is the same in Kuwait; no communications to anyone outside the hotel, locally or out of the country. The news (CNN) stated that the Iraqis did collect some twenty or so Americans from hotels and sent them to Baghdad – do not think they were from the Meridien Hotel.

Today, looking out of the hotel window, I see a lot of people, Iraqi and others, looting and pilfering. It is a total shame. The Iraqi soldiers are looting. When they see others (non-Iraqi) doing the same, they become angry, violent, and even harmful!

Our anniversary was very 'quiet'. I was not able to give Deborah anything – but I did request and was granted a cake by the chef at the hotel. A candle was on it with writing on the top…' HERE'S HOPING THAT YOUR 20TH WILL BE IN DIFFERENT CIRCUMSTANCES.'

We shared the cake and everyone ate it! Deborah is getting a 'little' anxious. Her medicine, oestrogen, is out and we have taken steps to try to get some refills.

August 8, 1990, Kuwait City, Kuwait
Some developments are intensifying our concerns and anxiety:

1. Telephone communication (except for CNN) is down.
2. Looks like many people are trying to leave Kuwait. Many cars/individuals are moving. Individuals are carrying luggage and/or boxes that appear to contain clothing.
3. CNN has reported 'foreigners' leaving Kuwait and

entering Iraq. Some individuals are/have left Baghdad (capital of Iraq).

4. Women, in the hotel, are now asked to dine in the basement.

5. At 4 p.m., Kuwait time, President Bush is to address the nation and explain his position (present and future).

6. At 6:30 p.m., Kuwait time, the military leader of Iraq, Saddam Hussein, is to make an announcement to all the world. The rumour is that he has 'annexed' Kuwait to be part of Iraq.

7. Comments and rumours about strengthened Iraqi forces at the Saudi Arabian border and planes being loaded with chemical weapons has caused much nervousness and concern. Many individuals in the hotel are trying to be optimistic but also realistic. Last night we had some discussions with another American, Wayne Corbin, about contingency plans – possibly going to either the Soviet or Canadian Embassy.

THINGS DON'T LOOK TOO GOOD!!

August 9, 1990, Kuwait City, Kuwait
We have been in Kuwait for a week. Although we are safe, have food and a lot of comforts, I still consider ourselves as hostages. We are NOT allowed to leave. Looting continues in an increasing mode! Some individuals have escaped to Iraq (Baghdad) but are now not allowed to leave there. Others have fled to Saudi Arabia and have arrived back in the USA. Deb is out of medicine (oestrogen) and we

have not been able to get any refills. Her emotions are very sensitive and quite volatile, at times. (My son) Preston doing pretty good. He is quite stubborn and thinks he is invincible (typical 17-year-old) but I think he is scared and trying to cover it up.

My personal thoughts are that I am very uncomfortable about our position and concerned about the safety of my wife and son, but am not concerned about my own safety. I am not, at all, second-guessing my decision. I feel the Lord ratified my decision to come to Kuwait and this will be a growing experience and something good will come out of it.

*

At the Meridien Hotel, Deborah Saloom had her first sight of the invading army. Often she saw Iraqi soldiers outside, taking advantage of shady spots in the hot August sunshine. Every day, there seemed to be more and more. The hotel was running short of food and some of the Indian staff were sent out to see if they could buy or scrounge any more. It was felt they were less likely to be attacked.

Reports came in daily of rapes and other assaults on women by the Iraqis. Several Filipinos who lived nearby had been attacked. At the hotel, the women were told not to leave their rooms, and so were no longer able to eat their meals in the basement.

On the morning of 12 August, Deborah woke up feeling quite ill. Soon she was in intense pain. It felt like kidney stones. There was no choice but to get her to a hospital. She put on Arab robes and went to the hospital with George in the hotel bus. 'George looked like an Arab already, he didn't need a disguise.'

At the hospital, the Salooms saw several injured Iraqi soldiers, and there were patrols everywhere, but they managed to get in and the nurses hid them behind some curtains. Deborah was treated with a supply of drugs that had been secreted away. Afterward, the Salooms made it back to their prison.

August 16, 1990, Kuwait City, Kuwait
A really scary day. The morning started off 'as normal.' Later in the day, we received a statement from the American Embassy as follows:

'We have been informed by the Iraqi Government that in order to better protect Americans, they desire all Americans in Kuwait to be located in one location. Americans are to move to the Kuwait International Hotel (the Hilton). We advise you that it is your option to move to the hotel. The Iraqi government has said that if Americans do not voluntarily move, they will take unspecified means to locate them into one location. If you choose to move to the hotel, take your food and give it to the hotel manager. You should only take one suitcase per individual.'

We had a meeting of the Americans in our hotel and decided not to move at this time.

Later this day, we then received communication from the Embassy stating NOT to move, that soldiers and the Kuwait International Hotel were not expecting or ready for individuals to go to the hotel.

Had some very anxious moments. We heard rumours that Iraqi soldiers were ordered to shoot all foreign nationals in the streets after the curfew. The curfew is from 7 p.m. to 7 a.m. We were also told that the soldiers would be going to individual homes, residences, and hotels to 'collect' them to one location.

Had a fairly restful night. Had some pains from kidney stone. Deb's kidney (or bladder) infection is still there and causing her a little pain. Nerves are tight. Emotions are high! Our family had several family prayers today seeking not only peace and protection but also direction of what we should do and how we could get out of this situation.

August 17, 1990, Kuwait City, Kuwait
No news today concerning movement to Kuwait International Hotel. Things very quiet today. MAYBE CALM BEFORE THE STORM!

August 18, 1990, Kuwait City, Kuwait
News/rumours today that Iraq would move 'retainees' to certain key civilian and military installations. I contacted the embassy. They are checking it out. Had a wardens' meeting at 10:30 a.m. at the embassy. Following information was provided:

1. Iraq said no one could be forcibly taken from residence.
2. Non-Westerners were going to Jordan and getting in pretty easily.
3. Individuals who are trying to escape would be shot!

*

Deborah had packed the family's bags in preparation for three types of evacuation: an orderly one where they took everything; a two-bag scenario (less orderly); and an emergency evacuation where only one bag would be taken, in which what little money they had stashed and her jewellery were hidden in her makeup bag.

Deborah saw the general manager of the hotel preparing to depart. She wondered if he was deserting them. Soon after, she got a call saying that now was the time to make their escape to the embassy. Apparently, the hotel manager Deborah had seen departing had persuaded the embassy to let them come.

Deborah was told they had to leave now, using the same hotel bus that had taken them to the hospital. Rumours started to circulate that Iraqis were rounding up Westerners. Deborah decided she must risk leaving the room to find George and Preston, who were down in the dining room. She saw a cleaner by the elevator who told her to go back to her room, but she made up a story about feeling ill again and needing to go to the hospital. She asked the man to fetch her husband and son to help her. Deborah didn't trust anyone enough to tell him the truth.

She saw a fellow American in the corridor. 'We are getting out of here,' she told him. 'Get the others.' More Iraqi troops were assembling outside as they prepared to leave. The bus driver was reluctant to drive Deborah back to the 'hospital' again. So she got on it and grabbed the keys from the driver so he could not leave, then went to look for her husband and son. They and the others came down and piled on board the bus. 'Are you all going to the hospital?' the driver asked, incredulously. 'No, take us to the embassy,' he was told firmly.

The driver had been out foraging earlier in the day and knew exactly where the checkpoints were, so he managed to reach the embassy gates without being stopped. On the way there, the horrified passengers saw the macabre sight of a body swinging from a communications tower. Cars were turned upside down, burning unattended in the streets. As they drove through the embassy gates, the hotel manager was waiting to meet them.

*

Fred Hart, a member of the USLOK military liaison team, had stayed at home in the early days of the invasion. He prepared his family for the potentially hazardous trip to the embassy, twelve kilometres away, right through downtown Kuwait. They packed all the foodstuffs they could into the car and waited for the order to leave.

Fred Hart:

We all knew there would be Iraqi roadblocks to traverse and the embassy was encircled by Iraqi troops. We had also monitored over the radio several other families' drive into the embassy and so far, they had all made it without incident. When early morning came we received no instructions to leave, so we continued our routine of inventorying our property. We would only be allowed two pieces of luggage, so we had to decide what we could carry out and what had to be left behind. This was a difficult task.

A civilian man, Westerner in appearance, showed up at our villa gate, announced he was from the US Embassy, and had come to escort us in. I had been assigned at the embassy for a year and I knew all the personnel assigned to the post, and I did not recognise this individual. I immediately radioed the embassy and they verified his identity.

I then recognised the foreign national driver who was with him, so once we got that straightened out I called a close neighbour to coordinate a link-up with him and his family so that we could all convoy in together. The USLOK administrative NCO, who was a neighbour of ours, also joined in the trek. We began our journey into the embassy with great trepidation of what was waiting for us. Our plan was to use foodstuffs, cigarettes, and alcohol as bribes to get through the roadblocks.

I had also taken the precaution of hiding the American citizen listing that had been brought to me. The list contained over 500 names and addresses of US citizens living and working in Kuwait.

As we pulled out of the Salwa neighbourhood, my wife and children were shocked at the destruction that was so close to our house. Now they could understand all the shelling, booming, and rattling of windows for two days, and most importantly why they had to remain away from windows. As we rode in, almost every official Kuwait government building along the route had been shelled, torched, or destroyed. Wrecked and smouldering vehicles littered the highway, some with the charred remains present. The once well-manicured and green medians were now brown, dried up, and trashed. As we came to First Ring Road, Iraqi soldiers and tracked vehicles formed a checkpoint but our lead vehicle, with the Palestinian foreign national who worked for the embassy, spoke with what appeared to be an Iraqi officer. After the brief stop and exchange, the Iraqi road guards waved us through.

We turned off First Ring just short of the Kuwait International Hotel and went down a backstreet to the embassy's rear entrance. Iraqi soldiers and combat vehicles had the entire compound surrounded. Strangely, the Iraqis were now manning the guard post the Kuwaiti National Guard troops had previously occupied. Our embassy foreign nationals told me that the Kuwaiti guards literally stripped off their uniforms and fled when they spotted the Iraqis on the morning of 2 August. We were allowed to proceed but

the anxiety did not subside until we crossed over the steel
barrier gate and into the enclosed parking lot.

Once inside the embassy, Hart and the others were billeted with the
five marines who guarded the compound.

Hart and others from the USLOK team began collecting
intelligence reports on Iraqi movements to feed back to Washington.
They also made an alarming discovery at the embassy. Classified
files on the work of the team had not been destroyed, including
personnel files and maps. 'If the embassy had been taken,' Hart
later wrote, 'the Iraqis would have had a wealth of information
on our organisation and the location of all USLOK personnel.
We immediately shredded all classified files contained in four
filing cabinets.'

The embassy was surrounded by troops, and the Iraqis had
watchers on high buildings to look down into the compound
and placed electronic surveillance equipment to listen in on
conversations. Initially, there were about a hundred people in the
embassy (including women and children), among them a doctor, a
teacher, and a minister who led a religious service every night.

Ambassador Howell asked everyone to prepare a panic bag to
keep next to their desks to grab in case the Iraqis stormed the
building and captured them. In it they should keep essential items
such as passports, medication, and a change of clothes, as well as
any important personal items.

Two people at a time were on rotating twenty-four-hour guard
duty. They also took on various other jobs, such as kitchen duty and
trash burning. Barbara Bodine was the Deputy Chief of Mission,
the chief operations officer of the embassy. She was responsible
for work assignments while they were in the compound. Bodine
was also the embassy official who routinely spoke with the Iraqis

on the telephone or other missions linked by the emergency radio network. She could often delay making responses to Iraqi demands by insisting that she must ask the ambassador before a decision could be made. In the event that Howell was captured by the Iraqis outside the embassy or somehow incapacitated, Bodine would take over.

Everyone prepared for a long siege. Security measures were put in place such as reinforcing the roof, building a bunker, and reinforcing the walls. Preparations for rescue included making sure the car park was free of obstructions so that a helicopter could land safely. Cars were ready to drive straight out if this became a possibility or a necessity. There was quite an extensive stockpile of food, including eight thousand cans of tuna and plenty of rice, although whether it was enough for a long siege was unclear. There were two date palms out in the compound. Once the water pump was up and running, a vegetable garden was established to provide healthy salads.

The hostages did not want the Iraqis to know details of their supplies, so when they were asked what provisions were needed, Barbara Bodine conferred with Howell and they decided to give nothing away. They asked for fresh fruit, soft drinks, and cigarettes rather than staples to give the impression they were stocked up on the basics but needed only luxury items.

Ambassador Howell had stocked up on pipe tobacco beforehand, but people kept stealing it to make roll-ups when the cigarettes ran out. He had to hide a stash for himself.

The heat was almost unbearable. It was an unusually hot summer and many of the hostages had never experienced heat like it. Their thermometer, which was kept in the shade, read 140 degrees on some days. The humidity was close to 100 per cent. But despite the heat, the bored hostages organised a tennis tournament, and also refurbished a pool table. The compound had a VCR library, so they voted for and watched different videos every night. They also had what Howell described as 'typical hostage tournaments' – time wasters such as fly killing.

But their relative peace was disrupted one evening, without warning, when automatic weapons fire arced over the compound.

Fred Hart described it:

> The Marine guards immediately alerted everyone to head for the Chancellery vault. Apparently, the embassy was being caught in a crossfire between Iraqis and Kuwaiti resistance fighters. However now the feeling was the Iraqis were attempting to take the compound.
>
> Once in the vault, we […] realised that there were no embassy or USLOK personnel at the Marine House in which most of the women and children were being housed. We asked the ambassador for permission to leave the vault and go to the Marine House. He approved and we headed out of the Chancellery building. The weapons firing had slackened but tracers were still criss-crossing the compound. We raced across the compound. Once inside the Marine House, we noticed the wives had followed the instruction we had given to them, to turn off all lights and assemble everyone in the games room for safety. Most had settled down; but several maids were in a state of hysteria and it took several minutes to calm them down. Their fear was particularly unsettling for the children.

This incident led Ambassador Howell to decide to destroy all the weapons in the compound. He did not want to give the Iraqis any excuse to invade the compound. Any attempt by the hostages to defend themselves with their small detachment of marines would have been bloody and futile, he felt.

Howell was very worried about the US citizens who had decided to remain on the outside. There was one family in particular who got their little girl to answer the phone in Arabic to avoid casting suspicion. But their security was less than perfect. When Howell would tell her, in code, that 'Margie's husband was on the phone', the girl would run off shouting to her parents, 'The American ambassador is on the phone!'

The hostages used a fuel-powered generator to make telephone contact with Washington daily. They were very worried that the fuel would run out and gauged the level with a stick each day. At one point, they thought they had organised a truck to bring more fuel to them, but it was blockaded by the Iraqis.

Other hostages used a 'message board' system to stay in touch with their loved ones, by which they could send three-line messages to staff in Washington, which were then relayed to the appropriate person. Responses were reported back in a similar fashion.

The Iraqi guards outside the compound and the marines in bullet-proof sentry boxes inside could see each other. One night, the Iraqi soldier who was regularly posted opposite one of the Americans signalled to him, miming a hand slicing his own throat and then shaking his head and smiling. He appeared to be indicating that he had no intention of killing any Americans.

In fact, the Iraqi soldiers had a rough time and were not treated very well. They were fed only once a day – a meagre meal of rice around noon. The hostages inside certainly had a better diet for a while. The average guard, most likely a conscript, seemed to want to be somewhere else. A number of Iraqi soldiers even came to the embassy gates offering to trade their weapons and uniforms for civilian clothes, presumably in order to escape the army.

The USLOK men – Fred Hart and a colleague, Chief Dave Forties – organised food runs from the embassy to various parts of the city that were still not fully under Iraqi control.

Fred Hart:

Each morning, Chief Forties and I would set out in his Chevy Blazer to canvass Kuwait City for food stocks. Chief had several Kuwaiti contacts who helped arrange a clandestine meeting with the Kuwaiti who owned the largest supermarket chain in Kuwait, known as the Sultan Center.

The Kuwaiti owner had gone underground and was attempting to get his assets out of Kuwait before the Iraqis could find them. After several days, we finally managed to link up with him at a discreet location. We then followed him to an underground warehouse in the vicinity of Kuwait International Airport. Chief Forties struck a deal with him for credit payment via the State Department, but we had to act quickly since it was only a matter of a few days or a week at best before the Iraqis would discover the warehouse.

That evening, the ambassador agreed to Chief's plan and payment was arranged. We returned the next day and surveyed the warehouse; the primary food stocks consisted of canned tuna and frozen turkeys. We also took everything he had in the way of medical supplies, paper products, canned drinks, and cereals. Most of the products were near the limit of their shelf life or had recently expired dates. We spent several days hauling the food stocks to the embassy.

During one of our last visits, an Iraqi patrol showed up at the underground entrance way. The Kuwaitis quickly moved us to a back storage area, bribed the patrol with

Pepsi Cola and canned tuna. Shortly after our last trip to the warehouse, the owner decided to abandon it and make his way out of Kuwait. We had one day left to get all we could from the warehouse. Chief Forties briefed the ambassador on the situation and we got the approval to make one last run using the embassy's stake bed truck, which could haul three times the amount of the Blazer. We rounded up tarps to cover the cargo and made three trips.

During our last trip back, we were stopped at an Iraqi checkpoint. We managed to convince the guards that this was a relief mission to the Philippine Embassy, and handed them some cigarettes. They agreed to let us pass. We did in fact make one additional run for the Philippine Embassy, since they had literally several thousand Philippine nationals camped outside their embassy compound.

Hart's team also linked up with the increasingly bold and well-organised Kuwaiti resistance. 'One Kuwaiti in particular, named Adel Safar, was brought into the embassy for debriefs,' Hart recalled'. 'Through Adel we also shared information and provided him with techniques for sabotaging Iraqi equipment and positions. Kuwaiti resistance grew stronger every day.'

CHAPTER 10

WOMEN AND CHILDREN FIRST

In occupied Kuwait, Saddam Hussein's new nineteenth province, behind every door, every gate, every entrance, there was a different way of life. The occupation had become a thing of random terror and mismanagement, where your future was determined by where you happened to be when the Iraqi army swept in, or where you chose to go in the days afterward or who you ran into or missed meeting up with, or which country's passport you carried.

There were Westerners – those from Flight 149 and those who were already there – now scattered all over the map. They were under siege at the American Embassy, on the way to Baghdad in convoys, already taken to Iraq as human shields, and in hiding in Kuwait City itself, in their own homes, in captivity, with the resistance, or in camps under guard by Iraqi soldiers.

As bad as things were for the human shields, they were worse for the Kuwaiti people. The hostages had front row seats to the growing horrors of the occupation.

One day, Charles Kristiansson and fellow hostage Mike, an Irishman, were hanging up their washing on the long line on the roof of their guarded villa in the city when they heard screaming. They saw a young veiled woman running down the road, pursued by six soldiers. She looked up and saw the two men on the roof.

Mike waved frantically at her, shouting: '*Leave her alone! Leave her alone!*' and then he ran downstairs and into the yard.

'*Come here!*' he screamed at the top of his voice. '*Come here! It's safe!*'

The young woman suddenly stopped in her tracks and looked at him, but seeing other soldiers guarding the villa, she fled into a looted and abandoned high-rise apartment block and disappeared.

Charles Kristiansson recalled his desperate effort to protect the woman: 'Running downstairs, my heart beating in a mad mix of fear and excitement, I could hear Mike's deep low voice bellowing, his fists battering against the garden wall.

'*Stop them! Stop them now!*' he yelled, now hysterically, at one of the guards who stood idly by. The guard looked slightly perturbed by what he regarded as a tiny but inconvenient 'disturbance'. Mike, now trembling, became frantic about the fate of the young woman. It was sickeningly obvious what was going to happen to her.

'The guard shrugged his shoulders slovenly, dismissively, and then to our horror, we watched a broad grin spread across his face. He spat on the ground, before roughly and exaggeratedly rubbing his crotch. I recoiled in disgust.

'*Jesus, no!*' shouted Mike. '*No!* Please, if there's a god then, please leave her alone!'

'Mike, don't provoke the guards! Keep calm!' I pleaded, fearing that one of the guards might panic and lose control.

'She's run into that building and the bastards are going after her!'

he shouted, banging his fists on the perimeter garden wall of the villa, pacing up and down. '*Do something! Do something! We can't let this happen… ! Please God, please God…* '

The woman appeared on the roof of the apartment block. She moved towards the edge, still pursued by the soldiers, who closed in on her. She screamed at the men, waving her arms, but they kept coming.

'*No! No! No! F**k please, no!*' Mike was yelling, cupping his head in his hands. '*No! No! No! Stop it!*'

He dived for the wall, trying to climb over it. A guard fired a warning shot into the air.

The young woman on the roof screamed again and then she jumped. Charlie and Mike heard a sickening thud.

Charles: 'The men who'd chased her looked gingerly over the edge of the roof top before scattering, their voices chattering in cries of panic. A few minutes later they scuttled away.

'*Bastards! F**king bastards! You killed her!*' shouted Mike. He ran towards the villa and lashed out at one of the guards with his fists for his refusal to intervene, starting to beat him.'

He was pulled away. Mike slumped to the ground and started crying bitterly and uncontrollably.

'They did nothing! Nothing! We did nothing! She's dead!' he continued sobbing bitterly on the ground. 'Those bastards wanted to rape her! Bloody soldiers!'

Another hostage in the villa was angry with Mike: 'He could've been killed! He was hitting the guard! We could've been killed. It's crazy here, anything could happen to us and there's nothing we can do!'

Later, when things had calmed down, Charles tried to keep up the morale of the group: 'Our lives could be extinguished at any minute and somehow, we had to accept this reality but at the same time keep it at bay by unflagging, unrealistic optimism that we would ultimately prevail.'

*

Sir Peter de La Billière, the newly appointed commander for the British forces gathering in the Gulf, was very worried about the hostages. A rescue operation could go wrong and result in hundreds of deaths, but equally, what if they were left in place and the bombing started? 'I do not want the RAF or other coalition air force to be responsible for blowing them into oblivion when attacking the Iraqis' bases,' he wrote in his diary.

At the IBI camp in Kuwait, where the Chappell family, others from Flight 149, and other Westerners were now being held, relations with the Iraqis deteriorated after an attempted escape. Two men were caught trying to cut a hole in the fence. The prison officer on duty was furious. He told the hostages through an interpreter that if anybody escaped it would be his neck that would be stretched: he would have to report the attempt to his captain. In the subsequent crackdown, a roll call was introduced. The hostages had to gather in the main square of the camp at 4 p.m. each day to be counted, to make sure that nobody had escaped. But still the hostages' defiance continued. They christened the square St George's Square and made a flag, England's cross of St George (a red cross on a white background), to fly above it. The Iraqis never realised the significance of this, as they only recognised the more familiar Union Jack. So each roll call was held under a flag that marked the camp as a little piece of England.

The hostages found a couple of radios that they tuned to the BBC World Service, and they gathered in secret each night to hear the news. They were not encouraged by what they heard. The news was full of reports of the huge build-up of allied forces – George

Bush's grand coalition of nations – and the defiant response from the Iraqis. There was going to be another Middle East war, this time involving the British and Americans, and they were going to be right in the middle of it.

But one broadcast did carry some good news. Saddam Hussein suddenly announced that he was going to let all the women and children leave and return home. At the various camps, the hostages were told whether they were in one of the groups designated for departure. At the IBI camp, the news was passed excitedly from bungalow to bungalow. All the families were to be let go as well.

John and Maureen Chappell prepared to leave with their children. On departure day, they and the others assembled in a hall to reclaim their passports. One of the officers took John aside and told him the heartbreaking news: 'The men can't go now. They have changed their minds and say the men can't go with their families.'

John had to make a difficult decision. He still wasn't convinced the women and children were going to be allowed to leave either; it might be a trick, like the day they were told they were going to Basra and then Baghdad but ended up at the camp. This time John gambled that the dictator would keep his word. He gathered his family together to give them the news.

Jennifer Chappell remembers her own hesitancy on leaving the camp: 'I didn't want to go because I didn't want to leave my father behind. I remember thinking rather childishly that I was annoyed, couldn't we go another day because we had just got the swimming pool sorted out and filled and I wanted to go swimming – not thinking of course that I could go swimming when I get home. And then I started thinking I didn't want to leave my dad behind on his own. But obviously there was no way I could stay behind.'

At the same time, her brother, John Chappell Jr., considered staying with his father: 'Once I heard that it was going to be the women and children and not the whole family, I was thinking in terms of perhaps Jenny should go with Mum and I'd stay. But Dad said, "No, I'll be a lot happier knowing that my family is out safe than having to worry about you here. And I need you to make sure that Mum and Jenny are okay. You know you've got to stick together and look after each other and make sure that you get through to Baghdad and get out." I said, "All right.'"

Maureen didn't want to go at all. She wanted the children to leave while she stayed with John, but she realised that was impossible. Her children needed her and she had to go.

The family packed in silence, gathering together some water and food for the journey. The children cried. John Chappell told them, 'You have been given the chance to go and you need to take it. I will have more chance of escaping after you have gone. I won't have to worry about what happens to you.'

Maureen and the children shuffled onto the coach, pressing their faces to the window and waving as the coach pulled away. Jennifer thought she would never see her father again. Next to her, John Jr. was more confident, believing his dad would be okay. John ran along beside the coach, tears rolling down his cheeks, until it sped up and finally disappeared. Then he walked back into the camp. Now he was truly alone.

Maureen and the children set off on the sixteen-hour trek north to Baghdad in tears, armed only with a couple of oranges and some water. The journey began with a trip around Kuwait City to pick up other women and children. At one stage the coach stopped by the docks and sat there for two hours. The guards told everyone they weren't allowed to get off, but the children needed to go to the toilet. Maureen marched off the coach, pushed the guard out of the way, and said firmly, 'I'm going to the toilet in there.'

The trip was a hungry one. No food was provided and there were no stops for provisions. Eventually some of the guards took pity on the passengers. They stopped and used their own money to buy their passengers bread and Kraft cheese triangles. The Chappells got four bits of bread and a couple of cheeses. They finally arrived in Baghdad at their new home, the Mansour Melia hotel.

Back at the camp, John struggled to cope with his family's departure on a coach he had thought he would be on, too. 'We decided we'd open the bar a bit early. And we went out and got drunk to be quite honest. And we spoke about it and convinced ourselves that everything would be all right with them.'

In Baghdad, Maureen and the children lined up to pick up their passports as the Iraqis called out the names. They called Maureen Chappell and then Jennifer Chappell – but no John. Maureen stood there with the two passports in her hand, asking for her son's passport, as well. The Iraqis kept trying to hurry her along but she refused to move without her son. Behind her, a few feet away, the children saw the guards suddenly train their guns on their mother. She was creating a scene and the passport process had ground to a standstill. But guns or no guns, Maureen refused to budge. 'I wasn't leaving there without my son's passport because he was fourteen and in Arab countries they are considered men at that age and I didn't know whether they were going to hold on to him and not let him out. There was no way I was leaving the room without my son.'

Eventually, the Iraqis caved in and emptied a carrier-bag full of passports onto the table. Maureen quickly pointed out John's and it was handed over. *Go now, go now,* said the soldiers. Maureen didn't need telling twice – she and the children were out and down the steps and on the coach in a flash. It headed off to the airport but the plane was delayed.

Back in camp John heard on the BBC World Service that the

women and children had left Baghdad on an Iraqi Airways plane. Soon afterward, he and others in the camp were watching Bahrain Television when it showed a plane landing at Heathrow. The cameras zoomed in as the passengers left the plane and stepped onto British soil. There in the centre of the shot was John Jr. coming down the steps. Three thousand miles away in captivity John Sr. couldn't take his eyes off his son – so much so that he missed seeing Maureen and Jennifer leave the plane, although others in the camp spotted them. John may have still been in captivity but he felt his life had changed for the better.

'I knew they were home and that was it for me. The rest of the stay took a different turn for me altogether. I had nothing to worry about for them.'

*

The Middle East nightmare of fellow passenger Henry Halkyard had come true. He and his wife, Daphne, had been worried about travelling on Flight 149 at all, as Henry's past experiences as a soldier made him anxious to avoid the region. They were moved from their comfortable hotel in Kuwait into Iraq, where they were held in a rat-infested tin shed near a nuclear plant somewhere outside Baghdad. Their decision to travel on their British, rather than their New Zealand, passports had backfired. New Zealanders were allowed to leave. The Halkyards were not optimistic about their fate.

'I think it was quite obvious that our lives depended on the actions of the Western governments,' said Daphne. 'If Saddam had his way, we would have been released within a few days. But we didn't anticipate that things were going to go the way that Saddam would like and so we realised that we might be there for the long haul.'

The Halkyards were among the first victims of the ruthless new policy by Saddam – the Iraqi High Command defied world pressure and decided to use all the Westerners in custody as human shields. The hostages were now ordered to be placed at various strategic locations, not only in Kuwait but in Iraq, including at nuclear, chemical, industrial, and military installations. The aim was to prevent allied bombing of those potential targets. At the Halkyards' site, living conditions were squalid and food was scarce. The septic tank, right outside their living quarters, was black and overflowing. It had no top on it, so a black, soggy mess oozed out constantly, and the smell was everywhere. But while the mess could be avoided, the fear was a different matter.

Daphne Halkyard: 'Chronic fear became a way of life for us. Every day there was something on which we would focus. We were afraid of being bombed by the allies. We were afraid of illness. We were afraid of being lynched. We were afraid of the breakdown of some of our fellow hostages. We were afraid of letting something slip that could have jeopardised members of our little group. We were watching our backs the whole time. But there was nothing we could do, nothing we could do. Our lives were on the line. We had no illusions whatsoever about that.'

Back home in Warkworth, New Zealand, the Halkyards' children had no idea where their parents were. They knew that they had flown into Kuwait and then disappeared. They guessed of course that they were probably hostages. Daughter Rowan hung on every scrap of news: most of it was bad. 'One day, we would be told that the hostages were having their rations cut, which was absolutely terrifying. The next thing, there was talk of a third world war. The chances were very high that we would not see them again.' When the news came through that women and children could leave, they thought that they would be seeing their mother soon. But at the nuclear site, Daphne was in an agony of indecision. She could leave but she might never see Henry again. Henry left the decision to her.

Daphne Halkyard: 'Every woman had a very difficult decision to make. I decided that it was right for me to stay. But I often had misgivings because if both of us were to be killed then our children would be bereft.' Henry Halkyard: 'I felt very humble. I shall always be indebted to her for staying with me.'

CHAPTER 11

SIEGE: PART II
THE DIARY OF GEORGE SALOOM,
US EMBASSY SECURITY OFFICER

George Saloom and his family felt they were on a long journey but they were not getting very far. They had arrived on Flight 149 and seen out the first days of the invasion at the Meridien Hotel. Now they were in the US Embassy compound, a safe haven, but one surrounded by Iraqi troops. How long would the compound's diplomatic status protect them? They would soon find out.

August 19, 1990, Kuwait City, Kuwait
We did some work around the embassy compound today. News is that after August 24, this embassy in Kuwait will no longer be recognised as an embassy with diplomatic privileges (from the Iraqi government's perspective). Therefore, more than likely, power and water will be cut off by that date. We are starting to make preparations to store water and make other preparations for that particular circumstance, if it occurs. Word is that individuals in the Regency Hotel were forced to go to Baghdad by the Iraqis

around 2:30 a.m. this morning. Things are continuing to heat up! Night was fairly quiet.

August 21, 1990, Kuwait City, Kuwait
This morning worked on the Water Task Force. The purpose of the task force is preparing/implementing necessary contingencies for water usage/supply if the water supply is cut off by the Iraqi government. I personally climb on the elevated tanks to:

1. Measure them.
2. Establish the present water level.

I did not mind at all, although it was quite scary on a couple of them. I also coordinated, again, the telephone switchboard crew. All went well last night and this morning. This is so important since this is the only source of contact or communication for most of the American citizen population in Kuwait. Deborah took the 0800 to 1200 hours shift.

Preston, doing well. He has found two friends – one fifteen and the other is nineteen years old. He is also working hard with the water emergency contingency task force. Most people are in good spirits. Seems everyone has good days and not so good days. Fortunately, the good days and 'bad' days are not occurring for everyone at the same time! Most people's concern now is the potential closing of the embassy and the transporting everyone to Baghdad.

August 22, 1990, Kuwait City, Kuwait
THINGS GOT HOT!!!

Today we were told by the Ambassador (Nathaniel Howell) that the President of the United States ordered all official staff that were non-essential (only minimal staff) to travel to Baghdad and then to Jordan. All individuals with diplomatic passports are to leave (again with the exception of eight or nine official diplomats) by convoy as soon as possible. This announcement was given at 8:45 a.m.

We [the hostages] were told that we were to assume full responsibility for the respective functions when the convoy (for all non-essential diplomatic personnel) left for Baghdad at about 5 or 6 a.m. the next morning, Aug. 23. UNFORTUNATELY, we were thrust into these roles around 5:30 p.m. today (Aug. 22) due to the non-essential personnel preparing for their trip. This included the Marine staff as well. Richard Atherton and myself had to 'jump in with both feet' and assume the entire security function for the embassy at 5:30 p.m.

I worked until about 0100 hrs (Aug. 23); slept for an hour or two and went back to 'work' at around 0430 hrs. With a lot of false starts and uneasiness, which has been the norm 'dealing' with the Iraqis, the convoy left at 0600 hrs. Everything went well except one of the individuals, Odessa Higgins, suffered a dislocated hip due to a car accident in the convoy. She had to be brought back to Kuwait and underwent surgery.

Utter chaos, disorganisation was the result of the action/ convoy leaving. It is a wonder that anything got done. Government people in general (although there are some sharp ones) are not at all 'on the ball'! It was like 'every man himself' with no regard for the embassy or the individuals staying behind. No smooth transition, or effort even attempted for redeployment, or an organised hand-off to the remaining individuals in the embassy. The convoy also left the embassy in an absolute mess! But our makeshift organisation and coordinated efforts were and *will be* fruitful.

August 24/25, 1990, Kuwait City, Kuwait
A very interesting day!

First, during the morning, we lost our power. We were planning to do more testing on the generator and identifying circuits and locations that were supported by the generator. (The test was the REAL thing!) Just as we were finishing our briefing and planning to test, our power was cut off by the Iraqis. Things worked pretty good. We did not have some areas covered by the generator. We were planning to move some freezers from certain areas not covered but too late. But, we then rewired certain areas and placed them on the generator – works well. Major concern, though, our supply of diesel fuel for the generator. Only have about 2,000 litres. Estimate is this can be stretched for about ten days. Staff at the embassy not that prepared. Did not get additional fuel. We had some scheduled and was actually near the gate (a 22,000 litre truck disguised as a water truck) but the Iraqis early in the morning had put a restriction of 12 noon, I believe. At 11 a.m. the truck was at the embassy, BUT, the Iraqis did not let it pass through because according to THEIR (Iraq) time (Iraq normally one hour ahead of Kuwait) it was 12 noon and since they had said Kuwait was annexed (19th Province) as part of Iraq, the Iraqis were using Iraq time!

Second, mid-afternoon, the Iraqis came to the gates

of the embassy and wanted us to tell them where water
lines were in order for them to cut off the water!! Of
course, we did not. They dug in two places where they
thought the lines were. They, evidently, had an individual
from the Ministry of Water with them to show them
where the water lines were. They were able to cut one
line off completely. They thought they had cut both
off, but as of today, one is still working. Power schedule
for the generator (now driven by the communications
requirements with Washington) is:

0630 to 0830 hours
1300 to 1700 hours
2100 to 2400 hours

There is a smaller generator also used for communications.

August 26, 1990, Kuwait City, Kuwait
Very difficult and frustrating day for me personally. I
have been working extremely hard in security about
twenty hours per day, literally; also changing/modifying
schedules and particular functions due to the impact of
no power. Even with the generator, much of the electronic
surveillance equipment is non-operative. In the morning,
I was finalising the schedule for the work and over the
radio requested a meeting with the Administrative Officer.
I immediately received a message over the radio to me
(Ramblin' Wreck) chastising me concerning improper radio
procedures and breach of security from the DCM (Deputy
Chief of Mission – Barbara Bodine). I then *immediately*
went to her and tried to explain to her that I was attempting

to find the Administrative Officer to make it easy to go to the individual instead of him coming to me. She proceeded to tell me how inadequate the security functions are, how that I spend three times the time on the radio than everyone else, that I walk around trying to be a big shot in my marine hat and that I treat the radio as a 'weenie toy'. She said, if I didn't get it corrected, she would take it away from me. At that point, I explained to her that her accusations were inappropriate, not to threaten me, that I didn't ask for this responsibility, and that she can have my radio! I then resigned as the 'security officer'.

August 28/29, 1990, Kuwait City, Kuwait
I worked a lot getting the snack bar/commissary organised. Cleaning and disinfecting the area was also necessary. Deb having difficulty sleeping due to her medicine not being the right kind (not Tegratol). The substitute she is using for Tegratol is okay but she must take 120 grams a night or she still has seizures. When she takes that dosage, she is really emotionally affected. Running out of fuel for the generator. Having to cut the number of hours for refrigeration, which is causing more spoilage of food.

Inventory has been completed:

- We have a great deal (6,336 cans) of tuna.
- Fairly good supply of other canned goods
- 750 kg of rice
- Low on flour and sugar: 1,000 kilos
- Fair supply of dry cereal and juices
- Water is STILL running. We also have a supply of potable water and 1,000 liters of boxed water

August 30/31, 1990, Kuwait City, Kuwait
Reverend Jesse Jackson came to Kuwait on a peace-making
mission. Not much has resulted in this visit as of to date.
Losing more meat from freezers. We are throwing some
away (burying) and consolidating freezers. We are also
trying to preserve the meat in four different ways:

1. Smoking
2. Cooking
3. Drying (Jerky)
4. Salting

Announcement over CNN was made that all women and
children would be allowed to leave. Excitement at first,
now just waiting and seeing.

September 1, 1990, Kuwait City, Kuwait
News today about a possible medical evacuation. Deb may
or may not be included this round. Two considerations:

1. Deb's seizures
2. Nathan's mental/emotional state

Deb says she will not leave Preston behind... If there was
a chance, I will do all I can to get her out and Preston, if
possible, at the same time. There appears to be a lot of
'politics' in the embassy about who will be 'allowed' (or
eligible) to go.

*

Deborah Saloom was eventually released with her son, Preston, leaving her husband, George, behind.

Deborah:

'We really didn't say goodbye to each other,' Deborah explains. 'You can't, you can't really do that, you're so concerned at the moment with what you're doing... What you must do... I was just very torn as a wife and a mother... If I had not had Preston I would have never left George... But we both agreed that it was important for me to go home as we had two sons together. We were not seeing any other way out.

'I don't think it is possible to prepare yourself for that kind of separation. We hugged a lot... When we walked through the gates and I saw my husband looking through the window blowing kisses at me I thought, *Well, then, this is it. I will never see him again.*'

She left a letter:

Dear George,
I don't know what to say – My heart is full! I love you
with all my heart. I will do my best to care for Preston and
Nathan and I'll never rest until we're all together again. I
know you'll be fine. I'll work to get you out any way I can!
My love and my heart are here with you. See you Home.
My beautiful Ramblin' Wreck.

Love Deb xxx

CHAPTER 12

DECISION

By the end of August, an allied army had assembled in Saudi Arabia. Forty thousand American troops and two hundred US aircraft were joined by Moroccans, Syrians, Egyptians, seven thousand Kuwaiti soldiers who had managed to escape, and forty-five thousand men from the Saudi army. On Saddam's northern border was another army, of seventy thousand Turkish troops.

All over Kuwait and Iraq, and in the capitals of the West, decisions were being made that would change the fate of the hostages. The hostages were not just at the mercy of Saddam's whims, but at the attitudes of their own governments, too. The French passengers had initially hoped for special treatment because their government had helped to train the Iraqi army and had made major commercial deals with Saddam's regime. But their hopes were dashed when President François Mitterrand committed France to supporting President Bush's growing allied coalition, which was dedicated to expelling Iraq from Kuwait. France committed a force of 8,500 troops.

Mitterrand's decision was a blow to French passenger Paul Merlet and his family who had hoped for an early release: 'Initially, we made friends with the Iraqis. For a while we felt that the bad guys were the Kuwaitis. So we hoped we would be released. But then Mitterrand joined the allies, and our hopes died.'

The Merlet family were at Ramadi, at an armaments factory. They arrived at night and some of the women burst into tears when they saw the grim factory surrounded by barbed wire. But it was even worse in the cold light of day: soldiers with Kalashnikovs, barbed wire everywhere. Their psychological state was up and down, from crazy bouts of euphoria (such as the day they fooled the Iraqi guards into believing that the French celebrated Christmas in August) to debilitating depression.

The mood of the Iraqis seemed to vary, too, according to the pressures on their country from the outside world. Initially they gave the French plenty of food and a television, once even feeding them masgouf, a typical Baghdadi dish, and an expensive one. But each time the UN voted for sanctions against Iraq, the treatment got worse, and when Mitterrand backed an air embargo, the Merlets and the other hostages were moved from the bungalows around the factory to the interior of the factory, where living conditions were much worse.

The French began to develop their own escape plans. At one site, the women sewed large French flags and laid them out on the ground, hoping that satellites would spot them and the allies would send a rescue mission. Escape committees were formed at many camps, and detailed plans made. But for the Flight 149 passengers, now scattered all over Iraq and Kuwait, the Brunyate escape had left its scars. These hostages felt they had come close to being executed after the pilot and some of the crew had fled, and some of them wanted a ban on any further escape attempts.

An American at the IBI camp cut through the outer wire fence, and then returned to his hut to bide his time before escaping. But the hole was discovered and an Iraqi officer went to see the hostage leaders. They confronted the American. A cut piece of wire was found in his possession. He denied everything and started shouting. 'You are crazy!' he screamed. The officer drew his gun and pointed it at the temple of the American. 'I am not crazy!' he shouted back. The others begged the Iraqi not to shoot. One of the hostages put his hand on the officer's wrist and pulled the gun down. The officer glared at him and then at the shouting American. Then he shrugged, holstered his gun, and walked away. A 'war' broke out between the British and the French at the IBI camp. The French were unhappy with the British attitude to the Iraqis and vice versa. One of the Frenchmen even threatened to visit a British villa in the middle of the night and cut the occupants' throats.

One of the cars in the compound had been set aside by an Iraqi officer as his spoils of war. But one night three of the French, students in their early twenties, got drunk on the brew from an illegal still and trashed the car.

John Chappell, held in the same camp, remembered:

We had had some problems with them [the French] for quite a few days. They had been drinking heavily and they were just being argumentative and they just didn't want to conform.

In the early hours of the morning, they decided to demolish a car that one of the Iraqi senior officers had brought into the compound for safe keeping, waiting for transport up to Baghdad. The three of them set about this car with baseball bats and something else. They set about really bashing this car. Every bit of glass was broken, they jumped on the bonnet [hood], they jumped on the roof, and they just ruined the car. It was a nice car, not old. Then they went off to sleep around 5 or 6 a.m.

The hostages gathered for the daily roll call. Numbers would be counted by the guards to make sure that no one had fled. This took place at 4 p.m. in St George's Square, in the centre of the compound. By this time, the Iraqis had seen the damaged car. They demanded the culprits be given to them to be 'dealt with'. It was quite clear the Iraqis knew who had trashed the car – the Frenchmen missing from the roll call.

John Chappell: 'They wanted to know where the Frenchmen were and where they lived because although they knew that the Frenchmen were in the compound they didn't know where individuals actually lived.'

Despite their anger with the French, the rest of the group refused to give the guards any information. The guards left but said they would be back.

John Chappell: 'A couple of hours later, these three young lads got up out of bed and we told them that they were in trouble and that the Iraqis were coming back to speak to them about the car, and again they were very argumentative. They said it's got nothing to do with you, it's got nothing to do with them, it's not their car, we can do what we want. Eventually the Iraqis came back in but this time it wasn't the just normal guard. There were three others that came, too, they had red berets on and these were Commando-looking soldiers – they looked rough and tough. They wanted to take these three lads away. We argued the case saying, no, you can't take them away. You take them, you take all of us.'

The show of defiance and unity worked. After a tense stand-off the red berets left without the Frenchmen. The rest of the hostages promised to keep them out of trouble. But there was a warning.

John Chappell: 'They left saying that if these three cause any more problems, then they'll be in any time they want and just take them, whether it's day or night, they might be asleep but they'll just come in and take them and nobody will ever see them again. I don't think these three lads realised how close they were to being murdered.'

One of the French students became very depressed. He felt he was being bullied by his older companions, he felt he had lost his chance to go to university back home, and he felt he could not face life in the camp any more.

John Chappell: 'One evening, the three French guys had been invited to my place and we sat round and we had some drinks, we played cards, and then when it was time for them to leave I said I would walk with them to their bungalow. They lived about fifty yards away across the compound. We were having trouble with some dogs and I used to carry a stick so I said I will walk you back to your place with this stick.'

At the Frenchmen's home, John decided to stay for one more drink. *I will see you in the morning*, he said, as he got up to leave. *You won't see me*, said one of the young men. *I have taken some pills.*

John and the other two went into his bedroom. They found an empty bottle of barbiturates. John yelled at the other two to keep their companion there and then sprinted out of the bungalow to raise the alarm. He banged on the door of his friend Eric Watson. Watson went across with a glass of salted water to make the Frenchman throw up.

John grabbed an empty kettle and went to the camp gates and began banging on the metal gates. He hammered away, again and again, for what seemed like hours. The kettle had practically disintegrated when a guard finally came. But he would not approach to talk to John until he had put what remained of the kettle down and backed away.

John Chappell: 'He just kept saying [to] go away from the gate; I just kept saying, "Doctor, doctor, bring the doctor," so, eventually, he understood what I wanted. He ran off and after ten minutes, came back with a doctor.'

When they got to the bungalow, Watson had succeeded in making the French student drink the salt water, and he had been sick. The doctor gave him an injection – 'To calm him,' he said – and he went to sleep on the sofa.

The next day, they went to see the student, to sit him down and talk things through. The young man poured his heart out. He had been on his way to India on Flight 149 and now he was miserable because he had lost his university place and would have to wait a full year before he could rejoin his course. He was somewhat calmer after the talk and there was no more trouble. The other hostages made a point of talking to him often from then on and kept a careful eye on him.

*

Life for the hostages became grimmer by the day. The allocation of human shields to strategic sites across Iraq and Kuwait was random. But for a lucky few, they found a captor who defied Saddam's orders and treated them with kindness.

Shammon Roel was the resident engineer of Dokan Dam when the invasion happened. A Christian Assyrian and Anglophile, he was living in a small villa overlooking the lake with his young family when orders arrived from on high in Baghdad. He was going to receive some 'guests' and would be responsible for the practical arrangements, under the watchful gaze of a secret police contingent and an assortment of poorly disciplined conscript soldiers. The orders were to confine the guests twenty-four hours a day, seven days a week.

Fortunately for the group, Roel's understanding of the word 'guests' was rather different. He persuaded the guards to allow the hostages out for a walk as often as twice a week, in the early days, and ensured they were properly fed. On one occasion, they were escorted by the guards to his house for tea on the lawn. His youngest daughter, age six and dressed in her best clothes, passed around a tray of sweets. It was a very human gesture and not without personal risk to Roel. Roel told his guests that the local schoolchildren wanted to come to the dam and sing for them, but suspecting a regime propaganda stunt, they declined the offer.

He also helped in one very important way – he got hold of a battered but still serviceable shortwave radio so they could listen to the BBC World Service – although hearing British Prime Minister Margaret Thatcher in Parliament suggest that the human shields were expendable, a sacrifice to the greater cause of removing Saddam from Kuwait by force – did not exactly improve morale.

Roel's kindness was not matched by his guards. The hostages were moved to huts on the top of the dam, they assumed to make them visible to the satellites. One evening, while they sat eating, a drunken guard came in, took out his Berretta pistol, and held it against the head of hostage and 149 passenger Barry Manners. 'America come Iraq, I kill you first, Mr Barry.' He then repeated the procedure among three or four others before getting bored.

*

Back in the UK, plans for a hostage rescue were finalised. The SAS commanders were not confident about the intelligence they were getting on the hostages, despite having pinpointed some of the locations where they were being held. There were just too many of them. Intelligence officers began watching CNN for any references or footage of the hostages, analyzing it frame by frame.

The plan called for a joint operation, with the Americans mounting a diversion and the SAS parachuting into the areas where the hostages were held using a HALO descent – high altitude, low opening. They would then force their way into the camps and free the hostages; helicopters would fly in for the extractions.

There was a plan B too, with members of the SBS infiltrating into Kuwait and Iraq to map out potential escape routes if the hostages had to flee on foot. The prospect of hundreds of civilians moving on foot across the desert, pursued by vengeful Iraqis, was not a happy one. *Hundreds are going to die*, one SAS officer told his colleagues.

Thatcher had been urging President Bush to act tough ever since their first phone call after the Iraqi invasion. But concerns over the fate of the hostages weighed heavily on the allied war planners. Saddam's decision to release the women and children was seen in some quarters as a step towards a settlement. Thatcher saw things differently. In an interview on the Sunday-morning *Breakfast with Frost* show on 1 September, she made it clear to David Frost that the hostage issue would not stand in the way of military action to free Kuwait. 'If you allow the taking of hostages,' the Prime Minister said, 'terrible as it is, to determine your own action against a dictator, he has won, and all he will ever do or anyone else with similar ambitions will do, is to take hostages, knowing that other people will never take the requisite action to stop such a dictator. So, I am afraid, we would have to take the necessary action we feel vital to stop a dictator, even though he still held hostages.'

Many of the hostages watched on television as CNN and Kuwait stations broadcast quotes from her interview. Her comments about the hostages made them feel 'sick to the stomach', one remembered. What followed made them even more fearful. And angry. Thatcher threatened Saddam and the Iraqi military with prosecution over war crimes:

If anything happened to those hostages, then sooner or later, when any hostilities were over, we could do what we did at Nuremberg and prosecute the requisite people for their totally uncivilised and brutal behaviour. We are all making due note of the people who do it because these days they cannot say they were only acting under orders. If they are doing something which is totally cold and cruel and brutal, then they could in fact be prosecuted later. I don't want them to think that they are going to get away with it because they won't.

I do not regard Saddam as mad. I regard him as totally calculating and brutal and having no regard whatsoever for the dignity or rights of the individual. None whatsoever. We do know that a person who has taken hostages cruelly, brutally, and a person who has hidden behind the skirts of women and children, is now manipulating them and using them, and although he has let some of them go – and they should never have been taken – he is obviously using their husbands and sons and not letting them go.

In other circumstances, some of the hostages might have cheered Thatcher's principled stand against blackmail and tyranny. But now, to most of them, it felt as if they were being sentenced to imprisonment. Or perhaps death.

CHAPTER 13
SAFE HOUSE

The grand escape planned by Richard Brunyate and his crew had gone wrong. Instead of all his crew getting away, just six people had escaped from the Regency Palace Hotel – Brunyate, his first officer Gordon Gault, purser Malcolm Butcher, engineer Brian Wildman, and stewardesses Jacqui Hunter and Maxine Woods.

After being cooped up for three weeks, Hunter found leaving the hotel a strange experience. The outside world looked very different from the luxury of the Regency Palace. They passed lots of burned-out cars and houses; everywhere were signs of war.

The group's destination was a safe house organised by the Kuwaiti resistance, a three-storey home in a quiet residential neighbourhood. The house had been abandoned by the previous occupants for reasons that were never clear. When they arrived, the housekeeper, from the former Portuguese colony of Goa in India, was still there. It was an awkward encounter. Post-invasion Kuwait City was a place of fear, a city of informants, spies, soldiers and resistance fighters. You did not want to be caught in the middle. If you wanted a peaceful life, you did not want to know the whereabouts of a group of Westerners on the run.

The housekeeper knew the Kuwaitis would harm her if she turned the Westerners in to the Iraqis, but she also knew the Iraqis would treat her even more harshly if they discovered she hadn't turned them in. The group had to be very careful how they treated her. They were polite and in general left her alone, but Jacqui Hunter felt very sorry for the poor woman, who soon left and did not return.

Brunyate had made contact with a key resistance leader named Fahad, who risked everything to help them despite his brother having been killed in the very early days of the invasion. Fahad turned up at the house to greet them.

He made a strong impression on Jacqui Hunter:

He was very jolly, saying things like Aunt Thatcher is sending her boys and Uncle Bush is sending his… Come in, you are welcome. But he was also a very serious Muslim, so he wouldn't touch, wouldn't shake our hands. He observed all the local customs. He was very, very Arabic in his ways. As we walked in, we could see that people had just left and there was a trail of ants where they had been eating, they'd just cut and run.

The house would now belong to us and we could stay there. Fahad said it must be our home and we are his family and he will look after us and he will get us home and get us back and he'll get messages out and he will make sure that nothing bad happens to us. All these [safe] houses, they all know that we're in there and they're all going to look after us, but we must stay in and he would do whatever it was that was needed.

There was certainly plenty of space. Hunter and Woods ended up in their own room with a double bed. The house was nicely furnished. There was a mosque just outside. For entertainment they had Dubai Television, Scrabble, and Uno – and Fahad, who liked to joke and keep them happy. Fahad believed that as the British had soldiers in Kuwait, he and the resistance had an obligation to help British hostages.

Brunyate was the group's leader, both by dint of rank and personality. He had led them to relative safety but, alone with his diary, he agonised about this decision.

August 18
The good news is that the apartment we are hiding in
has air-conditioning, running water, and plenty of food.
We seem to have fallen on our feet. However, I am very
nervous and constantly worried at the decision I have
made. Sleep is difficult. There is a lot of shooting in the
area with tracer fire lighting up the night sky.

August 20
I have slept badly again. I seem to be plagued by nightmares
and all of us, though we don't say it, wait for the knock on
the door which would end our freedom. I worry for Fahad,
our Kuwaiti benefactor, who is extraordinarily brave. He
risks his life daily to bring us supplies. Each night he takes
out Iraqi soldiers by the most awful methods.

*

All the crew hid their BA uniforms and took lots of precautions. Not only did they have to worry about Iraqi patrols but also gun battles between the Iraqis and the Kuwaiti resistance. Fear was a natural but not always useful emotion, they found. Jacqui Hunter, for example, felt that they had to try to stop being so afraid, because the fear just made them useless and impractical. Instead, she thought, they needed to be strong and even unemotional.

For the BA crew, the highlight of the day was Fahad arriving with the latest news. Often he had a gun, too.

Jacqui Hunter: 'Sometimes he had a red-hot gun because he'd just been involved in an exchange of fire. He said how they were picking up Iraqi soldiers all the time because they didn't want to fight and told us other stories about what was going on outside.'

Maxine Woods: 'We ranged from feeling safe to feeling completely terrified. There were Iraqis all around and we had the curtains closed all the time. We'd taped the windows in case of bomb blasts and so we had to crawl onto the roof for fresh air.' They could crawl out through a sort of doorway and lie next to a wall, keeping low on their stomachs to avoid detection. Despite the heat, the fresh air was a relief.

Jacqui Hunter:

[One day] we heard that there was going to be this display of civil disobedience. And so all the mullahs were calling, you know, which they'd been banned from doing – you know, 'Allah Akbar! Allah Akbar! [God is great!] – and there were people on the streets screaming and shouting and the whole of this area was just filled with this constant 'Allah Akbar!' And the air was filled with tracer and the Bam! Bam! Bam! of bullets, it was like fireworks. It was the first time that I'd really been outside properly, and I heard this noise, this whoosh, whoosh! And I thought that was a bullet. I said that's it, we will go back in now. I'd have been really annoyed to have been shot.

A new arrival at the house was an expatriate lady, Irene, with her cat, Pearl. The group liked the lady but hated the cat.

Another day, a bang on the door turned out to be a group of Palestinians trying to get in. The Palestinians were distrusted because their leadership had sided with Saddam, and in Kuwait itself, some of them had become collaborators and informants. The women had heard gruesome stories of rapes in the city and refused to let in anyone they did not know. In fact, they were scared most of the time, and hot all the time as it was the middle of the Gulf summer. But at least they could have showers. They felt they were better off than most people hiding in the city.

One afternoon, Fahad came to the stewardesses with an escape plan. Danish citizens were being allowed to go free, and Fahad would try to smuggle them out as Danes. Irene did not want to leave but Jacqui and Maxine, both blondes, felt they could pass as Danes and were keen to give it a try. Fahad arranged for their photographs to be taken and for someone to forge Danish passports. The stewardesses hid their genuine passports in the house and waited for his call. But the plan fell through. They never found out why.

Another plan involved them dressing up as Arab women and getting out to Saudi Arabia across the desert. They sewed together some clothes and shaved their arms and practiced applying makeup to change their appearance. But that plan fell through, too. These constant ups and downs wore them down. Their minds often turned to thoughts of home and family.

Jacqui Hunter: 'I used to go out and look at the moon and the stars and think gosh, my family can see that and so can I, that's really strange. And I can remember sitting with Gordon one night and we talked a lot about family and home and what they'd be thinking.'

Brunyate used to go out first thing in the morning and at night to check and survey the area. On his travels, he had managed to steal a car by hot-wiring it, and brought it back to the house so the group had transport in case of an emergency. Fahad seemed to move around at will, sometimes dressed up as a garbage collector.

On Dubai Television, they heard Saddam Hussein's announcement that he was letting all the women and children go. Brunyate said, 'That's it, you've got to go, we've got to get you out of here. We've got to find a way to get you out of here.' But *how* were they going to get out? Jacqui and Irene then heard a follow-up story on the World Service. A large group of women, including British nationals, were going to be taken to Baghdad and then to the airport and sent home.

Jacqui Hunter:

> I just knew that they were the crew, I just knew. So I got Maxine and said tomorrow on the television you're going to see something – you are going to see our cabin crew and they are all going home. That was a really black moment. There were no hysterics or anything, it was just kind of, oops, we jumped the wrong way. We're now in a worse position stuck in this house somewhere. Of course, the next day, that's exactly what we saw – we saw our cabin crew member, Claire Palmer, who we'd been with, queuing up and going home. Dick [Brunyate] was really upset.

Brunyate was determined that 'the girls', as he called them, should have a chance to go home with the other women and children. But Fahad was not optimistic. He warned them that the city was becoming more dangerous and the roadblocks harder to get through. Many of them were now manned by Palestinians who had sided with Saddam.

Brunyate had by this time grown a beard and had taken to moving around in Arab clothing. He also spoke enough Arabic to get by. One day, he told the women, 'I've made contact with somebody and you're going to go home, I have to get you home.'

Between them, they worked out a cover story. Maxine and Jacqui would pretend they had been staying at Irene's house and that they were Australian nurses who were going to join a convoy of other nurses. Fahad's team would travel with them, one car in front and one behind, to come to their aid if anything went wrong. To add to the risks: for the first time in her life, Jacqui would have to drive an automatic car.

The men in the house all wrote letters to their wives and loved ones back home, but in the end it was determined too dangerous to take them. If the women were taken prisoner by the Iraqis, the letters would compromise Brunyate, Gault, Wildman, and Butcher.

At the last minute, there was another change of plan. There was a convoy of women and children leaving for Baghdad, organised by the Indians but with British citizens allowed to travel with them. They would try to join that. This meant they could travel with their British passports after all.

The women packed for the trip. They each packed a little bag containing some rich tea biscuits, dates, and water.

Maxine Woods: 'We covered our hair because obviously being blonde in an Arab country is not a good idea. And we tried to look as ugly as possible, which was very easy, because we looked very drained.'

The women left at 5:30 a.m.

Jacqui Hunter: 'It was an automatic car about the size of a tennis court that we had to get into. I'd never driven an automatic car in my life. I felt like I was driving through back lanes and through people's gardens. I'd have to slow right down and crawl and then we'd go really fast.' Jacqui also had to keep just behind the vehicle in front being driven by a resistance fighter named Samir as well as look out for Fahad's car behind her. It felt like a very long journey, the most memorable car ride of her life, but it was over in just ten minutes. The convoy reached the rendezvous point on the seafront just outside the city. Some coaches were waiting in an area surrounded by barbed wire; lots of women with baggage and lots of children milled around. Many of them appeared to be Indian nationals.

Jacqui Hunter: 'My heart was in my mouth when we got there. I said to Fahad, "What are we going to do with the car?" ... He said, "Let me have the keys." And I was so afraid that I thought that if they see me giving him the keys, they are going to know. There were Iraqi soldiers all around us. So he walked close to me and I handed him the keys. He said, "Cars are at a premium, you know, in these situations." ... I passed him the key and he sort of melted away. Then an Iraqi guard came up almost immediately and said, "Are you nurses?" I said, "Teachers." So, he said, "Where have you been?" I said, "Oh, what a situation, I can't wait to get home, how has it been for you?"'

As she talked to the guard, Jacqui noticed that Fahad had appeared and was standing right behind him. For a moment, she thought he was going to kill him. But he just listened and watched and when he was satisfied that the girls' cover story was holding up, he just disappeared. Jacqui and Maxine went off to register for the long coach ride north, to Baghdad and then home.

Before they left the villa, instead of letters, the male crew members gave Jacqui and Maxine personal messages for their loved ones back home. And Brunyate had one startling message for one of the women. He gave a number and told her to call it when she reached London. 'Tell them you have been with me and I've had to blow my cover.'

It was a number for MI6, British intelligence, he said.

Brunyate it seems was an MI6 asset – his Middle East background and flying career had made him an ideal candidate, a fact he had already confided in his co-pilot, Gordon Gault.

He had been given Kuwaiti resistance contacts in advance of the flight to use if they got into trouble. This was a highly secret mission, but the one person the planners had to have on their side was the pilot: pilots of passenger planes had the power to stop or alter flight plans in the event of danger. They had to ensure that Brunyate landed the flight as planned in Kuwait and put the team in place.

Brunyate was their insurance policy.[6]

---

6   An MI6 source later explained to me the cozy relationship between British Airways and the intelligence services, a relationship that was at its height when Lord King was chairman and his close friend Margaret Thatcher was in Downing Street. BA was known to the service as 'Bucks Fizz' and any mission would always involve co-opting the pilot. An asset was an individual the intelligence service could call on if needed – not an actual employee of the secret service but someone who was 'on the books' because their job could come in handy during a mission. Other examples would be people working in private security in hotels to assist with surveillance, or, on rare occasions, journalists or aid workers in war zones. When I reviewed my notes of my Brunyate interviews, I was struck by the fact that he told me in the first interview that there had been no group of men boarding the plane at the last minute even though he had been told of this by his crew.

CHAPTER 14

AT THE MERCY OF SADDAM

Kuwait City had become a city of violence and fear, with a growing number of bold resistance fighters, Westerners in hiding, POW camps, Iraqi conscripts patrolling the streets, secret police, random shootings, collaborators, looting, and food shortages. Into this heady mix came Ali Hassan al-Majid, the man known to the world as 'Chemical Ali' for his gassing of the Kurds. As the newly appointed governor of the Iraqi province of Kuwait, he ordered a brutal clampdown. All Westerners were to be rounded up.

One of the first to have an up-close-and-personal encounter with the feared governor was Jerry Blears. Blears had been separated from his wife and children when he was driven off from the IBI camp with other British soldiers from REME (Royal Electrical and Mechanical Engineers) just after the invasion. The last their families had heard was the sound of gunfire as the men were taken away. No one knew whether they were dead or alive.

In fact, they were driven around Kuwait for a couple of hours before being taken to a headquarters. There Blears met a senior figure who turned out to be Chemical Ali. He told the men, 'We know who you are.' (Until then they had tried to convince the Iraqis that they were normal civilians.) After about four hours of questioning, the men were put back in the bus with an escort of four armed Iraqi soldiers. They were then paraded around in several locations, shown off as if they were 'booty'. After that, the bus headed north into Iraq. This was the first of many such journeys; one of the tactics the Iraqis had developed for the human shields was to keep them moving from place to place, to keep them disorientated as well as harder to find.

The British captives arrived in Basra at about 1 p.m. and were taken to the Basra Sheraton. The men were all deeply frustrated. Their superiors had ordered them to stay in Kuwait after the invasion, when they could have activated their escape plans, and now all thirty-seven of them from the REME unit were in enemy hands. They discussed overpowering the guards, killing them, and taking over the bus, as the guards looked like complete amateurs. But they felt it would be too risky, not for them but for their families who were still being held back at the compound in Kuwait.

At the Sheraton, the men were given lunch. It all seemed quite civilised. Then they were put back onto the bus and driven to the airport. They boarded a cargo plane, which seemed similar to a US Hercules but Russian-made, and flew under armed guard to Baghdad. These troops were much more professional.

The men were taken to the fifth floor of the Mansour Melia hotel. There were several men to each room but it was relatively comfortable. The Iraqis had first described their prisoners as 'guests of peace', but now they were aware that they were British soldiers, part of Margaret Thatcher's army, and they were treated with a great deal of suspicion. Each man was photographed.

The British military attaché in Baghdad visited them in the hotel. He said he would contact local aid agencies to get clothes for the men, but nothing came of his promise. Their stay lasted eight days. Alex Boyd – a colleague who'd been looking after Blears's son – was brought to the hotel with another man. They had been picked up in Kuwait City while wearing the Kuwaiti military uniforms supplied to them when they were on secondment. The Iraqis became quite hostile after Boyd and the other man arrived to join the rest of the unit in Baghdad. Blears was at least able to find out that his son, Colin, had been sent back to join his wife and daughter. He did not know where they were but at least they were alive.

Next, the men were sent by bus to Mosul in the north of Iraq. They thought they might be thrown out of the country into Syria, but instead the thirty-nine prisoners were taken to a refinery in Mosul, where the conditions were very unsanitary. They understood immediately that they were there as a 'key point defence'. They were not chained up but were confined to small rooms and were fed. Curiously, the guards did not confiscate any of the men's belongings (watches, wallets. etc.). Every effort was made to overhear the guards' conversations, who clearly didn't really know what was going on. One unpleasant guard took a particular dislike to Jerry Blears and told him that when they got the orders, he would kill him first.

The stay in the refinery lasted for five days. The men were then split arbitrarily into two groups and half of them – including Jerry Blears – were sent back to Baghdad. It was very difficult to leave the other men in Mosul. Morale was low and the situation seemed to be getting worse and worse. But back in the Mansour Melia hotel, there was a wonderful surprise: their families were there. On the fifth floor of the hotel, Jerry Blears was reunited with wife Jackie and his children. His elation was short-lived, though, when Jackie took him aside and told him about Colin. The ten-year-old had seen men being hung from cranes and was severely traumatised when he returned to his mother and sister at the hotel. He had become morose and uncommunicative. One day, Colin was in their room when he suddenly cried out, ran out to the balcony, and began to climb over the rails. He was grabbed before he could jump to what would have been certain death, but he remained depressed and withdrawn for a long time afterward.

Jackie went on to describe what had happened at the IBI camp after Jerry and the other men had been driven away. One of the wives, had been molested but not actually raped. There were various other incidents of harassment. In desperation, one of the wives at the compound had called the house of one of the officers who had not been captured, to tell him that the men had been rounded up. However, when the officer's wife answered the phone, she told her never to call again. The women felt totally abandoned. The Blears family were angry that all the REME soldiers had been told that they were now back under British military law and had to obey it, but nobody took responsibility for the families.

An embassy official had visited them at the IBI camp. They were still free to travel around in the early days of the occupation. He had collected all the British passports and had them shredded to get rid of the evidence of them being 'service personnel'. This meant the Blearses had no passports and the Iraqis would not let them out of the country without them.

When the women complained to the embassy official about their conditions, they were told – in front of a gathering of all the women and children – 'I don't know what you're worried about, the worst that can happen is that you'll be raped and shot.' They did not appreciate his so-called sense of humour. He returned to the embassy, and the women were left to their own devices. Eventually, the British Embassy arranged a convoy to take the families from their compound to the Kuwait International Hotel, the clearance hotel for hostages in Kuwait. Effectively, the families were then 'handed over' to the Iraqis.

The REME officers who were left in Kuwait moved into vacant embassy housing. The embassy tried to obtain Norwegian passports for them but to no avail. Colin had been among those moved to the new housing – it was felt he would be safer there – but later they were told he was 'not the son of an officer' and could not stay. He was returned to his family.

The woman and children had eventually been moved north and ended up where all the hostages went at some stage: the now infamous Mansour Melia.

Four days after the Blearses were reunited at the Mansour Melia, the Iraqis announced that the families were no longer guests of peace, they were now hostages. They were no longer going to be well fed, except for the children. Adults were given bread and water. The Brits heard an ugly rumour that a group of French hostages also held in the hotel had stolen some food from the children.

The Iraqis started farming their 'hostages' out to different locations. The Blearses were sent to the Dora refinery. They were handed over to the engineering manager of the refinery, a man whom they knew as Quas (which they pronounced 'Case'). Initially, they were kept in a comfortable area of the refinery. The Iraqis had prepared for the arrival of the hostages by installing Western toilets. Quas made every attempt to make life comfortable for them. They had 'lucked out' with Quas – other families suffered a great deal at the hands of their captors. The Blearses spent one night at the refinery itself and were then allowed to stay in the house next door, which belonged to the refinery engineer. Quas did not want the armed guards to share the house with the hostages, so he had a portable cabin installed in the garden.

They stayed in Quas's care until August 28 – Rachel Blears's sixth birthday. The families had stayed up late the night before to make birthday cards for her. The following morning the guards woke them up and took Jackie, Rachel, and Stan Roberts away. Jerry Blears protested that the guards had got the families mixed up, but the guards insisted. It was their way to minimise the security risk – nobody would risk anything if half the family was held separately. Blears spent the day with Laura Roberts wondering what was happening to their other halves and children.

Jackie was taken on a bus with blacked-out windows. She and the others arrived at a palace. They recognised what was happening as there were television cameras all around. She realised they were there for Saddam Hussein. Jackie had already seen several media stunts involving hostages. Jackie asked the crews if the footage was going to be shown in the UK. They didn't know. She asked the crew to focus on Rachel so that her grandparents in the UK could see that she was alive on her sixth birthday.

This conversation was overheard by Saddam's interpreter. Jackie was asked if she wanted to have a party for the children. She couldn't see why not and a party was duly thrown for the children. Saddam himself turned up and the whole thing was filmed. Jackie was photographed with Saddam.

After a long tirade, Saddam took questions from the hostages. Another British woman, Jackie Joyce, whose husband was also a member of the British military liaison team, stood up and addressed him. She asked, 'Why are you hiding behind the skirts of women and children?' At the end of the session, Saddam approached Jackie Blears and the kids and said, 'As a special treat I'll release you.' Jackie said, 'What about my husband?' She explained that he was at the Dora refinery. Saddam agreed to free the whole family.

Back at the refinery, Jackie found Jerry and told him they'd been released but he didn't want to leave the Roberts family. The guards told him he had to go: it was a presidential decree. So the Blearses gave all they had – a radio to listen to the BBC World Service broadcasts, which had become a lifeline, and £8,000 in cash – to the Roberts. They were then taken back to the Mansour Melia.

They had no passports so they had to contact the consulate to obtain new ones. Bizarrely, the Blearses were allowed out of the hotel to find a photo booth in the city to provide new passport photos. Later Jerry Blears went round the hotel collecting the names of every Brit there. He compiled a long list of hundreds of people to give to the consulate. He tried to give this list of hostages to the embassy staff, but to his dismay they refused to take it. So he kept it to take back to the UK himself.

The Blears family ended up on a plane home with Jesse Jackson, the American politician, who had gone to Baghdad to bargain with Saddam for the release of hostages. Not all the hostages, however, were happy with the Reverend Jackson's efforts, among them members of USLOK, the US military liaison team in Kuwait, who were now also being held in Baghdad, including Fred Hart:

> The Reverend Jesse Jackson came to the embassy... he also requested a meeting with all of us to inform us that he was going to meet with Saddam Hussein in an attempt to secure our freedom. We informed Rev. Jackson we wanted no part of his release plan if it involved compromising US principles, position, or any requirements by us to make statements. Needless to say, no one from Baghdad gained release under Rev. Jackson's deal with Saddam Hussein.

Rev. Jackson did manage to get a few out from the American Embassy Kuwait, and the woman who was injured during our convoy to Baghdad. Prior to Rev. Jackson's departure, he met with us one last time in an attempt to get us to understand the Iraqi position vis-à-vis the rich Gulf Arab states. We argued with him for an hour or so, and his group decided we were a hopeless cause and they left. This would become a typical drill in the months ahead as various foreign dignitaries came to Baghdad to get their nationals released. It became so commonplace we referred to it as 'bargaining for bodies'. Generally, Saddam would release a few to each dignitary, who would issue a statement prior to his/her departure condemning the US and UN resolutions.

Jesse Jackson was one of a seemingly endless line of Western politicians who trooped off to Baghdad to ask Saddam to free hostages. These missions were mostly undertaken by politicians no longer in positions of power and who were opposed to a 'military solution'. Usually, they had one other thing in common: their trips were undertaken in defiance of the wishes of Western governments, who did not want anyone negotiating with Saddam Hussein until he withdrew from Kuwait.

The visits were thus highly controversial. Many of the human shields and their families welcomed the trips as a chance to get people out. Others called the VIP visitors 'grovellers' who were being used by the Iraqis for propaganda, and that they only got out hostages who were going to be released anyway, some of them because they had taken ill.

Former British Prime Minister Edward Heath arrived and had a high-profile televised meeting with Saddam. He left with thirty-three hostages. He was followed by Tony Benn, a British MP, who wanted to get hostages out but also saw the visit as part of a grander strategy to prevent a war. The Iraqi Embassy in London invited Benn to visit Baghdad and he agreed. Benn then went to see Douglas Hurd, the British Foreign Secretary.

Tony Benn: 'I went to see Douglas Hurd… and it was all rather awkward. And he said, "I'm afraid that if you go, it might give Saddam the impression that we're weakening." I said "Oh, not at all. I'm going to tell Saddam that you're going to invade him and attack him." And then he got frightened the other way: "No, no, no, you've quite misunderstood it, no, no, no, no, no." So, he was very uneasy, it was a very uneasy meeting. But I didn't get much help from the British government.'

In the event, Benn went to Baghdad without the support of the government. On arrival, he was driven around the city until he was suitably disorientated. The vehicle finally stopped at an ordinary-looking house in the suburbs. He had no idea where he was.

Tony Benn:

I was shown into this room. And there was Saddam sitting there with a revolver in his belt and there was a television unit there… and we sat down and began talking. And it was three hours with a break in the middle for a short period. I began by saying, which I very much felt, that it was a great honour to come to the country between the Tigris and the Euphrates, where all the world's great religions came from: Abraham was from there, Jesus was born there, Muhammad was born there, and I wanted to make the point that I respected the civilisation of the country I was visiting. And then, I said to him, 'May I speak quite frankly?' And he said, 'Yes.' And I did.

I then went into the whole political background and

indicated at one stage that I thought holding the hostages made it more difficult for those who were working for peace, and that he should take that into account. I called them the British residents... I think he thought that it would make people reluctant to bomb them because of the British people. But I knew it wouldn't make the slightest bit of difference. And I also knew that the plight of the hostages was the big question that had been built up, which was whipping up the will for war in Britain.

At one stage, Saddam took his revolver out of his belt and, for a moment, Benn thought, *Perhaps I have gone too far.* But the dictator just put the weapon on the table. The meeting ended and Benn returned to his hotel, when he suddenly remembered he had forgotten to ask Saddam how many hostages he would release.

He also met some of the hostages in Baghdad and a group were allowed to go soon after his visit. Benn hoped he had helped in their release.

But for most of the human shields, such visits were a false dawn. They were hostages, with little hope of release.

Dr Paul Dieppe, the consulting physician from Bristol whose last-minute change of plans led him to cancel his Air Malaysia flight for a ticket on Flight 149, was with a group that included the flight's chief purser, Clive Earthy, and Charles Kristiansson, a BA steward who had befriended Jennifer Chappell at the Regency Palace Hotel. This group was being held in bungalows on the University of Kuwait campus, near the docks.

Paul Dieppe:

Most of it was just crashingly boring, because there's nothing to do. You're in limbo, you're kind of cut off from life. And although we had some contact, a little bit with the outside world through radio or whatever, we actually knew nothing about anything that was going on around us. We didn't really know where we were or anything... And what do you do? I had three main defences to the boredom: one was exercise, one was the various games that we played a lot – we played a lot of bridge, we played quite a lot of backgammon... and I'm a naturally competitive sort of bloke, that's always good. And the third was to write things. There was a computer in the house that strangely had not been trashed by the Iraqis.

Dieppe began to write, working most of the morning, every morning, on a journal of their activities that everyone could add to, or put comments on. Then he set himself a more challenging task: to write a medical textbook and a student booklet about the examination of muscles, joints, and bones. He had no access to any reference material, just what was in his head, but he found it easy to work, and very helpful to his survival.

Paul Dieppe:

I think the writing to me was important because I could forget about everything around me and where I was, particularly when I was writing about things I already knew something about. I knew a bit about a few things to do with arthritis... I wanted to educate others about it, and I could just lose myself in that whole thing. And for a period of a couple of hours or something at a keyboard I was lost, I could have been anywhere. And it was almost better than that in the sense that I wasn't thinking, oh, I should go and check the reference by X to see if I've got that right, or I should ring up Y and find out what's going on, because that wasn't on... there's a purity in just having to do stuff, just from what you have within your mind.

And all you have to keep you going in a situation like that is your memory, that's the only thing there is. It does make one realise that that's actually what human beings are about, and what distinguishes us from all others in this universe is our memories, that's all we've got going for us... I was involved in those subjects like arthritis and I could write about them authoritatively from memory, and it was gold dust to me to be able to do that.

There were constant visits by Iraqi officers who told them Kuwait belonged to Iraq. But the Iraqi soldiers guarding Dieppe's group were mostly young and scared. Clive Earthy took on the role of negotiator. Initially the guards would not let them out of their accommodations, but one day they just said, 'Bugger it, we are going for a walk,' and the guards followed them around the bungalows with their guns. Gradually, by talking to the guards, Earthy and the others were able to negotiate more concessions. First, they developed a running track to keep themselves fit and later had a game of cricket in the back garden, although the game ended when they lost the ball over the fence and were not allowed to climb over and get it back.

Some guards spoke a smattering of English. The hostages would show them pictures in old magazines, say, of a banana, point to it, and ask, 'Can we have this?' Sometimes the guard would write down their request in Arabic and take it away. Little luxuries, like fruit, would then appear.

As the prospect of having to fight a US-led allied army, which was planning to retake Kuwait, grew, so the soldiers grew more nervous and depressed. Some shot themselves in the foot to get sent home.

Paul Dieppe: 'And you know these young lads... were actually much more frightened than we were. And we also learned we could order them around and have some control of them, because they were just frightened kids. When one guy tried to shoot himself in the foot, and he was so incompetent he couldn't even do that very well and just grazed his toes a bit, he was brought to me to be patched up.'

As it turned out, the soldiers who shot themselves were not being sent home but to the front line, at the Saudi-Kuwait border, where they faced American tanks.

The Iraqi guards were essentially teenagers with Kalashnikovs. One evening, they decided to make a bonfire with all the bits of rubbish that was scattered around the docks in Kuwait. Some of this was plastic, and when it caught fire there was a massive bang. On hearing this the young Iraqi soldiers panicked: they thought it was a Kuwaiti resistance attack and made a run for it. They soon realised their mistake and came back, but the incident gave the hostages a rare laugh.

Food was a constant preoccupation for the hostages. They would often go for twenty-four hours without anything to eat. Sometimes they just got rice. Earthy felt this was Saddam's response to the pressures on his regime, including sanctions.

Getting news from the outside world became another obsession. Rummaging through the mess left at the bungalow when they arrived, they found a telephone socket, and later they found a telephone handset, which they plugged in. To their amazement they got a dial tone.

Paul Dieppe:

There was a wardrobe, a big wardrobe, in one of the rooms. And I actually sat myself in the wardrobe with the telephone for periods of time trying to see if I could make contact with people, because it seemed wise, because we were just a bit worried that if the lads saw us on the telephone they might storm in and rip it out of the wall. It was connected and it was the only contact we had with anything, our only means of contact. So, we wanted to preserve that means of contact. So, I sat in a wardrobe with a telephone.

And, to this day, I've absolutely no idea how this happened, but I actually made contact with the British Embassy, and I was so pleased with myself. I said, 'Really, are you the British Embassy? Oh, fantastic, can you help us out? We're in this place somewhere in Kuwait, don't know where, but I know who is here and they're mostly British. I'll tell you who we all are and give you the names and addresses and then you can get the message out, you can tell our wives and girlfriends, and in one case boyfriend, that we're all fit and well and everything's fine. We haven't got much food or water but we're okay.'

That seemed a good thing to do, and I was really pleased with myself. And so I went through the list, which I'd prepared in case I got through to someone sensible. I read out the names and he said, 'Yes, jolly good.' As far as I knew, he was taking it down on the other end of the telephone. And I said, 'You will get that out, won't you?' And he said, 'What do you mean, "get that out"?' I said, 'Well, don't be silly, radio it out, you're obviously in contact with the outside world, I am not, so radio it out. He said, 'How do you know we're in contact with the outside world? I said, 'Look, sunshine, I wasn't born yesterday, get a grip! Just do this, will you? And, if you can, help us out, now you know roughly where we are. We're somewhere near the university and the docks, but I'm not quite sure where.' And that seemed fine, and I remember emerging from the wardrobe and telling the others how well I'd done and being pretty pleased with myself and they thought it was all grand, you know, got the British Embassy onto the case, that's fine.

And so, the next day, I thought I'd just check through again. So, I went back into the wardrobe with the telephone and I rang up the British Embassy again and I eventually got the same chap on the phone and I said we just wanted to check that you'd been able to get some messages out to our loved ones. And he said, 'Tell me who you are again. I seem to have lost the bit of paper that I wrote it down on, old chap. You couldn't give me the names again, could you?'

I pretty much lost my temper then, but I sort of regained myself enough to tell him who we were again.

Then he said to me, 'What are conditions like?' And I said, 'Well, they're okay, we've got water, we haven't got much food, but we've got enough to live on. It's okay.' And he said, 'Yes, you know, it's pretty bad for us here, too – we're getting quite low on the gin.' I lost it then, I just lost it, that was it. I slammed the phone down and I told the lads I'm never ever phoning that embassy again. I lost it.

However, the group did make contact with the embassy again, later on, and also with others hiding out in the city, including some who were living nearby. They kept these conversations short. They were afraid the Iraqis were listening to any calls through the exchange so they devised a simple code to show their outgoing calls were from 'friendlies' – two rings, then put the phone down, one ring, hang up again, then call. For incoming calls from contacts in the city the code was four rings, hang up, then a single ring.

The hostages could only make calls within the city – international calls were not an option – but they no longer felt so alone, so isolated. They did have to be careful not to be caught by one of the many snap inspections, though.

Clive Earthy:

One afternoon, we were on the telephone and the front door of the bungalow was kicked open. The phone was very carefully lowered to the floor. This guy came in with his gun and just stared at us. He didn't speak or anything, he just wandered from room to room. And as he was walking out of the lounge into an adjacent room, our telephone actually rang, which frightened us absolutely sick. Very carefully, but very quickly, we kicked the receiver off with a foot under the table. And the guy stopped and looked around and we just looked up in the air… and he didn't twig it. We don't know why but he didn't twig it. He walked through into the kitchen and of course as soon as he was gone we whipped the telephone out of its socket and put it back in its bag and cardboard box quickly out of sight. He actually came back, thinking, 'I wonder if I did hear a phone,' but he didn't find it. We had it well hidden. So we were very lucky. Very lucky.

The phone provided most of what passed for excitement. Earthy burned garbage and did sketches on the roof to make the time pass. He was also in charge of building a bomb shelter inside the bungalow. He made a red cross for the top of the building with the bungalow's red carpet and notified the embassy of this. The idea was that the Allied bombers would know their position from the marking and not bomb them while attacking the docks. But the Iraqis spotted the cross, took it down, and nailed up the door to the roof.

Earthy became friendly with one of the Iraqi guards who spoke English. This man admitted to being a Christian although he had not dared to tell his fellow soldiers. He was training to be a dentist in Baghdad.

Clive Earthy:

One evening, I was out on the veranda, talking to this guy, and about eight or nine soldiers in our garden were digging this massive great hole in the sand. And it went on and on and, eventually, it ends up a hole about ten feet by eight feet I suppose, by about three feet deep. And they were piling the sand up over the wall and piling it everywhere and I said to this young guard. 'What are they doing? What are they doing? What are they digging a hole like that for?'

And he said, 'Oh, Mr Clive... Mr Clive... nothing to worry about. It is – it is a latrine.' And I said, 'A latrine? We've got toilets that are at the moment working, after a fashion. But you must have those in your guard house too next door. It's not a latrine is it?' And he went a little bit coy and he said, 'I'm... no,' he said, 'I think maybe it's for burning the rubbish. All the rubbish, we burn it in there.'

And I said, 'That's quite near the house there. Besides that you're burning all the rubbish against the wall over your side of the fence. All of the rubbish is burned every day. It isn't for rubbish is it? Now tell the truth. Tell the truth.'

And he looked away slightly, he couldn't actually look me in the face, but then when I basically insisted on eye contact he said, 'Well, Mr Clive,' he said, 'we've been ordered to dig this hole in which to bury you people in the event that any of your friends come in and try to retake Kuwait. We've been ordered to dispose of you. We'll kill you, basically.'

Earthy was shocked. Only that afternoon, they had watched a television news item saying the allies would land on the beaches of Kuwait, near where they were being held. 'Surely, you could take us with you if you move to get away from an invasion,' Earthy asked the guard. The reply was brutal: 'No.'

Earthy decided not to relay this conversation to the others. Morale was very low and he was afraid that one of them might attempt something reckless and 'go over the top' if they found out. But keeping the secret was an awful burden. He spent hours brooding about it, wondering if he would ever go home again. The others became concerned about his state of mind because he was usually so cheerful, but he kept his secret. They did not seem to notice that when they talked animatedly about being liberated in the event of an invasion, he kept very quiet.

*

Earthy and Dieppe did not know it but they were part of a rapidly expanding human-shields programme. By the end of October, Saddam had 661 hostages, including 260 Britons and 103 Americans, placed at seventy sites throughout Iraq and four in Kuwait.

The British were the largest group in captivity because those on Flight 149 had fallen into Iraqi hands, and because, unlike other embassies, British embassy staff did not warn their citizens before the Iraqis began rounding everyone up from the Kuwait City hotels. The Iraqi government television station still referred to the hostages as 'special guests'. Various individuals were used on television as a weapon of propaganda, despite the revulsion this caused in the West. A low point was a staged meeting between a group of twenty-five hostages, some from Flight 149, and Saddam. The dictator launched into a long speech defending the handling of the hostages and then called over five-year-old Stuart Lockwood, whose father was a member of the British Liaison Team. Stuart had been living at the IBI camp in Kuwait before being taken to Baghdad with the other women and children.

Dressed in summer shorts, Stuart was a picture of innocence. An outraged world television audience saw Saddam patting Stuart on the head. Stuart kept glancing over at his parents and then folding and unfolding his arms nervously as Saddam stroked his hair.

Later, away from the cameras, another British child kicked Saddam hard in the ankle. The dictator demanded to know whom his parents were. But there was no reply, and the child and his family lived to tell the tale.

The Halkyards were also forced to appear drinking tea with Saddam, on a programme called *Guest News*. The programme's production teams were touring the hostage sites and eventually turned up at the university bungalows.

Clive Earthy:

> An Iraqi officer arrived and one of these politico guys, to tell us that they would be bringing in a film unit for us and it was for us to talk to our families at home if we so wished, and tell them how well we were being looked after. I'm afraid this did not go down very well with most of us. Within an hour a lorry pulled up outside and all manner of goodies arrived. Boxes upon boxes of food, bottles of drink, a massive great radio, stereo… Blankets were put out. Bundles of clothes were put out. There were things like milk, cartons of milk.

A number of what we would have termed as luxurious things. Books, all sorts of things. And they were placed at strategic places in the kitchen and in the lounge and in the bedroom and all the way around. A fan arrived, you know a big portable fan, to give the impression of coolness and that we were being well looked after.

This was followed by the camera team then turning to us all and saying, 'Who would you like to represent you?', at which just about all my colleagues disappeared. I found myself alone in the lounge with this camera team. The director fellow said, 'Well, Mr Clive, how are you? We see you have plenty of things in your bungalow,' to which the man with the camera on his shoulder was escorted through to the kitchen and the fridge door was opened and he panned in on all the cupboards and the food and everything, through the rooms and then back outside.

Then they sat down and said, 'Mr Clive, okay, and how are you? Have you had a doctor to see you to make sure you are all fit and healthy, and have you been able to send letters home?' and things of this nature. And I said, 'Well, the only thing I'd like to say is up until now we've had absolutely sod-all from you until an hour ago when you brought all the stuff in – the fridge, the cupboards, the blankets, everything.' To which somebody shouted the equivalent, I presume, of 'Cut, cut.' And he said something in Arabic to me, which I don't think was very nice, and they all went out of the door.

Most of the goodies disappeared with the camera crew, but at least some of the food was left behind.

Some of the Westerners in hiding were critical of their countrymen when they saw them on the television. Why were they helping

Saddam? But they did not understand the pressures placed on those in Iraqi custody, nor appreciate the subtle ways that some of the stars of *Guest News* used to show their defiance, among them John Chappell, who was interviewed at the IBI camp in Kuwait.

We were given the opportunity to appear on what the Iraqis called *Guest News*. We were very reluctant to do this because of the propaganda that the Iraqis would get from it, but we were promised that we would get a lot of food and so we agreed that we would do it.

We also agreed that so as not to give any propaganda to the Iraqis, we would each form our own story so that our families would know that we were lying and that what we said was happening was really an absolute load of rubbish. At least it would give them the opportunity to see that we were fit and well.

A television personality from Iraqi TV sat opposite us. He had a big microphone and he introduced himself in Arabic and then said will you introduce yourself… I said my name's John Chappell, quite often known as the Yorkshire Terrier – a complete fabrication.

He said 'Would your wife be able to take advantage of His Excellency Saddam Hussein's offer to come over and be with you at Christmas' and I said 'Well, unfortunately we have two young children… so she would have to stay to look after them, but I have two aunts and I'm sure they would love to have a good time in Baghdad and they'd love to come, providing Saddam Hussein can guarantee them a good time.'

The interviewer said, 'I'm empowered here and now to guarantee that your aunts will have a good time,' so I said 'I'm sure they would love to come.' And he said 'We'll give them a week in a good hotel in Baghdad.' I said 'Ten days, okay.' 'Ten days,' he agreed. What they didn't know is that my two aunts had been dead for ten years so my family would be able to see that I still had my sense of humour.

*

The group at the docks was told they were going to be transferred to Baghdad and then home. They packed their bags but the next day there was no trip to Baghdad. Just as well, most of them thought, as they were not in a fit condition to travel. The uncertainty lasted for several days until finally they were moved north. A long coach ride ended up at the Mansour Melia hotel, the way station for hostages travelling through Baghdad. There they met Tony Benn and staff from the British Embassy in Baghdad, who did not cheer them up much but brought them tracksuits that were supposed to get them through the upcoming winter. To his relief, Paul Dieppe managed to give the embassy staff some floppy disks on which he had saved his precious medical text. It was a relief to know that all his work would not be wasted. He had worried that it would just end up sitting on the hard drive of an old-fashioned computer in the home of an academic chemist from Kuwait University. But he had managed to find some disks on which to copy his work, as well as the literary efforts of the others. Soon after the meeting, it was clear to the hostages that they were not going home. They were transferred to what they thought was a poison gas factory in the then little-known town of Fallujah. They promptly named their new home Chlorine B.

Paul Dieppe:

We had single rooms shared between two of us… compared with where I'd been it was luxury really. I was held with an

American called John, whom I had not met before. He had had the most appalling experience.

He had been working in Kuwait and living in a flat there. Shortly after the invasion, most of the Westerners had been flushed out of the place and captured. But he'd hidden in a lift shaft... And he got to know some Palestinians who were working in Kuwait and they fed him and kept him alive dodging the Iraqi military presence. He mostly slept in the lift shaft and did whatever, exercising and peeing, on the roof of the building. Until one day one of his Palestinian friends who was delivering food to the building for him was caught by one of the Iraqi soldiers and murdered in cold blood, with John watching from the roof. After that he gave himself up to the Iraqi soldiers and then found himself living with me in a poison gas factory. For the first two days he said nothing. It was only over a period of time that I was able to coax him into speaking and then slowly to get the story out of him. I guess I was debriefing John really, and allowing him to get his act together again. He was deeply traumatised. His experience dominated that part of my captivity. We did not keep in contact, but I'd like to think I did some good for John.

*

Athens-born American computer specialist Apostos 'Paul' Eliopoulos had been picked up by the Iraqis in the early days of the invasion. He had survived the sexual advances of an Iraqi soldier and confinement at a torture centre, had witnessed an execution, and been assaulted. Now he found himself at a phosphate plant near the Syrian border. It was a hellhole but at least he was with a group of other Americans, including Jan Bhatt, who was a passenger on Flight 149.

Bhatt, an engineer, was not in good health. He suffered from diabetes and high cholesterol but his medicines, including allergy medicine, antigen injections, and the cholesterol-reducing drug Mevacor had all been in his checked baggage in the hold of the plane. He never got it back. He had been taken from the Airport Hotel, loaded on a bus, and transported straight to Basra, a six-hour trip without food and with little water. It was a grim journey.

Jan Bhatt:

> I looked out of the window at the mass destruction to property and human life caused by the Iraqi invasion. Buildings had been bombed to rubble, stores had been looted, and dead bodies and garbage were strewn all over the city, covered by swarms of flies. We noted no human activity other than the omnipresence of the soldiers and the tanks rolling by. As it became obvious that we were journeying to Iraq, the instigator of all this destruction, all the hostages on the bus became increasingly upset. Grown men wept at what we saw outside our windows and the uncertainty of what awaited us.

The bus arrived at Basra at approximately 8 p.m. and the passengers were taken to the railway station, loaded onto a train, and transported overnight to Baghdad. Upon their arrival, they were taken to the Al Rasheed hotel and detained there for the following nine days. Bhatt still had no access to any medication.

On 16 August, they were once again herded into buses and driven out of the city.

Jan Bhatt: 'We had no idea where we were bound for, but as we drove near the airport our hopes rose, and I thought that perhaps we were going to be put on a plane to freedom and be released from this awful nightmare. I was devastated when we continued past the airport. We drove for another eight hours, stopping only once to relieve ourselves in the scorpion-and-snake-infested pits beside the road.'

The phosphate plant that Eliopoulos and Bhatt found themselves in was protected by two ten-foot-high barbed wire fences with armed guards. The prisoners quickly dubbed the area in between the fences 'the killing fields', after they were told that they would be shot if they tried to escape or if they were ever found in that area.

Bhatt began to suffer from diarrhoea due to the lack of nutrition and clean drinking water. He and the others were forced to drink dirty water to survive. They were confined to their living quarters for all but two hours a day. The houses they occupied were situated in the middle of the plant and had been long ago abandoned. They had not been cleaned for months, or even years. The smell was almost unbearable, worse even than the giant cockroaches that were their constant companions.

The walls of Bhatt's room had been freshly painted with oil-based enamel, and the caustic fumes caused his eyes to burn and made it difficult for him to sleep. After a number of complaints, he was moved to a dilapidated bungalow, where he shared sleeping and bathroom facilities with three other hostages. He managed to see a doctor but never received any medication.

Bhatt, Eliopoulos, and others were soon on the move again. Eliopoulos ended up at a power plant, Bhatt at what appeared to be a biological research factory. The transfer point was once again the Mansour Melia hotel in Baghdad.

Jan Bhatt:

I waited my turn, as one by one, names were called by an Iraqi guard holding a pistol. Several hours later, I was separated from the rest of the group and put in the back of a car with a guard and an armed driver. I had heard earlier in the day of the release of a Palestinian American and, as we drove once again towards the airport, I was extremely hopeful that as an Indian-born American national, I had been separated from my fellow hostages because I too was going to be released. As we drove past the airport and onto a small dark road, every hope I had held onto vanished, and I experienced pangs of terror, loneliness, and utter desperation that plagued me for the remainder of my detention.

Many hours later, I arrived at a biological factory... The building was permeated by the stench of burning bodies, which we assumed (and hoped) came from the corpses of animals used in experiments. The air quality caused my allergies to worsen; as did the fact that I had to share my room with a heavy smoker.

Our living conditions were unbearable. The bathrooms were cramped, filthy, and unlit, and we had no hot water. Both the bathrooms and the kitchens were infested with roaches, mosquitoes, and vermin. The food was largely inedible – we were served unidentifiable soups with large chunks of fat floating on top. These soups were often so salty and disgusting that we spat them out upon tasting them. I became extremely agitated about my cholesterol and adult diabetes, given the diet that was being forced upon me.

After many repeated requests, I was taken to Baghdad General Hospital for a check-up. Upon arrival, I could not believe how filthy the hospital was and, after a brief and token examination, the doctor told me that my sugar and cholesterol levels (which I knew were extremely high) were normal, and that I was making too much of a fuss.

On another such visit to the hospital, a dentist gave me a filling without administering any Novocaine, which caused me extreme discomfort and stress... I became increasingly more agitated regarding my physical health, knowing that there was no recourse available to me if my condition deteriorated.

Six weeks later, Bhatt's guided tour of Iraq continued. He was loaded into a car with a British hostage. They were going to another 'home', they were told. The two men were then split up and Bhatt arrived at a large multi-storey military complex with heavily guarded gates.

As winter drew near, the cold set in at night. The hostages, lacking heating or warm clothing, found sleep increasingly difficult.

Jan Bhatt:

I rarely slept for more than a couple of hours at a time owing to the difficult conditions and impending sense of doom that were forever occupying my mind. I existed in a state of constant fear and extreme anxiety, as the idea that US hostages might be killed on international television in a theatrical warning to the United States continuously plagued me.

I also understood from the beginning of my detention as a human shield that, owing to the nature of the locations at which I was detained, I would be among the first to die in the event of an allied aerial bombardment. I tried hard to remain in a positive frame of mind, but the longer I was detained, and the more physical hardships I endured, the more hope I lost and the more depressed I grew. The brutal and unexpected manner in which I had been seized from my British Airways flight contributed greatly to my extreme disorientation in the initial phases of captivity. One moment, I had had a good life – I was financially secure and on my way to India for a family vacation, and the next I was in captivity, attempting to reconcile myself to the fact that I might never see my family again.

Eliopoulos, meanwhile, had been moved to a power plant. The manager, knowing he was a computer expert, showed him around. Eliopoulos offered to help with the computers in return for some fresh fruit. He worked on their computers for two days, and systematically sabotaged them, erasing back-up disks so that the systems were still running in memory but there was nothing on the disks.

The hostages were given some fresh pears in return for his work. Eliopoulos felt good about the pears and good about what he had done. But he did realise that they would discover the damage if the system was shut down or there was a power interruption, so he was glad to be transferred soon afterward. Though proud of what he had done he was scared, too: he believed he faced certain death.

Paul Eliopoulos: 'We were resigned to our fate. I mean, we were convinced we were going to be killed. We just hoped it would be done in a dignified way... my greatest fear was that they were going to hurt us before they killed us. We just wished we would go out fast.'

One day, the prisoners were given a couple of treats, olives for breakfast and onions for lunch. They thought maybe they were about to be visited by the Red Cross. Instead a priest turned up that evening and told them that they would be allowed to talk to their families, to call home. The news did not get the reaction the Iraqis intended, so bleak was the mood of some of their prisoners.

Paul Eliopoulos: 'We didn't like it. We were trying to forget that we had families. We were trying to stay away as much as possible from what could really get to us, which was remembering what we had… everybody felt the same. We thought it was a terrible thing.'

Eventually, Eliopoulos did call home and spoke to his wife and his children. The conversation was almost physically painful for him. It brought him no relief.

Paul Eliopoulos: 'It hurt. I mean that was the part of us we were trying to shield from these guys, that was the part we didn't want them to touch. It was cruel. They did exactly what we were trying to protect ourselves from… Anything that made you remember your family made the situation much more difficult… It made me remember that I was a human being and that was bad.'

Life for many of the remaining human shields had become primal. It was no longer about grand strategies and political manoeuvres, alliances and escape plans, or even thoughts of loved ones back home. It was about getting enough food and staying alive. For some, though, it was very much worse.

British Airways steward Charles Kristiansson had been befriended by an Iraqi officer he had met at the Embassy Palace Hotel in Kuwait. The officer started visiting Charles at the apartment where they were held in the Kuwait City.

The officer said he was glad to see Charles. He told Charles he had been thinking about him. He liked Charles's blond hair and he wanted them to be friends. He had studied in Europe and he was a civilised man; they would have a lot in common.

Charles Kristiansson:

> I was raped by an officer familiarly called 'Al Alemani' (the German) – he was an officer older than me but I'm not quite sure by how many years. He came to visit me several times… at the El-Dousouqui's villa in Shuweikh. I needed

to have some dental care and he offered to take me there. It happened at a building in Shuweikh Port area. I just remember it being on the third floor and I jumped when I thought he was going to do it again. I fell on some mass of matting or carpets and then I was sent back with a driver.

He did it to some other young men.

Later, he was taken to the Mohammed Salih missile base, a prime target for an allied air raid. It was deep inside Iraq, just forty miles from Baghdad. He was being held with some RAF men in adjoining cells. The men could see a trench had been dug nearby and left open. They were fed airline food, two meals a day consisting of cabin service trays from Iraqi Airways. They slept in beds with one sheet and a rough pillow. It was very cold.

Charles had been transferred to Iraq by the secret police, but then other guards took over. He lived in contact fear of being raped again. One of the drivers who brought him to the camp had tried to kiss him and touch him.

Charles was suicidal. He dreamed of death. The captives were told that if they attempted to escape they would be shot. 'I couldn't stand it. I wanted to get shot, sometimes I felt I just wanted to go outside and run and get it over with,' said Charles.

CHAPTER 15

CRACK-UPS AND
ROUND-UPS

Maureen Chappell and her two children, John and Jennifer, tried to adjust to life back home in the UK, but every day was filled with fear for the husband and father left behind in Kuwait. They felt alone and abandoned by the government and also had to contend with a strangely uncaring British public. The whole country seemed to be caught up in the excitement of the preparations for war and the allied coalition being assembled by President Bush to drive the Iraqis out of Kuwait. The plight of the hostages was no longer front page news: sometimes it seemed as if they had disappeared from the news altogether. John and Jennifer were sent back to boarding school. Their mother felt she could cope better with them at school, but her children were angry with her as they struggled to adjust to school life after their haunting experience as hostages.

Jennifer found her fellow boarding school pupils indifferent to her ordeal. Some were even hostile, and those with parents in the armed forces bizarrely blamed her for the upcoming war:

I started my school late and it was an all-girls boarding school. Obviously, you need to be there at the beginning to make friends within the group at the beginning, otherwise the whole thing doesn't work. I hated it. When I got there all the groups had already been formed so I was always stuck on the outside of them. I was ringing my mum up crying down the phone every night; just get me out of here. I found it worse to deal with that than to deal with Kuwait. There were some girls there who'd got fathers who were in the forces and they seemed to want to get into the stupid 'Oh, my dad's in more danger than your dad' rubbish. And I wanted to say just leave me alone, at least. The thing I kept saying to them was at least your father's there by choice, your father chose to go into the forces, my dad's not there by choice. And trying to explain to them that half the reason why I was upset wasn't just because my dad was there but because of what I'd gone through as well. Oh, it was just – get out of my face. I hated it.

Maureen was on antidepressants, carrying on as best she could while she waited for news of John. She spent most of her time watching the news. She had no contact with anyone from the government, no regular updates on John's whereabouts or the negotiations with the Iraqis to free the human shields.

British Airways at least did keep in touch. Maureen and the family were invited down to London to visit the operations centre the airline had set up after Flight 149 landed in a war zone. The Chappells and other hostage relatives were given a full tour of Heathrow. They were shown what was being done to keep track of the hostages and how the information was collected, and they were briefed on the latest government level talks.

Lord King, the British Airways chairman, met the relatives' group in the operations centre. He was all charm, until Maureen asked him a question.

> He was quite chatty and telling us how they track the planes and they know where things are and I asked him, 'Why did you allow the plane to land in Kuwait, then?' At which point, he went very quiet. He said nothing… and then, 'I think it's time for lunch,' and that was sort of the end of the visit.
>
> There was increasing coverage on the news about the build-up, about troops and the alliance, to do something about what had happened in Iraq. This worried me an awful lot because I didn't know what would happen to John should our forces attack Iraq and I didn't know what the position of the hostages would be. Saddam was playing games with these hostages, saying that he would put them at strategic installations – which we knew he had done because we had been at one. I just was very anxious as to what would happen.

Maureen's fears were well founded. The Iraqis continued to dig in and defy world opinion. The allies had made it clear that they would bomb strategic targets even if there were hostages held at them.

*

As the prospect of an all-out war grew closer, relations between captors and captives at many of the camps were stretched to a breaking point. Life for those on the run, or in hiding, became increasingly fraught as Iraqi patrols swept the city day and night hunting for Westerners. Whether in captivity or in hiding, the Westerners felt they were trapped between two trains destined to collide.

At one camp in Basra, life had been relative pleasant, and the hostages were able to set up their own golf course and play every day. But a new officer arrived, a senior member of the Ba'ath Party, who hated Westerners. He took four of the prisoners away at night to a site where a deep trench had been dug. He forced them to kneel in front of the trench and lined his men up behind them. They heard the sound of weapons being loaded. But no shots rang out: it was a mock execution. The traumatised men were taken back to camp.

One of the hostages, an explosives expert, was actively helping the resistance using a phone the Iraqis had not disabled. He used the phone and his Filofax, which he still had with him, to call a member of the REME group who was working with the resistance. He would give information about where and how to set up the IEDs (improvised explosive devices): how many were needed for a certain operation, where to place the charges. In one operation, explosives were put into a Mercedes. It was then left, with its key, at a roundabout where Iraqi troops were stationed. The Iraqis' curiosity eventually got the better of them. The troops got into the car and it blew up as soon as one of them turned the ignition.

It was dangerous work. The Iraqis had collaborators in Kuwait. A Palestinian married to an English stewardess for Kuwait Airways nearly uncovered the phone operation and it had to be temporarily shut down. The woman had been picked up in one of the sweeps and was held hostage in one of the camps. One of the other hostages got in touch with her husband to tell him where his wife had been taken. When he arrived at the camp to find her, he revealed himself to be part of the Iraqi secret service. He turned up with a group of other Palestinians who were brandishing AK-47s and proclaiming their support for the Iraqi regime. They took the woman away but did not search the camp. The precious phone was never discovered.

*

Richard Brunyate, the captain of Flight 149 on the run with his small group of British Airways crew, was still being helped by resistance fighters. After the release of the women, they moved from safe house to safe house, often disguised as Arabs to avoid the Iraqi patrols. But Brunyate was a man in constant turmoil, still wondering whether he had done the right thing.

At one point, the group came close to cracking. One of the resistance fighters sheltering them was captured. 'Fahad says his boss has been taken in for questioning. This involved being beaten, strung upside down, and slices cut out of his legs with a knife,' Brunyate wrote in his diary. 'No one could withstand that kind of torture and Fahad fears our cover will be blown again. He is moving us back to our old house tomorrow. We will have to be totally silent with no lighting or air-conditioning so as to make the house look deserted.'

Life became even tougher at the latest refuge, with living conditions so much worse and little contact with the outside world. 'We are all ill at ease,' Brunyate wrote. But, occasionally, there was a little light relief. One day, the BA group found some resistance fighters digging in their backyard, and to the group's amazement, a stash of buried machine guns was revealed. The group hoped that the guns still worked: they had watered the garden for weeks in an effort to produce more food from the date palms. The fighters seemed happy with the guns, though, and took them away.

A female doctor who briefly housed Brunyate and his crew was later caught. She had all her hair torn out by Iraqi troops. She was then raped and beaten to a pulp. Her own parents were unable to recognise her. Such brutality by the Iraqis left Brunyate thirsting for revenge. 'There is a hatred of Saddam in me that is all-consuming,' Brunyate wrote in his diary. 'I would dearly enjoy assisting the Kuwaitis in their nightly killings. I worry for Fahad, our Kuwaiti benefactor, who is extraordinarily brave. He risks his life daily to bring us supplies.'

Hunger was a constant worry for Brunyate: 'Am like a stick insect. I am passing out when I stand up or move around.' And news from home provoked mixed reactions: 'Heard on the radio that Mrs Thatcher is in trouble. More to the point, we have run out of curry powder.' During the period of their captivity, Margaret Thatcher had resigned as prime minister after being challenged for the leadership of the Conservative Party by Michael Heseltine. She was subsequently replaced by John Major.

Hunger was also a worry for American Robert Morris, still in hiding in an apartment block elsewhere in the city: 'As the months dragged on and the US forces sat and waited, we began to worry about starving. We decided to store all the food we could get our hands on.' His group pooled their cash – several thousand dollars – and found a friendly Kuwaiti to go out and buy food for them and bring it in under the cover of darkness, between midnight and 2 a.m. 'On my computer, we began to keep track of the provisions. Now we could tell how many cans of tuna we had, how many kilos of dried beans. We even factored in how much protein we had, how many calories. We filled our bathtubs with drinking water. Every bottle we owned was filled with water – grape juice bottles, plastic clothes packets, garbage cans.'

Morris's group was receiving little information from outside. The embassies that they could contact told them very little and the major news agencies worldwide seemed to have lost track of the hostage story, or lost interest. Basically they were on their own, and had to protect themselves as best they could. Simple precautions, such as immobilising the lifts and removing door knobs, did not always discourage visitors and looters.

Robert Morris: 'One day, there was a banging on the door. I crept up and looked through the pinhole. Two heavyset men in dirty Arab dress stood there. One of them seemed to stare right through me. They were studying the nameplate on the door. I had posted the name of an Egyptian. They muttered something to each other and left.'

Morris began writing letters to the *Boston Globe*, his hometown paper, letters that were smuggled out of Kuwait and posted home from Amman, the capital of Jordan. He signed them 'R.E.M.'

September 21, 1990
We hear of weakness in the American Congress, of doubts that victory can be achieved. We laughed, ready to cry as we despair. The greatest fighting machine in the world – $300 billion a year for arms – cannot fight the rag-tag army of old men and children who pass by our windows, armed mostly with plastic bags filled not with arms but rather with food or a few stolen items of pleasure somehow overlooked in the initial plunder.

We hear daily of atrocities and deaths. They are not reported on the international news. Are the reports true? Are the news services paralyzed, unable to obtain any of these stories?

- Six to twelve doctors massacred in Ahmadi Hospital, presumably for refusing Iraqi orders.
- Three young children gunned down and killed in an Iraqi supermarket for wearing the Kuwait flag.

- Three teenage boys executed in front of their mothers for alleged resistance activities.
- Twenty-four Kuwait men machine-gunned in a diwaniya.
- A supermarket manager shot dead for refusing to put up a poster of Saddam in his shop.
- The Kuwaiti chief of the Red Crescent disappears when lodging a complaint over treatment of patients at the Amiri Hospital.
- An Iraqi doctor attempts to disconnect a wounded Kuwaiti from a life-support system in an ICU.
- Kuwait men arrested at the border and separated from their fleeing families to be presumably turned over to the Iraqi army and conscripted. An entire nurses' hostel sealed off and every nurse raped by marauding Iraqi soldiers.

R.E.M., Kuwait City

October 9, 1990
We are in the 69th day of the occupation and through the grace of God we have eluded the enemy and remained in deep hiding. We have increased our food supplies to hold out for another 130 days. Physically and mentally our group of 13 can survive although we are demoralized by the approach of my government and other governments to the hostages and the failure to rescue us.

Less and less is heard each day on the BBC, the Voice of America, Radio Moscow, or other shortwave stations on the Gulf crisis. We assume, correct or not, that we are forgotten, unimportant, and, as Americans, do not fit into the strategic deliberations of George Bush on Kuwait. We think back to Tehran and some 52 hostages; here, there are thousands of hostages with violence on a far greater magnitude…

International reports on local conditions remain vague. Only Amnesty International speaks out on the atrocities. Iraq piously denies all. We are visited this week by a Kuwaiti doctor. Three of us have health problems, all of which are controllable. One member has bronchial asthma – an attack might force a visit to the hospital and certain arrest. The doctor updates us on events in the country.

- A young Kuwaiti physician is summarily executed in front of his wife when caught with saline drips in his car – one bullet in the head.
- Some four Filipinos are executed for aiding the resistance.
- A bomb explodes in the Hilton lobby – several injuries are reported.
- An Iraqi commercial jet is attacked as it lifts off at Kuwait airport.
- A top agent of the Iraqi secret police has his head blown off by the resistance.
- Al-Adan hospital has 100 beds set aside for gas victims.

It is easy to be wise after the event but our early statements, predictions, and questions vis-à-vis US actions remain valid. The President should have ordered the immediate evacuation of all Americans from Kuwait covering the operation with helicopter forces, fighter aircraft, and amphibious craft. A relatively simple exercise has become a very difficult exercise with each passing day and may eventually be paid for in a lot of blood and tears.

R.E.M., Kuwait City

October 15, 1990
We are in our 75th day of deep hiding. Unfortunately, there are those amongst us with delusions of grandeur, invincibility, invisibility, and immortality. These delusions have led to breaches of security by 3 of the 9 in our immediate group. These 3, exposing the entire group to danger, are spotted by the barbarians too and are captured as they return to their unit after a match of bridge at my place. A Jordanian had betrayed the couple, reporting their presence to the officials in Baghdad. We had warned them, even placed them in a safe apartment, but their delusions of invisibility led to their capture. If good is to come of this, because of their age and Edward Heath's promised visit, they may soon return to England. The third member of our group was spotted departing on foot in the parking lot. He is a loose cannon, unable to think logically. Confronted by friendlies, told that he was seen, he illogically argued that since he saw no one that no one could have seen him… the group comes down hard on him, he had jeopardized all of us.

We intensify our secret patterns, reduce noise and conversation to a minimum, bathe and wash dishes at 2 a.m., presuming that the secret police must sleep sometime. We know they are some 100 feet away. Yet they do not approach our units. They are more interested in robbing empty units, we believe. It is now 8 days since the security breach, we believe we are over another hurdle.

Daily, we collect food. We are well stocked now except the Asians below are paralyzed. The women won't move. The men won't spend money on food. We have 5 more mouths to feed. We will face fierce shortages in 4 weeks if these people fail to act. We remain disillusioned. VOA [Voice of America] says little of us. Messages and letters are almost nil. Congress speaks not of us. We remember Grenada – the US attacked because of some students in danger at St George University Medical School; in Panama we attacked because a navy officer and his wife were accosted in the city. In Kuwait – with several thousand Western hostages and other hostages of friendly countries – the US fails to act.

We have taken it upon ourselves to survive each day. Hardly holding out hope that our great country will see the wisdom to bring its family home early. Rest assured, the psychological destruction of many hostages has already occurred, and there will be countless more tragedies – the results of Iraqis invasion and the US failure of will in August past.

R.E.M., Kuwait City

October 25, 1990
An eerie silence has come over the city. While Friday is the holy day, it does not account for the absence of activities. Our guards continue to watch the building and ignore us. Our 2 fellow travellers were taken away almost two weeks ago by the secret police. Since then, we have, if it is possible, increased our silence.

We had hoped that the 2 taken – because of age and illness – would travel with ex-PM Heath. [With the group of hostages whose release had been negotiated by former British Prime Minister Edward Heath.] They did not get on the plane. Others younger and healthier did and our group here feels that Heath and the old boy network came to secure the release of friends only – a sad commentary but apparently true.

Tank movement is constant out on the ring roads. 60+ tanks were seen moving north on Oct. 24; a similar amount on Oct. 23. The road south to Saudi is sparsely patrolled but no Westerner will risk it just yet. But we are all thinking and sending out reconnoitre parties.

The atrocities continue – 3 Kuwaitis strung up and castrated in front of their families – this happened after a military sweep that caught 8–10 Westerners. That is the punishment for protecting Westerners!!

R.E.M., Kuwait City

*

Although at times Morris wondered *Why me?*, his belief in God gave him the comfort and strength to live from day to day. He reread Homer's *Iliad* and *The Odyssey* and he 'felt that things would work out and that I would reach my family eventually, even if it took years.' Some of the others turned to religion for comfort. Morris recalled, 'Many of us turned to reading passages of the Bible and finding solace from the pages.'

In late November, Morris found solace through God in an unusual way. He was up late at night listening to Voice of America and heard that a prayer service was being organised in Boston for 16 December in the famous Old North Church, next door to his sister's apartment. He said, 'I knew immediately that she must have been involved in the organisation of this prayer session.' With this thought in mind he was able to consider surviving for another day, and another day after that. In the morning he passed this information on to the other hostages and was able to lift their spirits with the thought that people were praying for them.

The BBC and later Voice of America broadcast messages from home. These were sometimes responses to coded messages they had sent out via people leaving the country, telephone calls, or the embassies. Via the US Embassy, Morris sent messages of love and 'not to worry' to his family. When non-Westerners were leaving the country, those left behind tried to send letters with them. In early November Morris and the others managed to smuggle out a video describing their plight, feelings of abandonment, and potential starvation. This video was taken by the Kuwaiti resistance to Amman, Jordan; transferred to London; and played on independent television, Canadian television, and the ABC programme *Nightline* with Ted Koppel. Unfortunately, Morris's eleven-year-old daughter Anna saw the broadcast without warning and was devastated by it, becoming hugely distressed.

The Australians and the Irish were not nationalities wanted by the Iraqi authorities. This meant that two of Morris's group were freer than the others to move about and obtain food and supplies, as well as having the freedom to move around the country or leave and go to Iraq. Unfortunately, as they were within a group of Americans, Canadians, and British, they had to think about the safety of others.

One of them had 'a totally cavalier attitude about the safety of nationalities at risk,' said Morris. This man and others were trying to be heroic, Morris felt, but instead were putting everyone else in danger. As a result, there were arguments, threats of violence, and minor conflicts over daily chores. One member of the group, X, left the building although he had signed an agreement not to do so. He had red hair and a red beard, which were very conspicuous. After several hours, it was assumed he had been captured, but he returned that evening to be confronted by the group. He explained that he had gone out to get some food for some nearby friends in need. The others asked if he had got the food; he admitted that he hadn't, nor did he find his friends.

Robert Morris: 'We were angered almost to violence by his laissez-faire attitude. At this point Imad, using our secret codes, entered the apartment and was visibly shaken, his complexion pallid. He explained to the group... that X had been spotted leaving the building, putting all of us at risk especially Imad, who could be executed for hiding us as the Iraqi army had issued an order to execute conspirators. X remained blasé and we quietly made plans to remove him from the group.'

It was decided that the man should be asked to go and live somewhere else. He soon left to find another safe haven in the city.

Paul Kennedy said he had friends in the Palestinian community who could bring weapons for the group to protect themselves. This suggestion was put before the group, but Morris's opinion was that this was highly dangerous as it would put them on the side of the resistance: 'There was no way to use the weapons to escape, and it would put us in the middle of a fight between the Iraqis and the Kuwaitis.' Morris got his way and they did not acquire weapons.

Over time, Morris came to view his American passport as a death warrant. He realised he needed new documents, so he contacted the Kuwaiti resistance, who were already providing them with money to buy food and medicines. New ID cards were delivered to him, showing Morris as an Irish engineer working for the government. Morris sent a coded message to his wife via the US Embassy. She knew that he had earlier considered getting an Irish passport as he was a second-generation Irish citizen, but his grandfather's papers had been lost in the great fire of Dublin in 1920, so he could not prove the Irish connection at the time.

Jill Morris and the whole family began to lobby US politicians to get her husband an Irish passport. Senator John Kerry, a fellow Vietnam veteran and former naval officer, was able to produce immediate action from the Irish ambassador, who issued an Irish *laissez-passer* to Morris. It was hand-delivered several weeks later by an Irish agent. By this time, however, the Iraqis had changed their attitude towards the Irish. They were not being taken hostage but they were not allowed out of Kuwait or Iraq, either. Morris could not test this out locally, as he was well known in the community as an American. So he put the documents aside until he saw a chance to use them for an escape attempt.

There was another major row within the group over security. Shortly after, two more of the group were asked to leave. They were very upset at being kicked out and were especially angry with Morris as the group's leader. But they did agree to leave and signed a document to say that once they had left the building, they couldn't come back or compromise the safety of the group.

Eventually the hostages heard that the US Navy was in the Gulf. Morris desperately hoped that the marines would come and save him, as he was one of their own and had served alongside them. He had been with the 5th Marine Division, Da Nang, Vietnam, as a lieutenant in the United States Navy Dental Corps, responsible for the oral health of 1,100 marines of the 1st Marine Battalion as well as small Army of the Republic of Vietnam outposts. The navy had honoured him in 1970 with the United States Navy Achievement

Medal for bravery, outstanding professionalism, and humanitarian efforts to the Vietnamese people.

He was a man who understood the consequences of war. Even if they couldn't get the hostages out of Kuwait, Morris wanted the Americans to attack the Iraqis, even if it meant that he and others became casualties of war.

*

Brunyate's team, at the resistance safe house, were also under great stress. 'I have slept badly again. I seem to be plagued by nightmares and all of us, although we don't say it, wait for the knock on the door which will end our freedom,' he wrote in his diary. A neighbouring Palestinian did inform the Iraqis of their hiding place, and again the captain and crew had to make a frantic dash to another safe house. It was a close shave.

The group started receiving radio messages via the BBC *Gulf Link* programme. From September, it broadcast short individual messages from family and friends to people trapped in Iraq and Kuwait. The broadcast lasted for forty-five minutes a day, carrying up to ninety messages. The Americans had a similar programme, *Messages from Home*, on Voice of America. The broadcasts were the highlight of the day for most of those in captivity or in hiding. Brunyate got messages from his wife, Carol. With Brunyate living away from home, their marriage had been in trouble, but the loving messages brought hope and a major boost to his morale.

The poor diet was also taking its toll. The BA captain had lost about forty-five pounds on their diet of mostly boiled chicken bones and rice. The group started an exercise programme to try to ensure that they would be fit enough to run if they were discovered. They also followed a security programme that involved twenty-four-hour surveillance from their rooftop.

Brunyate: 'Gordon (Gault), my co-pilot, has measured out a running track in the middle flat. If you run a figure of eight between two rooms, you cover a distance of thirty metres, so four days a week I go into hamster mode and run 160 metres,' he wrote in his diary. 'I can cope with the hunger, the discomfort, the lack of sleep, and the constant fear, but what I find so hard is the apparent normality of life so close to the apartment. Fathers holding hands with their children, families together.'

Brunyate's group was one of dozens of Britons still in hiding: some who had ended up in the middle of a war zone on Flight 149, and some who were already living in the city. The house-to-house searches were becoming more frequent, although the searchers were not always competent. In one raid on an apartment where several Flight 149 men were hiding, a British serviceman, David Dutson, hid under a bed. All his colleagues were taken prisoner. As they were escorted into the room to collect their baggage, they noticed Dutson's foot poking out from under the bed, clearly visible. In a moment of inspiration, the captured men burst into song: '*Your foot's sticking out, your foot's sticking out, pull it in!*' they sang. The soldiers looked bewildered but they did not understand English. Everyone left the room and Dutson escaped.

Among other Westerners in hiding was Briton Cliff Lindley, who had travelled to his job at Kuwait's airport as usual on the day of the invasion and had been forced to go under cover. He was one of hundreds whose lives were in the hands of locals who had taken them into their homes or hidden them in empty apartments.

Lindley and others had gone into hiding in an apartment block. They befriended a Syrian, who ventured out into the city regularly to buy them fruit and vegetables. He was one of their lifelines.

The group dug in. They built a wall across the entrance to their apartment block and wired up all the doors to make the building look abandoned, or ready for demolition. Any Iraqi patrol would have to force its way in.

The Kuwaitis, mostly women, who supplied Lindley and his friends with food had to negotiate a series of checkpoints between the apartments and the stores. One day, they were stopped by a patrol, arrested, and taken to a secret police unit where they were interrogated for hours until one of them gave up the hiding place.

At eight in the morning, Lindley was drinking coffee as he looked out of a lounge window onto the street below. Armed vehicles raced down the street and pulled up, and red-bereted soldiers with AK-47s leapt from them and ran into the apartments. They snatched the British men from one apartment and dragged them out into the square. Lindley and a colleague sprinted up the stairs to an empty flat above, where they had constructed a hideaway – a wardrobe fitted out with pillows, blankets, and bottles of water, with barely room for two men to squeeze in. It could be locked from the inside. They crouched in fear, hardly daring to breathe, as they heard the sounds of the Iraqis moving through the apartments.

Lindley and his friend huddled together in the cupboard. The door rattled as a soldier tried to open it. His footsteps receded. Then other soldiers came in and started banging and pulling at the door, trying to open it. Any minute now, the door would be torn open or bullets fired into it. But they were lucky. The Iraqi troops gave up trying to open the door. For four hours, the men remained in their refuge until they could no longer hear any sound. They emerged to find that they were the only ones left in the apartments block. Everyone else had been caught.

CHAPTER 16

RESISTANCE

The menacing raids by Iraqi troops increased as the resistance grew stronger and gained popular support.

Initially, most of the resistance was passive, such as men growing their beards whereas previously most Kuwait men had worn only moustaches. (The Iraqis ordered the beards removed, pulling them out with pliers if the men refused. The beards were a sign of religious devotion and therefore opposition to Saddam's secular regime.)

A few days after the invasion, Kuwaitis took to the rooftops in a mass display of defiance, shouting 'Allahu Akbar!'

Beard-growing and shouting was quickly replaced by armed resistance with weapons and other ingenious methods.

Hostage John Levins, an Australian-born accountant, recalled a visit by a colleague who asked if he knew where they could get cyanide to inject into oranges to offer the hungry Iraqi troops (the Iraqi conscripts, as opposed to the elite Republican Guard, were poorly clothed and fed).

Levins refused but the Iraqis quickly learned not to accept any food from the Kuwaitis. On the streets, there were more gun battles and more casualties. As the Kuwaitis took their severely wounded resistance fighters to the hospitals, sometimes they were only steps ahead of the Iraqis. To begin with, the resistance had consisted of simple things, such as taking down street signs and changing house numbers to confuse Iraqi special units as they searched for Westerners, Kuwaiti officials, and military officers. Now it was more serious.

The resistance groups were mostly organised by groups of Shiite Kuwaitis. At the beginning, they were a nuisance to the Iraqi army, but now their campaign of sabotage, shootings, and bombings began to undermine Iraqi morale. However, it also led to savage reprisals.

Many of the most successful resistance fighters were women with a passionate belief that after the invaders were defeated, they could change Kuwaiti society and improve their status. Women with astonishing courage and tenacity.

Asrar al-Qabandi was a confident young woman who had studied in the United States, wore jeans and T-shirts, and had an American accent. Born in 1959, Asrar, the sixth-born, had devoted her life to gaining a good education. She was educated in Kuwait up until the age of eighteen, when she went to England for an English-language course, and then to a high school in Colorado in the United States. An ASA [College] computer major back home, she went on to earn three master's degrees in education, economics and handicap rehabilitation. Asrar worked in the Ministry of Foreign Affairs at the information centre, established a nursery school, and regularly volunteered at the Khalifa Pearl Association (a non-profit organisation) to take care of autistic children. She loved volunteering and enjoyed devoting her time to charity immensely.

Described by friends as a pint-sized powerhouse of energy, she was five feet tall with a fiery temper. She usually had her dark hair in a pony tail and wore large glasses. She was vocal in declaring her support for democracy and women's rights – controversial opinions in Kuwait even before the invasion.

At the beginning of the invasion, she and a female friend moved into the abandoned school in an old villa on the coast. There, they plotted Iraqi positions to help in what they hoped would be a quick allied invasion. They used a satellite phone to establish a connection to the Kuwaiti government-in-exile in Saudi Arabia and the Kuwaiti Embassy in Washington. She threw herself into resistance work. She smuggled weapons from Basra in Iraq to Kuwait, money and more weapons from Saudi Arabia, single-handedly destroyed some of the monitored telephones and communications set up by the Iraqis, provided targeted Kuwaitis with new IDs to protect them from harm, provided foreign families with food and money, and took care of sixty-five foreign hostages, risking a guaranteed execution.

Disguised as an Indian domestic worker, she was able to breach the heavily guarded Ministry of Civil Information and steal computer disks and smuggle them to Saudi Arabia. She then managed to come back over the border, past the Iraqi guards, with the new identity of 'Sara Mubarak' to continue her resistance work. She bombed cars and killed many Iraqi soldiers and continually sent reports about the condition of Kuwaiti families to the make-shift Kuwaiti government headquarters in Taef, Saudi Arabia. She was also able to acquire and preserve all the information on Kuwaiti accounts from the Central Bank of Kuwait in order to prevent Iraqis from hacking into the accounts themselves and stealing the money. She was the first to discover that the Iraqis were planning to taint the petrol reserves with a phosphoric material, and she managed to get a map of their targets. She set up safe houses, distributed fake IDs, arranged passports for escapees, even sprayed anti-Iraqi graffiti in the city.

She was due to be smuggled out to give evidence to the US Congress on what was happening in her country. She would make a powerful advocate for Kuwait in front of the cameras in America – a star witness. But after she crossed the border at Khafji, she looked back at her country and decided to turn back. Her resistance colleagues pleaded with her to go on, that she had done enough for the cause and had taken enough risks. They suspected the Iraqis had learned of her false identity, but she thought they were too stupid to catch her. Asrar did not want to leave her country while it was occupied. She decided to stay and carry on the fight.

She hitched a lift back into the city. Later she called her brother on the satellite phone. 'Guess where I am,' she laughed. 'Back in Kuwait.'

Even though her ID had been compromised she tried to run one roadblock too many. On 4 November, she was arrested at a checkpoint. That night the Mukhabarat, the Iraqi secret police, raided her family home, arresting her father and brother.

They beat Asrar in front of her father. Attempts by the resistance to pay a bribe to get her out of custody failed. She was brutally beaten and tortured for seventeen days but she would not give up her friends and resistance colleagues. Her captors later said she refused to give them any information at all, despite the torture.

In January, she was murdered with four shots to the chest and one to the head. Her hands were bound with a plastic tie and her head sliced in two with an axe. Her body was dumped outside her family home with her head in two parts. She was still wearing the same clothes as when she was captured.

A later autopsy revealed she had been raped. The doctor stated her body was completely mutilated.

The Iraqi death certificate claimed she had died in hospital.

*

When the Iraqis first arrived in Kuwait, they set up a perimeter facing out towards the sea, from where they expected the allies to attack. However, the resistance campaign meant that many of the troop units eventually switched the position of their guns, to face towards the city with their backs to the sea. For the moment, the sea seemed less threatening than the resistance in the streets of the capital.

Among those helped by the resistance was Australian Gaela Tolley, who was living in the city when the invasion begin. Gaela, twenty-nine – New Zealand-born and raised but holding an Australian passport – was alone in her Kuwait City apartment with her three children – Nicholas, seven, Jesse, three, and Sam, two – while her husband Mark, a petroleum engineer, was in Amsterdam on a business trip.

Soon after the invasion, she heard banging on the door. Seconds later, she was face-to-face with a detachment of soldiers from Iraq's Special Forces, wearing their red berets. Pushing past her, they went racing through the apartment and ransacked it, ignoring her pleas and the screams of her children. They went into her bedroom and tipped everything out of the drawers, going through all her clothes and stealing her underwear. On their way out of the complex, they also took all the keys to all the apartments in the building. Later, Gaela was standing in her kitchen when a soldier tapped his gun on her window and gestured at her to let him in. Much of his face was covered with a red and white cloth but she could still see his eyes. She didn't like what she saw. She felt a chill. She ducked down beneath the window and half ran, half crawled out of the kitchen. She grabbed her children. Three-year-old Jesse had taken his clothes off so she hoisted him naked onto one hip, grabbed his clothes, and hoisted two-year-old Sam onto the other hip. Together they were a heavy burden but she was a mother and her children were in peril.

Nicholas, aged seven, was complaining because he had to leave his toys behind. Gaela screamed at him to move. She looked through the peephole in the front door. There was no sign of the soldier. She opened the door and went outside, dragging her children with her, quickly locked the door behind her and then ran to her neighbours' apartment. She banged desperately on their door. The neighbours, a British man and his Irish wife, let her in but they were not impressed by her story. They told Gaela she had overreacted. She should calm down. The soldier was probably just looking for a glass of water. But Gaela was distraught. She knew she was in danger. She ran out to the street. The soldier had not given up. He broke into her apartment and searched it. Unable to find her, he turned his attention to the upstairs apartment where a German couple lived, friends of Gaela's. The soldier tied up the husband at gunpoint and then forced him to lie face down on the floor and listen while he raped his wife. Out on the street, Gaela took stock. She was on the run, alone, with three small children, in a war zone.

For the next few weeks, she moved around the city, from apartment to apartment, her children and dogs in tow. She soon realised the dogs were a dangerous liability. The Jack Russells were excellent guard dogs – every time someone came near their hiding spot they would bark and growl. Gaela was terrified that they would bring a patrol down on their heads so she decided they had to be put down. She could not bear to do it herself but a group of Australians agreed to help. They wrung the dogs' necks in a deserted apartment several floors beneath Gaela and her children.

Gaela's next problem was to keep her children entertained

during the long days in hiding and make sure they did not make too much noise, either to be heard outside or to disturb others in hiding. The days were long, the children usually rising at 5 a.m. She and her children were provided with a series of hiding places by the resistance. From them, she learned that there was a team of 'British Commandos' on the ground from the start of the war, and that they were still operating in the city. Gaela twice tried to escape across the desert, stocking up a four-wheel-drive with food and water and dressing all three children in nappies to avoid toilet stops. She stuffed the front of her overalls to make herself look pregnant, to avoid being raped. The first time she was turned back by friendly Iraqi soldiers. She then tried to join a convoy leaving the city but was phoned by a man who told her the convoy was off. Later, she was stunned to see the very same man on television in Saudi Arabia, telling reporters how he had escaped.

Gaela's second escape attempt did not even make it out of the city. The British in the convoy were arrested but Gaela was allowed to go. Once again, she was helped by the resistance, hiding out with her children in a basement for a day until new accommodations were found. Finally, with the help of a male friend, she dressed as a Bedouin and drove to Baghdad. She bluffed her way through twenty roadblocks on an epic two-day journey and finally arrived at the Australian Embassy. She was debriefed by a senior embassy official. He warned her she must never talk about the team of 'British Commandos'.

*

Those 'Commandos', the Inc team that had landed on 149, were working alongside the resistance, gathering crucial intelligence for the military campaign. The teams were marking Iraqi targets for air strikes and assessing troop and tank positions.

Their intelligence was immensely valuable and awesomely detailed. It conveyed details of the deployment of individual units and their capabilities, artillery and tank positions, the map coordinates of headquarters units and the positions of individual generals, even the depths of the defensive trenches dug by the Iraqis (the depth being crucial to air planners deciding what sort of bomb would be needed to destroy them).

The intelligence provided by the Inc gave the allied war commanders an accurate picture of the opposition and saved hundreds of lives in the invasion. A US Delta Force unit was also in Kuwait; its members set up secret observation posts all over the country to monitor Iraqi military movements. And a unit from the SBS infiltrated the city from the sea to add to the intelligence-gathering operation.

The remaining two teams from the Inc, two men in each, moved from place to place by night, always staying one step ahead of the sweeps by Iraqi patrols. But one team was betrayed and had to flee on foot, then by car and finally truck.

The final team had been met at the airport after they landed on Flight 149 and taken to a pickup point where they were given their weapons and rations and driven to their observation point. They were able to stay there for more than a week, sending back reports on Iraqi deployments. They were kept supplied by a Kuwaiti support team, who were based nearby. But the Kuwaitis' movements aroused suspicion and they were compromised. Iraqi troops raided their house, just four doors away from where the Inc team was hiding. The Iraqis killed one man at the scene and arrested three others, one of them a woman. They were taken away and never seen again. They had to move, fearing their location would be given away under torture.

Their second location was compromised, too, this time by sheer bad luck. During their twenty-seven days in hiding, sending back daily intelligence reports and never leaving the apartment, the two men accumulated a lot of personal waste. This was kept in bags but eventually it had to be disposed of, outside. But one of the bags split, drawing the attention of locals and giving away their position.

On the move once more, they ran into a vehicle control point. It was close to the curfew time, dusk. The Iraqis waved down their car. They seemed to realise its occupants were European. They had only seconds to make up their minds. They did not think their cover as stranded engineers would hold up under questioning because they had weapons. It was six weeks after the invasion and their story would not add up.

They jumped from their car and ran towards the Iraqis, opening up with their weapons, spraying the Iraqi position. The Iraqis were unprepared for the withering, accurate fire. The two men killed five Iraqis and wounded several others.

The team abandoned their car and took to the streets. No one from the Iraqi vehicle control point was left standing to give chase. They eventually found cover in an old mosque under reconstruction and hid there for several hours, avoiding Iraqi patrols before eventually making their way on foot under cover of darkness to their next observation post, a high-rise apartment near the city centre. They were greeted by an elderly Kuwaiti couple and shown around their new home. It had a great view of the occupied city.

CHAPTER 17

SIEGE: PART III
THE DIARY OF GEORGE SALOOM, ARAB HOSTAGE

George Saloom had gone from Flight 149 passenger and banker to stand-in security officer at the US Embassy in a matter of weeks. His new job was hard work; he was taking the place of professional diplomats who had been allowed to go home while civilians like himself were still trapped. But he felt he was coping well with his ordeal, and the safe departure of Deborah and Preston had been a huge boost to his morale. He was momentarily optimistic about the future. Of greater concern to him was the attitude of the remaining embassy staff, some of whom seemed to expect the embassy to run as normal, even though they were under siege and surrounded by Iraqi forces.

September 2, 1990, Kuwait City, Kuwait
Got word this morning that Deb and Preston are already in London and, in fact, have left London for Washington, DC!! They should be in Washington, DC, sometime

around 6:00 p.m. Kuwait time. We were notified today that we will no longer have any power for food, electricity, air conditioning etc. Only for communications.

We are emptying freezers that have spoilage and trying to cook meals out of freezers in the order of which food needs to be cooked first.

September 3, 1990, Kuwait City, Kuwait
- We will be cleaning out more freezers
- Doing more preserving (or trying to preserve) food

Addendum: Cleaned out about 4 more freezers. Had to throw away a lot of food that was good for only TODAY or the NEXT! This food is potentially very dangerous to eat after 24 hours and we cannot afford to be sick or have an 'epidemic' throughout the compound. We have no real medical care or facilities.

Guard duty again, each day at 3:00 to 6:00 p.m.

Had a variety show tonight. Afterwards, we all (American citizens who were not embassy employees) signed personal services contracts for two reasons:

1. To Be Employees of the Embassy
2. If Desired, to be compensated for the work/services performed at the embassy during this time. Since I have no other income, at this time, every little (and I mean very little here) helps.

President Bush made a speech last night and said US is committed to Kuwait and will not allow IRAQ or Hussein to dominate the oil situation by force. Committed to whatever time it takes and will not allow hostages (guests) of Iraqis in Kuwait and Iraq to deter [him] from his mission.

September 14, 1990, Kuwait City, Kuwait
We are out of meat. I took an inventory of all food. We have, at this time, plenty of juices, cereal, rice, tuna, and milk to last for an additional 80 days. We are on a planning calendar (I discussed with the Ambassador) for a December 1, 1990, exit. We are short of meat (other than tuna!). I have collected all canned meat and we will use it very sparingly. I am physically, mentally, and (I think) spiritually well. I am concerned about a job and monies for Deborah; but I cannot do anything about it now. Trying to keep in contact with individuals in the States via cables.

September 15, 1990, Kuwait City, Kuwait
A new and serious development occurred today. NO MORE OUTSIDE WATER. We are beginning to experience some 'trauma' from certain individuals who are now just having a 'tragic awareness' that this is not a picnic and expectations must be modified (with respect to what may be required to sacrifice, team work and working together, tolerance of other people and their idiosyncrasies, and what is really necessary and what is 'nice to have') to meet/match/deal with the present and future situation. I went to the non-denominational church service tonight. It was nice. Tomorrow will be an interesting day. Establishing rules and guidelines for 'no water situation'.

September 20, 1990, Kuwait City, Kuwait
Had a problem in the kitchen today. xxxxxxxx was
suppose to work along with xxxxxxx, but xxxxxxxx was
late and xxxx refused to wash dishes. The interesting
thing about this incident is that it is not atypical. There
are several individuals in the compound that are not (in
my opinion) true team players and are only after what is
best for them, even if it is at the expense of others. As the
situation in the compound continues, time will bring out
<u>the true nature and character of the individuals in the</u>
<u>compound.</u> Had guard duty tonight 1800 to 2100 hours.
No problems.

*

Iraq announced a release programme for people with Arab names.
There were two such men in the compound. One was George
Saloom. It seemed like a way out of the siege but he was wary of
the Iraqis' true intentions. He wanted more information. But weeks
went by without any news.

September 27, 1990, Kuwait City, Kuwait
I pray that some resolution to this situation is imminent
so that I can be with my family in the United States very,
very soon. I try each day to be a better person and benefit
from this.

October 3, 1990, Kuwait City, Kuwait
My 'room' is now completely dark all the time since the
sandbags have been placed on the windows. Only had
one small row of windows near the top. All other sides
were walls, solid in the basement of the Chancery. I am

considering moving to another room where I will have some daylight.

I went looking today, around the compound, for more short pants or other pants to cut for shorts. Couldn't find much. Found one pair of swimming shorts that may work.

October 6, 1990, Kuwait City, Kuwait
This afternoon the Kuwait International Hotel (K.I.H.) was on fire! A very loud explosion. I thought the war had begun! I did see it as I climbed on top of the Marine House. Some people say it was a firebomb or something to that effect detonated by the Kuwaiti Resistance against Iraq. The fire was in the Kitchen! Spent the afternoon also sorting out and packing one emergency bag, in case of evacuation by the US Military. I have about an hour more of work left to straighten things out. I want to have this one bag available at all times.

October 7, 1990, Kuwait City, Kuwait
Had Brunch today. Unfortunately, the xxxxxxxx, in my opinion, was really off base. He rapped on the Kitchen door around 1045 hours and asked what was going on. I said, what do you mean, Sir? He said, 'The sign says 1030 HOURS (referring to when the Brunch was to be served) and some of Us have to work!' That really made me mad… my feelings are:

1. This is not a 'normal' embassy situation.
2. What does the xxxxxxx think that people who are getting up at 0500 hours to prepare the Brunch for HIM at 1030 hours are doing, playing?

223

3. The majority of the people on the compound are not embassy staff, but are volunteers and working on their own accord.

As for myself, I am probably one of (if not the only one) who is not being paid by a company. I do not have a company taking care of my family. Today I have to be in the commissary for eight hours to watch the ice machines and ensure all is well. That's not much fun, especially when the ice is for the individuals who <u>HAVE TO HAVE THEIR 'HAPPY HOUR' DRINKS!!</u>

I do not know how things will work out. Just do the best I can, but it is a shame to have this type of 'politics' or behavioural interplay in the crisis situation that we are all in. Here we are, not knowing if tomorrow we will be alive, much less if we will ever see our families again, and we have this type of 'petty' nonsense to contend with.

Upon reflection, I think because we are in this crisis situation, the type of petty nonsense mentioned above will play a more serious and negative role in relationships and survival than it normally would.

October 11, 1990, Kuwait City, Kuwait
Forgot to mention in my journal last night that we had a ten-minute meeting with the Ambassador, after dinner. He said:

1. Bunker (Chancery) is, in essence, completed; although there are some additional items that will be done.
2. We may use it if/when we have military activity in the compound or if there is an attack on the compound.

3. We may or may not have any warning or notice of (2) above.
4. If are notified or are aware of activity of (2) above, take one small bag and gas mask with you.
5. Don't make a lot of noise if you are awoken at night or asked during the day to go to the 'bunker'.

I have my one bag ready. Hope I can take all of my possessions, but that looks doubtful.

October 21, 1990, Kuwait City, Kuwait
Sunday, 81st day since the Invasion of Kuwait by Iraq.

Today, eight hours of power; so I was at work all day. Went to the non-denominational church service at 7:30 p.m.

Busy day at 'work'. I did make some ICE CREAM!!!

October 26, 1990, Kuwait City, Kuwait
DAY 86 – SINCE INVASION
DAY 70 – SINCE I HAVE BEEN IN EMBASSY

Became ill around 1030 hours with chills, aches, and fever. Went to bed around 11:30 a.m. and woke up at around 1500 hours. Had a sore throat, headache, fever and still ached all over. Dr Jim Carroll came by. My blood pressure was 110/80. Throat somewhat red. He gave me some Tylenol and then ten days worth of penicillin. I will stay in my room for a day or so.

October 28, 1990, Kuwait City, Kuwait
DAY 88 – SINCE INVASION
DAY 72 – SINCE I HAVE BEEN IN EMBASSY

Everything feels good as day progresses except my stomach. Every time I put something in it that's fairly solid, I get cramps and my stomach starts 'rolling', but not much diarrhoea.

Things are getting pretty edgy here, at the Embassy. More 'quarrelling and arguments' over such minor things. Last night and today arguments existed over a thermos to be either at one of the guard stations (Falcon II) for water or one of the individuals wanted it for coffee, for HIS guard duty!

Today, a meeting was held for the 'residents' of the Embassy. The word was given that no one was authorised to have a radio <u>EXCEPT THE EMBASSY STAFF!!</u>

October 29, 1990, Kuwait City, Kuwait
DAY 89 – SINCE INVASION
DAY 73 – SINCE I HAVE BEEN IN EMBASSY

Slept well last night. Will go to work today. Will take it easy; feel good, except stomach is queasy. Difficult to heal and be healthy without a proper diet.

Did not receive any more messages today, but found out that Mike Penniman taped Debbie's message from/on VOA (Voice of America) – 'HI GEORGE, THIS IS FROM DEBORAH IN SAN DIEGO. I HOPE YOU CAN HEAR THIS. I LOVE YOU. I MISS YOU. I PROMISE THAT YOU'LL NEVER HAVE TO EAT TUNA AGAIN.'

Boy, do I want to get home NOW!!

October 31, 1990, Kuwait City, Kuwait
It was a busy day with all the Halloween Activities, I dressed up as an Arab... Everyone said that I looked like

I could just walk out of the compound and not even be noticed. All I needed was a little Arabic. Most people said I looked like King Faisal, Saudi Arabia.

Had problems today with Kitchen detail, xxxxx <u>AGAIN!</u> xxx says xxx will not do dishes except that we bring them to xxx outside. xxx refuses to go into the kitchen to do any work.

November 5, 1990, Kuwait City, Kuwait
DAY 96 – SINCE INVASION
DAY 80 – SINCE I HAVE BEEN IN EMBASSY

Atmosphere in compound is one of tension and anxiety. A lot of arguments and dissension is occurring on very, very minute/minor items. One individual became extremely upset because he could only have two instead of four small packets of salad dressing on his tuna!! Stress is taking its toll. Many people relieve some stress by drinking alcohol (SO MUCH) during our 'Happy Hour.' We have about two more weeks of alcohol left in the store room, unless other people, which I suspect is true, have private 'stashes'.

No messages today from the outside. I am a little concerned (I am not sure if it is not just talk) but X said tonight that he will not see his family again. That he and others will be dead before this is over. This afternoon, he said that by the 28th, he will take his own life. I asked why; he responded, to get action for others. Very difficult to 'read' him and to know what he is really saying and/ or feeling. He is very moody and then domineering individual. I really like him. He is extremely talented and very, very intelligent. I hope and pray that all will be well with him.

November 8, 1990, Kuwait City, Kuwait
DAY 99 – SINCE INVASION
DAY 83 – SINCE I HAVE BEEN IN EMBASSY

I ran 24 laps around the 'compound track'. I am not sure how many miles this is, probably 2½ miles, maybe more. I did not read as much as I would like to have. All is fairly well. Still the minor disruptions of personality conflicts, 'verbal fights' and people being downright immature and unprofessional. Today, X grabbed a lasagne from the serving window and acted just downright rude, immature, and (childlike) selfish.

November 9, 1990, Kuwait City, Kuwait
DAY 100 – SINCE INVASION
DAY 84 – SINCE I HAVE BEEN IN EMBASSY

Had special meeting tonight (all the compound) with the Ambassador to:

1. Recognize this is 100th day since Invasion.
2. We all have diplomatic passports/status in case we need them.
3. The 'enemy' is outside <u>NOT</u> inside (implying we must work harder at getting along with each other).
4. Many ways this could work itself out, but we need to prepare for a long time siege. Will only have one eight-hour power day from now on. We must look at all the ways we can to save fuel for power. Looking at ways also to cook without using propane.

November 10, 1990, Kuwait City, Kuwait
DAY 101 – SINCE INVASION
DAY 85 – SINCE I HAVE BEEN IN EMBASSY

It looks like we will be decreasing power usage to save on diesel; which means fewer and fewer messages. I surely understand this, but it does not seem right for the non-diplomatic staff in the Embassy to be so negatively impacted while the diplomatic staff can and do physically call/talk with their loved ones on the communications system when the power is on!!

November 21, 1990, Kuwait City, Kuwait
DAY 112 – SINCE INVASION

November 22, 1990, Kuwait City, Kuwait
DAY 113 – SINCE INVASION
DAY 97 – SINCE I HAVE BEEN IN EMBASSY
THANKSGIVING DAY!!!

We have a special schedule with a special meal today. We have Tuna Lasagne and a Cold Salad (Greens from the Garden) scheduled at 1500 hours. Today I am thankful for my wonderful family. Especially thankful for my wife. I am thankful for my health and safety here in the Embassy. xxxxxxxxxx, didn't want to participate and neither did xxxxxx xxxxx!!! WHAT A SHAME!!

November 27, 1990, Kuwait City, Kuwait
I sit here in my room tonight, filled with a great deal of emotion. I was told this afternoon by Barbara Bodine (DCM) and Gayle Rogers (Consular) that Sergio and I will be leaving tomorrow on a flight to Baghdad at 11:30 a.m.!!!

We are to be ready to go to the airport at 9:00 a.m. We are supposed to stay in Baghdad only enough time to get exit visas and then travel to Amman, Jordan, then London and THEN to UNITED STATES!!!

I was told we would probably be at least a week in Baghdad. I asked Barbara and Gayle why we were allowed to leave. Barbara said that we were special cases – although we didn't fit completely the Arab-American criteria, we were also on a humanitarian list… talked briefly to Ambassador Howell, this evening. He said, as far as he knew, all was ok and if I had a chance, I should take it. I asked him, if I was questioned by the Iraqis what I should reveal, he did not offer much comments. He again re-emphasised that anyone that can get out, 'should get out now!'

Very mixed emotions, except very easy to make a choice. I do not want to feel or have the individuals here in the Embassy feel that I am deserting them, but my priority is my family. Not a second thought about staying with the group in the Embassy or going home to take care of my family.

I am so overjoyed and excited and THEN I am very remorseful for all of the individuals that are still here. I pray for them that this will be resolved for them very quickly!!! I know it will be very difficult to sleep tonight!!!

November 28, 1990, Kuwait City, Kuwait
DAY 119 – SINCE INVASION
DAY 103 – SINCE I HAVE BEEN IN EMBASSY

In the morning, around 8:00 a.m., I reviewed with Gayle again the situation. I asked her was my leaving coordinated through Washington? Did the US Embassy in Baghdad know all about this and approved? Was the Ministry of Foreign Affairs (Iraqi) involved? Is all the paperwork taken care of? She answered 'YES' on all of these. I asked her why we couldn't stay in Kuwait and have exit visas processed in Baghdad and then leave to Baghdad. She said we had to physically be in Baghdad to do the rest of the paperwork... I also asked all the diplomats in the Embassy <u>NOT to say anything about my leaving to go to Baghdad,</u> especially no communication to my wife until I PERSONALLY notify her. I wanted to insure that everything is/was legitimate and to not expose her to any undue/unnecessary anxieties. Received no messages today from anyone, even though it was a power day and others did receive messages.

*

On 29 November, 120 days after the invasion and 104 days since he arrived at the embassy, George Saloom finally walked out of the compound at 11 a.m., and promptly found himself being questioned by the Iraqi secret police. From his diary:

November 29, 1990, Kuwait City, Kuwait
Was asked the following items:

1. How many total people in Embassy?
2. How many diplomats and civilians?
3. How many women and men?
4. How much food do you have? How long will it last?
5. How much diesel fuel do you have?
6. What is the Pink Fabric in the garden used for?
7. Number of telephones and location?
8. Who talks and to whom on the radios?

9. Why TV is turned on and off?

10. What type of communication facilities do you have?

I never gave any straight or factual answers to any of the above questions.

*

He was taken to the military airport and flown to Baghdad.

Saloom then met the acting American consul, who gave him some disturbing news.

'She didn't know why we had left the Embassy in Kuwait! She said she had sent a message <u>yesterday</u> to Barbara (DCM) to tell us <u>NOT</u> to come to Baghdad! <u>ACCORDING TO THE AMERICAN EMBASSY IN BAGHDAD – NONE OF THE INFORMATION THAT WAS CONFIRMED IN KUWAIT WAS TRUE!</u>'

There had also been a message at Thanksgiving warning him not to come to Baghdad but it had not been passed on.

Saloom was held for questioning by the Mukhabarat, the Iraqi secret police. He refused to give them any information. But he had walked straight into a trap and had gone from siege hostage to human shield, a role that became much more dangerous after, at the end of November, the United Nations passed resolution 678, authorising the use of force unless Iraq withdrew from Kuwait. The Iraqis were given a deadline of 15 January 1991 to comply, six weeks away. In Geneva, US Secretary of State James Baker met Tariq Aziz, the Iraqi foreign minister, for six hours of talks that went nowhere.

Iraq wanted the discussions about withdrawal to be tied to wider talks about the conflict between Israel and Palestine. Washington viewed this as a smokescreen and a delaying tactic. They refused. The countdown to war continued.

CHAPTER 18

GOING HOME

The human shields had become, in the words of a British Foreign Office official, 'a difficult problem'. Initially, attempts were made in the West to downplay the plight of the captives. President Bush refused to discuss them or answer questions about their status. 'I want to see them out of there, obviously,' he told the world. 'But I am not going to try to heighten tensions by responding to hypothetical questions.' Across the United States, though, yellow ribbons were tied on trees in the hometowns of the hostages, in solidarity.

Iraq had 200,000 troops in Kuwait, well dug in and prepared to repel invaders. Facing them was George Bush's coalition, consisting of forces from the West and from Arab countries, that was eventually to total 250,000 men. The allied generals had detailed hostage rescue plans in front of them, but none seemed to have any great prospect of success. The chances were that the 'friendly' death toll in any rescue attempt would be high. Seemingly, the human shields were a problem without a solution.

Saddam Hussein, once again, fooled everyone. On the afternoon of 6 December, there was a short news announcement. Travel restrictions on foreigners in Iraq (the new Iraq that included the nineteenth province, Kuwait) were being lifted. Everyone quickly worked out what that meant: all the hostages were to be released and allowed to return home.

Whether all the trips by politicians to Baghdad had finally paid off, or the pleas of other Arab leaders, or whether Saddam felt the hostages were no longer useful, or that their release would help in the 'peace' talks, we will never know. It's possible he was looking for a way out – having misjudged the West's response to the invasion – but Bush was not about to let him off the hook.

John Chappell had been moved to Baghdad, through the way station that was the Mansour Melia hotel, and then to an armaments factory. There the hostages were allowed phone calls and John was able to call the UK and talk to Maureen, their first communication in months.

The men from the IBI camp had been split up and two of John's friends, Ken Best and Don Majors, were being held elsewhere. John received another phone call to tell him that the two had been on a run around their camp when Don, a fifty-seven-year-old expatriate, had suddenly collapsed and died of a heart attack in Ken's arms.

Soon afterward, John's mind was taken off this tragic news by great excitement as the news of the release of the hostages spread: 'Shortly after that, two young chaps with no insignia but in olive military-type uniforms came to our camp and they spoke to our guards and they told them that we had to be ready as quickly as possible and that we were being released... We were ready in minutes and then about two hours later a coach came to pick us up to take us into Baghdad.'

The hostages returned to the Mansour Melia hotel where they

waited for two anxious days before an Iraqi Airways 747 was organised to take the British home to London's Gatwick airport. John finally believed he was going home when the plane actually took off from Baghdad: 'I couldn't imagine then that they could do anything else with us other than really take us home, so I remember we gave a little bit of a cheer as we took off... but the real cheer was when we landed at Gatwick, that really nearly blew the windows out.'

The British return was carefully stage-managed. The plane carrying the human shields landed in a remote part of Gatwick airport. They were kept away from the waiting media, as were their families. Most of them were too overwhelmed by their ordeal, or too glad to be home, to complain or ask too many questions. Until much later.

As everyone disembarked, they were separated into two groups – British Airways staff and others. John sought out one of the intelligence officers who were waiting to debrief passengers. He had some valuable information. At his final location, the armaments factory, he had secretly noted details of the arms shipments by writing down what was on the outside of the containers. Job done, he made his way to the meeting point at the Gatwick Hilton, where his family awaited. The experience was overwhelming.

Maureen Chappell was waiting in a corridor:

He still wasn't coming and then I'd gone back into the room. The room was very crowded because everybody had arrived and it wasn't a very big room and we just watched and waited and he just came through the door... He was hobbling because he'd hurt his ankle so he was slower than other people.

He was obviously just very bewildered and he wasn't taking

anything in – we just clapped eyes on each other and hugged and Jennifer stood behind me crying her eyes out and John just stood there... but he definitely wasn't with it, as the saying goes. He was too emotionally drained I think to know what was going on and it was really quite a number of days afterwards before he was fully aware of what had gone on.

Paul Dieppe was also on the plane that landed at Gatwick, but he was not celebrating his return. He was grieving. After arriving from the prison they had christened Chlorine B to the Mansour Melia hotel, he was shown into a room where various British passports were strewn over a bed. His passport was there and he was told to take it. That seemed like a good sign, confirmation that his departure was going to be real. It was two days until the flight left but in that time his life was turned upside down. He learned in a phone call home that his father had died two months earlier.

For me personally that was terrible. The whole thing of getting back was wrecked for me by learning that my father had died and the way I learned it, which was cruel. So it was a very weird thing... there was no joy in going home for me.

There was a lot of joy and excitement on that airplane. Not for me but for the group. And people cheered and clapped when we landed at Gatwick. And we were told when we arrived at Gatwick that those people who had been on the BA flight should identify themselves or something. I can't remember the details. I was in a mess. When we got off the plane, somebody there recognised me, God knows how, because I looked very different from the man who went out there. I was about three stones lighter, a lot greyer and I had a beard.

We were all in a room and there was champagne and relatives, reunions, all seemed okay. And then I went home to Bristol with my family. And I was a complete mess at the time. So, where do you go from there? What's happened to me and why? And you know, after sort of a day or two, I started to pick those threads up. I got correspondence from BA saying they'd offer compensation for the luggage and would you please sign this piece of paper and never ask for any other compensation or ever speak to the press or something.

And I thought this is very bizarre and what's going on here? And we talked to a lawyer about it… and said look, we got this bit of paper from BA. And he said you must never sign anything like that: I mean, take the money for your luggage, but for God's sake don't sign up to any conditions. They are trying to gag you. And then he said, I don't know why, but it's very fishy, they are trying to gag you: don't go there. And we didn't. And I didn't sign anything.

From all over Iraq and Kuwait, hostages were returning to the UK. Some brought home grim tales from their captivity. Among the returnees was Stewart Griffiths, who had run straight into the Iraqi army on 2 August. He had been held at a dam for four harrowing months. For some of the time he had lived in cramped quarters next to a noisy generator. Then, he, and those held with him, were moved into steel containers on top of the sluice gates. Three to a container. No windows. The bedding was filthy. There were cockroaches everywhere. It was clear the dam would be a prime target for the allies. The only thing that kept Stewart going were messages from his wife, Barbara, who had been picked up and taken to the IBI camp, where the Chappells were being held.

She was released when the women and children were allowed to go. Back in the UK she had managed to send several messages to Stewart via *Gulf Link*.

The Americans were also looking forward to going home, among them George Saloom, who was facing up to the consequences of his apparent betrayal by his own people at the embassy in Kuwait. He had left the protection of the embassy to go to Baghdad only to find himself in the hands of the secret police. Worse, he discovered that the embassy had previously been sent a message warning him not to leave Kuwait:

December 1, 1990, Al Mansour Melia Hotel, Baghdad, Iraq
DAY 122 – SINCE INVASION
DAY 2 – SINCE I HAVE BEEN IN BAGHDAD

Good night's sleep. Not much news to report or event this morning. Did have the opportunity to take a hot 'shower'. Shower in quotes because of the European method of bathtub and hose; but surely cannot complain!!

Gave suitcase last night to Jim (Marine from Kuwait embassy) and Dutch (also Marine from Kuwait) who are 'assisting' as 'diplomats' at the US Embassy here in Baghdad. Also discussed with them steps that Deb has taken concerning documentation for me to certify I am an American of Arab descent.

Would like to get outside today. Either walk in the garden or go to what they say is a gym. Would like to get some sun, if possible, but do not really think it is. The weather is okay but surely not as nice as the weather in Kuwait…

Not much news except on the World Scene:

1. President George Bush has asked Iraq's Tariq Aziz (Foreign Minister) to come to USA and James Baker, Secretary of Defense, to come to Iraq (Baghdad).
2. Mohammed [*sic*] Ali (World Heavy Weight Boxing Champion) is in Baghdad to take about fifteen individuals to America. They will leave tomorrow at 3:30 p.m., local time.
3. I met with Jeannette Pina, US Embassy (Baghdad). She showed us documentation that was sent October 31, 1990, to the Minister of Foreign Affairs, Iraq, requesting our release. She is going to update the documentation and resubmit. She will also get me a copy of my documentation.

I talked with Deb again!!!! She sounded good but really lonesome. Nathan spent the night at home and did pretty good, she said.

December 3, 1990, Al Mansour Melia Hotel, Baghdad, Iraq
DAY 124 – SINCE INVASION
DAY 4 – SINCE I HAVE BEEN IN BAGHDAD

Today is a difficult day, as each day, at any time, the Iraqi Security Force could come to me and within thirty minutes or so move me to a camp as a human shield. About sixty Japanese came in yesterday. The Japanese government flew the wives over to be with their husbands. Also, tomorrow, a flight from USA with some wives and family; then the respective men will be coming in from the various camps. Not good for me; but, of course, good for those involved. This also means the Iraqis need more space here as well as more people at the various camps/sites. Hamid [a fellow hostage] will be released today or tomorrow, according to him. This leaves me sitting here 'ALL EXPOSED'! So, I feel I will be gone (to a camp) very shortly. Jeannette is supposed to be here at 10:00 a.m. to bring me copies of what she has.

I gave Jeannette my suit, shirts, and shoes to keep at the Embassy until I leave. If I go to a site, I do not want to 'lug' it around. Not much else new...

December 4, 1990, Al Mansour Melia Hotel, Baghdad, Iraq
DAY 125 – SINCE INVASION
DAY 5 – SINCE I HAVE BEEN IN BAGHDAD

Sometimes, no news is good news. In this situation, this is TRUE! It is 4:00 p.m. and no information concerning being 'reassigned' to a camp has been received. Jeannette did not come this morning. I believe she is tied up with a group that is to come from USA today or tomorrow. Hopefully, I will see her tonight.

Very frustrating and difficult sitting around. Feel helpless.

December 5, 1990, Al Mansour Melia Hotel, Baghdad, Iraq
DAY 126 – SINCE INVASION
DAY 6 – SINCE I HAVE BEEN IN BAGHDAD

I am very anxious today. Hamid is to find out at 10:00 a.m. whether or not he is released or if he will be going to a site, today.

Addendum #1: The Iraqis put me in the back of a small pick-up (like a BRAT with seats in the back of the truck facing opposite to the direction of travel). They took me to a complex, factory, medical supplies (maybe chemicals) etc. They drove around for about an hour or so; although, I was told by the other hostages there, it was only twenty-five kilometers from Baghdad on the road to the city of Kut.

Previous to the above events, I had called Deb to come to Baghdad as soon as possible. Also, I talked with her after I had entered the compound/complex. She was quite unsettled!! The State Department had called her and said, 'SORRY TO BE THE BEARER OF BAD NEWS, BUT YOUR HUSBAND WAS TAKEN TO AN UNKNOWN LOCATION AS A HUMAN SHIELD.' The place that I am now at is called/named 'Hotel California.' Note the song, 'You can check in but not check out!'

The individuals (other hostages) here are very nice, Eleven in all counting myself. Seem to have enough food… facilities are inadequate. Atmosphere appears to be relaxed and do as you please WITHIN the confines of the complex.

December 6, 1990, Factory Complex: Hotel California, Baghdad, Iraq
DAY 127 – SINCE INVASION
DAY 7 – SINCE I HAVE BEEN IN BAGHDAD
DAY 1 – SINCE I HAVE BEEN IN HOTEL CALIFORNIA

I was told last night that the 'bed' I have been assigned is the 'lucky' bed because the last several individuals assigned that bed have left Hotel California. I do not know how lucky because I do not know where they went!!!

A very, very interesting development has occurred today; an announcement over radio and television has declared that President Saddam Hussein has written a letter to his Parliament requesting that all foreigners be allowed freedom of travel!! If this is true, then I and all others who were/are hostages will be allowed to travel home!!! It sounds great; but, I am approaching this with very much caution and unfortunately, scepticism (especially as a result of my <u>MOST</u> recent experience) – but trying to be optimistic. We shall see what develops over the next day or so.

December 7, 1990, Factory Complex: Hotel California, Baghdad, Iraq
DAY 128 – SINCE INVASION
DAY 8 – SINCE I HAVE BEEN IN BAGHDAD
DAY 2 – SINCE I HAVE BEEN IN HOTEL CA

In the afternoon, was able to sun 'bathe' for a while. Then I continued my scripture study. Then I was able to run (around the parking lot) 200 yards = 40 laps = 8000 yards/1760 yards/mile = 4.5 miles. I am so anxious to get home.

December 8, 1990, Factory Complex: Hotel California, Baghdad, Iraq
DAY 129 – SINCE INVASION
DAY 9 – SINCE I HAVE BEEN IN BAGHDAD
DAY 3 – SINCE I HAVE BEEN IN HOTEL CA

Another day in Paradise!!!! I am going to try to at least do my various exercises, sunbathe and then run. Hopefully today we will have a little more information about Saddam Hussein's 'request'. Last night, we found out/heard on BBC that, if this is true, the individuals closest to Baghdad will be leaving first.

Addendum #2: We didn't leave until around 2200 hours. We were supposed to leave Hotel California at around 1930 hours. A group of military personnel came and searched us individually and our bags. The senior military official made a little speech (sounded like it was something he had rehearsed and/or was told to say). He expressed his apology for the situation and inconvenience that Iraq had to have the 'Guests' in order to protect themselves from attack by the Allied Forces and that now Iraq is ready to defend itself. Finally, got to Al Mansour Melia Hotel around 11:00 p.m. It was an absolute madhouse!!! Don Bradbury and myself roomed together in Room 427. Tried to call Deborah several times before going to bed at 3:00 a.m.

December 9, 1990, Al Mansour Melia Hotel, Baghdad, Iraq
DAY 130 – SINCE INVASION
DAY 10 – SINCE I HAVE BEEN IN BAGHDAD

Awoke at 0600 hours. Tried to call Deborah several times. Could not get overseas line. We are supposed to be packed and in lobby at 1300 hours today. A flight is chartered to leave Baghdad at 1600 hours. I hope we will be off on time, but don't think we will make 1600 hours!!!

Addendum: I received the following message from Deborah via the US Embassy in Baghdad:

'YOUR WIFE SAYS SHE HAS RESERVATIONS
TO WASHINGTON, D.C. AND IS PLANNING TO
MEET YOU THERE WHEN THE US GOVERNMENT
CHARTER ARRIVES FROM FRANKFURT.'

After a great deal of waiting and anxious moments (the Airport was horrendous and the Iraqi staff could not find the key to open the gateway to load the airplane), we lifted off from Baghdad at around 2130 hours. All civilians that were with Sergio, Hamid, and myself at the US Embassy in Kuwait came from Kuwait on a Boeing 707 and we all left from Baghdad together on a chartered Iraqi Airways Boeing 747.

The flight was very scary. Upon take-off, the whole plane rattled and shook AND the oxygen masks were all released. The smoke was unbearable. So many people were smoking and the ventilation was so very bad!!

We had a 'false' landing!! As we were about to touch down (I saw the tower, about eye level) we did a 'touch and go'!!! It was snowing and, evidently, the pilot misjudged and missed the runway!!!

We *finally* arrived in Frankfurt, Germany, around 0100 hours. Everyone at the airport was extremely nice. We are staying at the Sheraton Hotel at the airport. Government is picking up the tab, I think. I talked with Deborah. Left message for Preston. Went to bed around 0400 hours.

*

Paul Eliopoulos's wife had made the journey to Baghdad with a group of other American wives to plead for the release of their husbands.

Paul Eliopoulos:

The guards came in and said, 'We're taking you to Baghdad' – every time they would take us any place, they would say, 'We're taking you to Baghdad', so I didn't know what was happening. They put me in a car and I was the only hostage. On the way, they picked up other security people – armed security people who apparently wanted to go to Baghdad. So we drove for about four or four and a half hours and then they took me to the hotel. They took me up to one of the floors, and they kept me by the stairwell on the corridor and I was just sitting there for a while... I can't remember how long, but it was more than fifteen minutes and then I saw my wife coming up the stairs.

Eliopoulos did not feel anything when he saw his wife. He just felt numb. He did not rush over to her. He just asked the guard if he had permission to go and see her. The guard said yes and he went toward her, their first embrace in over four months. But he still felt nothing inside. He just thought his wife was now one more hostage and that she had just joined him in his living hell.

Paul Eliopoulos: 'That evening they had dinner for us at the restaurant in the hotel, I ate with my wife and some other people and I felt very sick, so we got in the elevator to go up to the room. As the elevator was going up, I started fainting, and my wife told the guard. So the guard stopped the elevator and took me outside and laid me down, and he got – I assume it was – the hotel doctor to look me over.' The doctor told Paul that he had probably become ill because he had had a full meal, his first for a long time. He was thirty pounds lighter than when he was captured.

Soon after this, Eliopoulos and his wife joined a group that were put on an Iraqi Airways 747 bound for Frankfurt. It was 11 December. With him was Flight 149 passenger Jan Bhatt, whose wife had also come to Baghdad, much against his wishes.

Jan Bhatt:

My wife also informed me that she had made arrangements to come to Iraq, as many wives had done, to attempt to secure my release. I was very reluctant about this trip, as I was extremely concerned that Saddam Hussein would capture her and hold her hostage the way he had held me these past months. I worried about what would become of our children in this eventuality and tried to discourage her. After some discussion, she held firm and we decided that she would journey to Iraq as she had planned. On 6 December, after over four months in captivity, I learned that I was to be released and was transported to the Al Mansour Melia hotel, where I was tearfully reunited with my wife in a hotel room. I was informed not to assume that I was free by my captors and was still confined to my room. My wife and I, while thrilled to see one another alive, were extremely concerned that our room might be videotaped or bugged and thus took extreme caution in what we said or did.

As had been my practice for the past 130 days in captivity, I slept with my shoes on, ready to run in case of an allied attack in the middle of the night. However, on 7 December, I obtained an exit visa and journeyed to the airport eager to get out of Iraq. Finally, after much anxiety caused by flight delays, I was able to leave captivity and flew back to the United States via Frankfurt.

Robert Morris was also on the flight. Through the efforts of the Irish Embassy, he was allowed to go to Baghdad, where he spent several days in the Al Rasheed hotel courtesy of the Irish Embassy. He was despondent and felt that if he did not escape by Christmas he would head back to Kuwait City and wait out the war. Throughout the ordeal he had lost almost thirty pounds in weight, was hollow-eyed and gaunt, and his red beard had mostly turned to gray.

But he soon found out he was going home. With his Irish *laissez-passer* in hand, Morris was taken to the airport by Joseph Wilson, an assistant to the US ambassador to Iraq. After a while, other hostages he hadn't seen for four months drifted into the airport. No exchange of words took place between them, only eye contact, out of fear of the Iraqis. After several hours of waiting and drinking whiskey, hostages from several countries boarded the flight to Frankfurt. There was no sense of euphoria or excitement. They still could not believe that they were free of Saddam Hussein.

The flight out of Frankfurt was a Pan Am 747, chartered to Washington, DC, with approximately one hundred and eighty American hostages on board. They feasted on champagne and McDonald's burgers on the plane, but only began to celebrate once the plane was airborne. As they climbed into the sky, the hostages' emotions soared too, with the knowledge that they were free at last of the clutches of Saddam Hussein. They gave whoops of delight, high-fived each other, and applauded, so happy that they would be home to see their families for Christmas.

When they arrived in DC and made it through the bureaucratic debriefing, the hostages were taken to a basketball gym where their families awaited. Morris quickly found his wife and two children and fell into their arms. His four-year-old daughter, who always said he would be home for Christmas, pulled out a small American flag from her coat and waved it at the watching crowd.

Paul Eliopoulos was adjusting less well to his return. The family went to Athens for a break, but even after two weeks with his wife and children, Eliopoulos could not even begin to feel normal. He was completely numb. He could not express himself. He could not tell his children what had happened to him. He decided he wanted to go straight back to work, to try to get his life back on track.

Richard Brunyate's group from Flight 149 came out of hiding and gave themselves up when they heard the news of the release programme. They stole some bicycles, peddled to an Iraqi position, and surrendered. They too were flown home via Frankfurt to a reception party that included Lord King, the British Airways chairman, and Brunyate's wife, Carol. His last diary entry read: 'I have seldom been unable to speak but this was one of those moments that I will remember for ever.'

All of the remaining US citizens in the Kuwait embassy compound – Ambassador Nathaniel Howell and four others – were also released and flew home. Howell received a formal welcome from US Secretary of State James Baker at Andrews Air Force Base. He was pleased and relieved to have lasted out the siege and to have got everyone home for Christmas. He and his family were invited to meet President Bush on 17 December and were given signed photographs of the president.

All the human shields were home by mid-December. They had many unanswered questions, as well as the trauma of their captivity to deal with – but the world at large moved on quickly. It would soon be Christmas and war was coming.

CHAPTER 19

THE COVER-UP BEGINS

At 11 p.m. on 16 January 1991, an attack squadron of Apache and Black Hawk helicopters from the 101st Airborne Division left Saudi Arabia and entered Iraqi airspace. Their target was a cluster of early-warning radar stations. Three and half hours later, they fired off twenty-seven AGM-114 Hellfire air-to-ground missiles. Within seconds, sixteen radar sites were wiped off the map. One hundred Tomahawk cruise missiles were launched towards targets in Kuwait and Iraq from the cruisers USS *Bunker Hill* and USS *San Jacinto*, out in the Gulf. F-117 stealth fighters attacked key government buildings in Baghdad, including the Ministry of Defense. B-52 bombers, flying all the way from Louisiana in the United States, fired off air-launched cruise missiles against other targets.

The air war, the first stage of Operation Desert Storm, the planned reconquest of Kuwait, had begun.

The Republican Guard positions, which had been pinpointed by the Inc intelligence operation, were pounded. Iraq retaliated by firing Scud missiles into Israel in an attempt to drag the Israelis into the war and mobilise Arab opinion on the streets to Saddam's side. But the Israelis refused to be drawn in. In the desert, Special Forces teams – including the now famous Bravo Two Zero patrol – were tasked with finding the mobile Scud launchers and calling in air strikes.

The early strikes were a great success, disabling important parts of the Iraqi war machine at minimal cost, although several allied pilots were shot down and subsequently brutally treated by the Iraqis.

The air war lasted over a month and the Iraqi military's ability to fight was, in the Pentagon's terms, 'badly degraded'. Saddam's reaction was to set fire to dozens of Kuwaiti oil fields, creating a major pollution hazard, as well as firing more Scuds at Israel and Saudi Arabia. The Soviet Union launched a new round of peace talks but still Saddam would not give in.

The allies prepared an estimate of the damage done to the Iraqis by the air war. At least 1,700 Iraqi tanks were destroyed (2,700 were still thought to be operational), 1,500 artillery units destroyed (1,700 remained), and 950 armoured personnel carriers wiped out (2,000 were still operational). There was never any proper count of Iraqi dead: numbers varied between 20,000 and 150,000.

The ground war began on Sunday, 24 February. There was a diversionary attack by US Navy SEALs on the beaches of Kuwait, suggesting that the main thrust would come from the sea, but, in fact, the main attack came in a sweeping tank movement from Saudi Arabia into Iraq itself, making an 'end run' around the Republican Guard and the forces dug into Kuwait.

Helped by detailed intelligence, careful preparations, and an overwhelming superiority in the accuracy and firepower of their weaponry, the allies achieved a quick victory. Kuwait City was liberated on 27 February. The city was a mess – most of its downtown area was destroyed, the port sector a shambles. The invasion, the looting, and the bombing had all taken their toll. More than six thousand Kuwaitis had disappeared, having either been killed or carried off to Iraq. Allied troops found makeshift torture chambers containing pictures that the Iraqis had taken of their victims. Fingers and toes had been jammed in vices; electric drills and electric hot plates had been used to maim and burn.

The ground war lasted just four days and ended with a cease-fire on February 28. The Allies took more than seventy thousand Iraqi prisoners and destroyed more than three thousand tanks. Saddam Hussein was bloodied but still left in power, a decision that would come back to haunt Western policymakers.

Among those liberated in the city were the last remaining team from the secret group from Flight 149. They had managed to evade capture for an extraordinary five months at their last observation post, the city-centre apartment, supported by the truly remarkable elderly couple who lived alongside them and kept them supplied with food.

Twice Iraqi search teams had ransacked their building. The first time the two men simply hid under the couple's bed; they waited out the second search by hiding in the main water tank on the roof of the building. Both times their elderly hosts kept their nerve under questioning. The men sent intelligence on a needs-must basis – every four to six days – rather than on a strict schedule, both to conserve their batteries and to avoid sweeps by Iraqi radio detection vans. As their confidence grew, the men dressed up as labourers and ventured outside the apartment, moving around the city to check on troop positions and strengths.

After five months, the two men were at last able to walk around freely when Kuwait City was liberated. But the entry of American troops into the city nearly spelled disaster. They encountered an

American patrol that promptly opened fire, narrowly missing one of the men who started yelling at the top of his voice that he was a friendly, as he dived for cover. Suddenly they realised he was shouting in English and stopped shooting.

They were finally evacuated by helicopter to Saudi Arabia, then Cyprus, then home. Their intelligence gathering had delivered a huge pay-off for the allies, helping deliver vital blows to the Iraqi war machine and save allied lives. But London and Washington had also ignored the intelligence that did not suit them – that the Iraqis had not taken up offensive positions in southern Kuwait, threatening an invasion of Saudi Arabia.

*

Once the war was over, the fallout began. A damaged but still powerful Saddam, a brooding and bitter Osama bin Laden, a newly invigorated American military that had finally shaken off the curse of Vietnam: the consequences of the Gulf War would stretch down the years.

Behind the giant stage of international politics, the human shields tried to make themselves heard. The French passengers were the first to start demanding explanations: why was Flight 149 allowed to land when it seemed clear that an invasion was coming? The Merlets were told by one French Embassy official in Kuwait that the reason the plane landed was to put a 'British Special Forces' team into the country. But when they started to make inquiries about this back home, they came under immense pressure, especially from the French Defence Ministry, to shut up and not make waves. There was a war on, they were told: better to say nothing rather than provide propaganda for Saddam. Thierry Parfenoff, another French passenger, was told upon his return by a friend of his in the GIGN (the French equivalent of the SAS) that there were Special Forces soldiers on board Flight 149. Later, as the French passengers considered legal action against British Airways, Parfenoff received phone calls from a so-called fellow ex-hostage, giving him friendly advice not to pursue legal action. The man left his number, but this did not work when Parfenoff tried to call him back. He never heard from the mystery caller again.

The plane itself, *Coniston Water*, had met an inglorious end, apparently blown up on the runway by Iraqi troops fleeing Kuwait, according to official accounts. On board were all the personal possessions and baggage of the passengers and crew. The image of the destroyed aircraft was broadcast around the world. But was this a cover-up to disguise why it had landed in a war zone at all? Some passengers asked themselves why the Iraqis would destroy a valuable possession, and an ideal propaganda tool such as a fully equipped 747, when they could easily have flown it to Baghdad?

The passengers focused on a statement made by Margaret Thatcher to the House of Commons just after the invasion back in August, a statement made while they were all still in captivity. 'The British Airways flight landed, its passengers disembarked, and the crew handed over to a successive crew, and the crew went back to their hotels. This all took place before the invasion. The invasion was later,' she had said. In fact, the invasion had started when the plane was still four hours from Kuwait, and there had been countless warnings.

The statement was a lie.

John Prescott, the then Shadow Secretary of State for the opposition Labour Party, began asking questions about Flight 149. Why had it been allowed to land? Who was on board? He demanded an inquiry.

The new prime minister, John Major, absolved the government of responsibility and supported the British Airways version of events. In a carefully worded letter to Prescott turning down a request for an inquiry, Major said, 'While it was clear that Iraq was massing troops on its border with Kuwait... the Government had no firm evidence that Saddam would invade, still less occupy, the whole of Kuwait.' The letter continued: 'BA are a private company and with the airport authorities have absolute control over operational decisions. The British Government did not attempt to influence BA's decision to operate Flight 149 on 1–2 August.' Major said the plane landed at 0113 GMT (4:13 a.m. in Kuwait) but it was not until approximately 0300 GMT that the government had 'clear evidence of a full-scale Iraqi invasion of Kuwait.'

The passenger list of Flight 149 was a commercially confidential document, 'which remains with British Airways. I understand it is their practice to respect the privacy of passengers by keeping such records confidential.' But, Major also said, 'I can confirm that there were no British military personnel on the flight.'

He ended: 'I am satisfied that there was no negligence or oversight on the part of the government. Accordingly, I do not intend to establish an inquiry into the circumstances surrounding the incident.'

His letter was immediately attacked by Prescott: 'There are a lot of weasel words in the letter. Why does he say 'clear' evidence and 'full scale' invasion? We have to ask whether the Government allowed that plane to land in Kuwait out of sheer incompetence or because they wanted some of the people on board to reach Kuwait?'

Others were also exploring the mystery. After his release, Clive Earthy, the Flight 149 cabin service director, heard that the group of young men who had boarded the plane had all been checked in by one member of British Airways ground staff. He set out to find her. She had told others that the group of young men turned up quite late, after everyone else had gone down to the Departures gate. The ticketing codes on the tickets, she said, were for a military account.

The woman's name was Carole Miles.

Earthy talked to her and asked her to make a public statement. She refused, but confirmed the story was true; she also said she would deny it for fear of getting into trouble.

When Earthy later contacted her, though, she denied all knowledge of the whole affair. She had left British Airways for a job with the Ministry of Defence.

Which of course meant she had signed the Official Secrets Act.

CHAPTER 20

THE SUFFERING

The passengers and crew from Flight 149 were in Kuwait because of a secret mission ordered by the British government at the request of the Bush administration, to get eyes on the ground before the anticipated invasion.

Many of them never recovered from their ordeal, their suffering made worse by the lies told about what happened to them, from the stories put out that they spent most of their captivity in luxury hotels to the cover-up of the mission.

Many suffered long-term health problems or needed psychiatric treatment. There have been suicides and attempted suicides. Two studies published in the *British Medical Journal*, by Turner and Easton at the Harcourt Medical Centre in Salisbury and by Bisson, Searle and Srinivasan at the Gabalfa Clinic in Cardiff, highlighted the trauma of the victims, a trauma that has been almost totally ignored by the public at large. More than half of the hostages lost their jobs and careers or homes or suffered other severe financial damage or long-term depression and illness.

All emerged damaged to some degree, Jennifer Chappell perhaps most of all. Jennifer was an outgoing twelve-year-old with a good school record and a bright future when she flew on Flight 149. She celebrated her thirteenth birthday in captivity. The ordeal took away her youth and her optimism and led to years of psychological problems and counselling. She tried to kill herself several times:

> It has had a big effect. I've spent many, many years now, pretty much since then, dealing with depression and having treatment on and off. Sometimes I do better than other times but August is never a good month. I think it's had a big effect... it has made me angry, very, very angry, always very angry and very aggressive. Since then I've always found it difficult to talk about feelings and face up to some feelings. Because we couldn't there, because if you acknowledged or spoke about your feelings there, all the mechanisms you'd got to help you get through the experience would have come crashing down and you wouldn't have coped. And that feeling has stuck with me, I don't let any of the walls down any more. Funnily enough, I've not been bothered about flying again but I don't like trusting people. I don't like relying on anybody but myself.
>
> There have been several times in my adult life when I have found it all too much for me, and taken steps to end it. It is something I'm still dealing with... I think we do deserve answers, real answers. I think we've been gypped badly... lots of people have got a lot to answer for... such as British Airways, the British government. You can't tell me they didn't know what was going on before they sent that plane in. It's rubbish, they knew. I think we were used. And I think that plane was used.

*

Charles Kristiansson befriended Jennifer during their ordeal, stood up for her, made her laugh. He was one of the British Airways crew due to fly the plane on to Madras. He spent 134 days in captivity suffering verbal and physical abuse and tried to take his own life. He suffered from post-traumatic stress disorder (PTSD) and needed psychiatric care. He had to give up his job with British Airways after an encounter with an Iraqi passenger on a long-haul flight to Caracas, which triggered memories of his Gulf War ordeal after he mistook the passenger for the officer who had repeatedly raped him.

His situation was made even worse by the nightly television pictures of conflict from Iraq after the US invasion in 2003. He became afraid of his British status and now lives in exile in Luxembourg. His anger and pain were summed up in a letter he wrote to British Airways complaining about his treatment, which said, in part:

> My disgust comes from the fact that the reason I am now no longer able to do the job I love is no fault of my own. Has BA forgotten that the 134 days that I and my fellow colleagues likewise endured in captivity and as 'human shields', being verbally and physically abused, were no fault of our own? I was on duty. I was doing my job. Fact. I was constantly told by the Iraqi Secret Police, that by working for BA, the UK's prestigious, national carrier, I was a 'special guest of Saddam Hussein'. It certainly seems like BA has completely forgotten me. Why is this so?
>
> Ever since Flight 149 happened, I have done everything I possibly could to negate those memories and be able

to function and grow in my job – leaving long-haul (and the considerably higher financial rewards many crew enjoy), moving down to London (leaving my family) and transferring (on medical grounds) to short-haul, going into training and getting promotion to Purser. I would never have done all of those things, had I not loved my job. The most important thing for me was to keep doing the job I love. This, it seems, has fallen on completely 'deaf ears'.

Where was BA when our lives were in danger every day? Our so-called manager in Kuwait, whose wife had, coincidentally and conveniently, 'left' a week or so before, did what is colloquially called a 'runner', and we were left to our own devices. BA has a very short memory.

Merchant banker Brian James, head of treasury sales for the Gulf Bank in Kuwait, was put in front of a firing squad several times during his captivity. Each time he was lined up and heard the order to shoot, and the weapons firing, only to discover that the Iraqi soldiers were firing blanks. James returned to work in the Middle East after the war but he was never the same man. He gave up his job and moved to New York, running up large debts. In April 1998, he tried to shoot himself while back in South London. He had apparently been playing a gruesome game of Russian roulette, mimicking his appalling treatment in Iraq. He suffered wounds to his chest, abdomen, and neck. A few days later, recovering from his wounds, he travelled to the Yorkshire moors near his childhood home of Bradford. Dressed in expensive clothes and wearing a gold Gucci watch, but without any money or identification, he took a fatal dose of aspirin.

*

Thelma Croskery, widow of Douglas Croskery, was haunted by his death and by nagging doubts about what happened to him. She went back to Kuwait to search for his body while the country was still under Iraqi occupation, and went to his apartment:

The door had not been forced, but every single item in the flat was gone. The only things left were an empty medicine bottle and a dead plant. Thankfully a good friend of Dougie's had risked his life to go over to his apartment soon after he heard what had happened and before it got looted. He managed to save all the photographs in the apartment and also Dougie's camera. We now have the photos Dougie took of the soldiers marching down the street at the beginning of the invasion. I then went to his office, even though I thought it would have been bombed. But it was just as Dougie left it, with papers still lying on his desk signed, just under a thin layer of dust.

Thelma went in search of her husband's body. With the help of the UK ambassador Michael Weston, she found the spot. Ignoring the threat of unexploded land mines, she looked for any sign of him, some ID, a bit of material from his shirt, anything. We didn't find any trace of him. I know it's irrational but I still wonder if he survived that gun shot. I have seen soldiers in Northern Ireland survive a shot to the head... Maybe he was still alive and they took pity on him and took him to hospital. The thought that haunts me is that he is out there still and that he doesn't know who he is or that I still love him. I still hold out a tiny bit of hope that he's still alive somewhere. Even a few years after he died I was repainting the garage and I insisted it was repainted the exact same colour as before, so if Dougie came down the street and was confused, he would know which one was his house. I visited my doctor when I returned home and told them of the angle of the bullet holes in the car. He told me it was more than likely he was dead. It's the not knowing that is so painful. I can't finish my grieving process, I haven't had a funeral.

The logical part of my brain accepted the fact that he must be dead, so I soon put my energy into trying to get his body back. I started writing letters to everyone I could think of, MPs, the Prime Minister, even the Queen. The Iraqi government never acknowledged they had anything to do with Dougie's death. Tariq Aziz said that Westerners shouldn't have been there in the first place. Over the years the letter writing has got less, but every now and then I have another burst of activity. I also regularly phone the Foreign Office here to remind them that if they ever find a body in the desert, please to remember to let me know.

I remember thinking after it happened, I can never be happy again. I will never laugh again... He was a good man, a family man, and he helped those Kuwaiti people. I had known Dougie since we were both fourteen. I wasn't allowed to go out with anyone until I was sixteen but he waited for me. We were engaged at nineteen and married at twenty-one. I knew Dougie inside and out, we grew up together. We would finish each other's sentences. I still feel like half of me has gone. Sometimes I get up in the morning and wish it was time for bed again.

Although I feel lucky to have known him at all, my life stopped on the day that Dougie died. I will keep going for the grandchildren but I will probably eventually just fade away until they finally cover me in clay.

*

Michael Cooper and Nikki Love, BA crew members who had become a couple in captivity, have both suffered from depression over the years.

In the early hours of 19 August, when Iraqi troops stormed the hotel and summoned all the Western guests down to the lobby, the first group they called for was families and married couples. Everyone was terrified and panic filled the room. Love and Cooper looked at each other, and deciding it was their only chance to stay together, Love quickly swapped a ring onto her wedding finger so the Iraqis would think they were husband and wife. It worked. They were herded onto buses at gunpoint with no idea what would happen to them next. Nicola and Mike were sent as human shields to the IBI camp.

The site had been recently looted and defaced by Iraqi soldiers. The couple lived in a bungalow with two other hostages. They were placed under twenty-four-hour guard, given only a spoonful of rice each day and dirty drinking water. Over time, mattresses were delivered, very occasionally a bit of fruit was sent. At one point, they were given a very large leg of meat, which was a vital source of food. Later, they discovered the leg had come from the only giraffe at Kuwait Zoo.

At the camp, a bus arrived to take the women and children away. But the Iraqis wouldn't give any guarantees of what was going to happen to them. Unsure which option was better or worse, Love stayed.

The couple were married in a blaze of publicity after they returned to the UK but the marriage ended after a few years.

*

Paul Dieppe came out of captivity with a medical textbook but mentally he was badly damaged. He was determined to get answers, after ignoring what appeared to be an attempt by British Airways to gag him and prevent him talking to the press:

I wrote a few letters [along the lines of] 'What's going on here? Why are you trying to gag me?' but I got no response... mostly for me, and I guess for most of the people in my situation, it was about trying to pick my life up and deal with the chaos at home and the fallout for the kids and my professional situation, which had been shot to bits... for me, personally, because I'm in a very privileged position, money and compensation wasn't a very important issue. It was about getting my life back on track. I think, subsequently, though, I have gotten more angry about that BA thing and about this concept that they were trying to gag me early on and they did underhand deals with Americans and French and others and never got back to me. I have subsequently gotten more angry about that. But I think what really bugs me is that nobody has ever told me the truth about this thing.

I have never received an apology from anyone. I've never received an explanation from anyone. I've heard nothing from the British government... I have had nothing. I have had no offer of help at all... Fifteen years later and I'm angry about that.

It's very hard to talk about the effects of this long term, because you never know where life's going to take you. What I can tell you is that various aspects of my life underwent enormous change as a direct result of this event. But perhaps more difficult for me, so did the lives of members of my family. My family's lives were altered irrevocably by this.

And in a sense, I resent that more than my own life being altered... I was sort of at my prime when I went out there. I was forty-four. I had been appointed a professor only two or three years before... And I never got back to that. Also I was practicing medicine fairly fully then. I've never been able to do that since I got back. I can't really see patients any more. I do a little bit, but I can't handle seeing patients much. So my trade, if you like, has been shot to bits by this. I can't really tell you why that is, but it is something to do with being too empathetic now with patients. I too easily identify with the troubles of my patients... I can't practice my trade any more because I'm damaged...

My daughters' lives were irrevocably changed by this. That's unacceptable. My father died and I feel guilty for that. So, I think I killed him and that's very hard... there is this very strange guilt response to any experience of this sort. So why should I be guilty for something that was done to me? I don't know. But I think that's a reaction common to a lot of people that have been through something very extreme. And this was extreme.

Dieppe still wants someone in the government to own up to what happened, to tell him that the suspicions he has held for all these years about why the plane was allowed to land are true – but more than that, he wants an apology: 'I think it would help and it would go some way towards [achieving] this strange and hackneyed concept of closure, which I think is important to many of us who were caught up in this thing because we have never been told anything... but it would help me a lot more if someone from the government or BA knocked on my door and sat me down and said, look, we're really sorry about this. This is how it was. Here's the paperwork. This is what we did. This is how it happened. And we've come to apologise.'

*

John and Maureen Chappell moved on with their lives. But it was a long hard road and it is not just their children who bear the scars. John feels that he has never fully recovered from his captivity. He is not able to recall everything that happened – some things he remembers only in flashback. He puts this down to the stress of his captivity: 'I don't think you ever can recover fully... even now, after all this time, so much emotion is brought out by remembering the events and it's uncontrolled, you can't turn it on and off. Some aspects I can relate to friends and I can tell them things that happened and there's no problem, yet other times you can tell the same story and all you want to do is weep. It can be very difficult and quite embarrassing.'

At the beginning there were nightmares, less now, but the couple worry constantly about how their children have been affected. Maureen grieves for the harm done to them:

> We really can't say how much damage it's done to them. At the age they were, it was their formative years, which I think has caused them a lot more problems. I mean they had all this to go through and then they were back at school, actually away at boarding schools so they hadn't got each other after these terrible events. They'd only got their friends to rely on and obviously they were missing their dad... We thought they were coping with it but with hindsight you can see the little areas where they weren't.
>
> I think it changed our son's nature in as much as he got harder. He was quite a sensitive person and I think he wasn't

as sensitive afterwards, he was a lot harder. Our daughter has been very angry, very angry about it for a long time and is still angry about it, so I think it did change her nature as well. John was always quite studious and academic but afterwards he didn't seem to be able to settle, neither of them seemed to be able to settle again to how they were. Jennifer didn't want to stay at boarding school any more which she had enjoyed up until that point. She came back home and went to a local school... but they don't really seem to have settled since.

John Jr. agrees that the ordeal made him a different person, angrier and less trusting, not the boy he was before Flight 149 landed in Kuwait. He now lives in Texas.

It completely altered my psychology after seeing that soldier killed... but, thereafter, I realised, actually, just how cheap human life is when it comes down to it. How easy it is to end it. How attached I am to my own and how little I care about anybody else's, if it's a choice between me and them. Or at least that's certainly the attitude I developed. And at school I was having problems with people who insisted on picking on me and I became a very, very nasty person really... If you single me out and beat me up, I'll single you out and leave you a lot worse. And when your mates aren't around you know you're not so big and heavy? Once, I shoved a bloke out through a window. He'd had a go at me, I don't know, maybe three hours earlier, with his mates or whatever, and he was just standing on the stairs while I'm walking past and before he knew it I'd grabbed him and just pushed him through the window, hung him out of it. I was going to let him go but somebody grabbed him. And then, they're asking me, 'Why are you doing this?' And I said, 'Why do you think? You know he's bullying me. They said my response was out of proportion but I didn't think so.

So, yeah, I think it did change me. I can't believe that I would have had that attitude otherwise. It took me a long time to get away from that and to come to a view which is much more useful for dealing with everyday life, not dealing with a combat situation. I seemed to approach everything as a combat situation, a war zone, because that's what my experience had been... how to cope in a war zone. But life isn't a war zone... and the frustration of it is that I had been shaped into this person who couldn't deal with life as it actually was because I'd been put into an extraordinary situation where that was the way to deal with it. It made me into somebody who was determined not to trust anybody else. I don't actually trust anyone.

*

Stewardess Maxine Woods, who escaped with Brunyate's group, did not return to work for a year. It was at least six years before she could even say the word 'Kuwait'. Her career was handicapped because she longer wanted to fly on 747s and then later, when she began working long-haul at Heathrow, she did not want to fly anywhere near the Middle East, not even to places like Athens. She would dread getting a roster that had a Kuwait stopover.

Through her union, she tried to find out whether she had a case against British Airways but it was an uphill fight: 'The solicitor said that there were no answers. They kept coming up against closed doors all the time and that we were not going to get any answers. In the end BA offered us an ex gratia payment, I think it was six thousand pounds. But I couldn't sign on the dotted line, because, in the small print it said this is in full and final settlement of any future claim against British Airways... I think it was some sort of wording that it was not a liability payment. To me they were liable, they knew, so I could not sign on that dotted line.'

After two years, Maxine finally signed the document and received a payment. She wanted to move on with her life. Shortly afterward, BA organised a Kuwait reunion and at the party, Maxine and others received a framed certificate commending them for their behaviour during the crisis.

Stewardess Denise Dyer found out that she was three months pregnant when she got home but the poor diet meant she was very light – only about eighty pounds. Thankfully, the baby was born safely. She never received any counselling from British Airways. She cut back on her work, eventually taking half pay and then leaving the airline.

Gabriel Chardin, the engineer for the French atomic energy authority, has suffered from severe psychological consequences, including panic attacks, nightmares, and phobias, which led him to consult a psychologist. In 2000, he made a speech on his experiences to a conference of the atomic energy authority in Saclay. It was called 'The British Secret Service, British Airways and a Physicist Prisoner in Iraq'.

*

Jan Bhatt has never recovered from his ordeal. Giving evidence in an American court case, he graphically described life after his stint as a human shield:

> My experience as a hostage took a tremendous toll on my physical and emotional health. The extreme fear and anxiety that I had experienced during captivity manifested themselves in the form of frequent panic attacks after

my return. I was later diagnosed with anxiety disorder, and prescribed medication to control my condition. My anxieties and fears made falling asleep difficult and, when I did manage to fall asleep, I was often awakened by horrifying nightmares of my experience as a hostage in Iraq.

For about a year after my release, I also experienced vivid and periodic flashbacks, usually triggered by violent and upsetting world events. For example, in the immediate aftermath of my detention, it was absolutely petrifying to watch every one of the installations at which I was detained be bombed to dust. For three years after my release, I was unable to board an airplane, as flying was the most obvious and severe trigger to my anxiety episodes. Additionally, I suffered from lethargy and depression – I had lost agency over my own life so suddenly that I felt powerless to control the events of my life after my release. I found it deeply upsetting to talk at any length about my experience, and could not bear to watch a television or news programme that dealt with the subject of hostages anywhere in the world.

After my return, I found my re-entry into the working world extremely difficult. Prior to the hostage-taking, I had been the manager of some fifty employees at Unisys in a high-pressure environment with responsibilities of a sensitive nature. When I returned, I found that I had been demoted, had lost my private office and secretary, and I was left with only five people to supervise. On the basis of nothing more than supposition, my superiors had decided that I was not capable of assuming the important position in the company that I had occupied before. My manager told me he was happy that I was back, but as a result of the emotional trauma inherent in a hostage crisis such as the one I had just lived through, he thought that I could not possibly handle the responsibilities and stress associated with my previous position. He thought that as a former hostage I would not have the aggressiveness and drive that I had had in the past. He feared that my trauma would make me prone to a nervous breakdown in the future.

As the year progressed, I found myself being awarded projects that were completely inappropriate for my skill set. This greatly demoralised me – I had lost all the prestige and responsibility that I had, and began to feel worthless. I had previously been considered a man of action, and while I was a hostage, I felt paralyzed. This paralysis was perpetuated by my demotion, prompting me to take an early retirement.

Bhatt took drugs for his frequent anxiety attacks but they did not always help. At one stage he suffered a serious attack while on a flight to India. He refused to get on flights that had a stopover in the Middle East. And he has always been reluctant to discuss his experience and the loss of his confidence and his love of life.

*

Paul Eliopoulos suffered from sleep disorders and nightmares of impending execution. He was diagnosed by a psychiatrist as suffering from PTSD. He had difficulty concentrating and he would often find his mind wandering back to Iraq. He tried to return to Kuwait in March 1991 with the intention of taking up his old job but it was a disaster. Visiting his old home, he found it destroyed and looted. He threw up when he entered the house.

He lost his job and had to find a new one, at half his old salary, in Greece. His relationship with his wife and children deteriorated. He felt disconnected and numb and his sleeping problems continued. He told a US court his life after Kuwait was even harder than being a hostage:

> *Question*: And I know this is a difficult thing to do, but could you compare the difficulty of your life in Greece during those four years to the period in detention as a hostage in terms of how easy the two were to cope with?
>
> *Answer*: It was easier being a hostage.
>
> *Question*: Why?
>
> *Answer*: Because they had taken away everything from me, so I didn't have to consider anybody else but myself. And I knew I was going to die, so it didn't make any difference.

Later, he told the court, he returned to the United States:

> *Question*: Have you experienced any changes in your emotional condition since returning to the United States from Greece?
>
> *Answer*: I think the worst thing is I have learned how to live with it.
>
> *Question*: Say again?
>
> *Answer*: The worst thing is I have learned how to live with it, sir.
>
> *Question*: Why is that the worst thing?
>
> *Answer*: Because I accept that I have a handicap.
>
> *Question*: And you accept that you cannot overcome that handicap?

Answer: I wish I could. I don't know if I can.

Question: You described a whole host of symptoms that you experienced in Greece. Have all of these symptoms continued to carry over while you have been in the United States?

Answer: Yes.

Question: How is your relationship with your wife?

Answer: It's very loving, but it's not a sexual relationship.

Question: It doesn't have the kind of intimacy that you normally expect in a relationship between man and wife?

Answer: No.

*

Dentist-in-hiding Robert Morris returned to Boston. He has suffered further flashbacks to his time in Vietnam (where he had served as a doctor). He felt that others did not understand his condition, or what he had gone through. He sought professional help from the veterans' hospital in Boston, which has a special unit for hostages and similar cases of PTSD. In the years since he was a hostage, Morris has suffered from an excessive fear of people and of authority, and has at times found himself overcome with anxiety, weepiness, and melancholy, a condition that 'has decreased gradually over the years but it never disappears completely'.

Morris managed to return to Kuwait to help rebuild the nation's healthcare system, joined by his family. He is now back living in Boston, semi-retired. He has written a book on his experiences in hiding.

*

For Paul Merlet and his family, the years that followed the events were hard. Among other things, Paul found he had a fear of fireworks and his son has developed psoriasis, due to the stress endured while he was held hostage: 'I learned something when I was a hostage. In a place like that when you are made hostage, no matter if you are white, black, yellow, communist, Muslim, Christian, worker, rich, we all have the same concern – it is being free, and all the material considerations don't exist any more. The people who are made prisoner together, no matter their social status, their religion... what's important is fraternity and solidarity. Freedom is important. We don't know how to appreciate freedom because we are concerned by the little concerns of everyday life. Material aspects have no value any more when you are hostage.'

*

The Salooms have lost their trust in governments. George believes that he and Deb and Preston were 'collateral damage' to a military operation that should never have happened. He values his freedom, more than ever: 'The first day I came back I went to the grocery store, sat in the parking lot for thirty minutes, and cried. I cried because I was able to drive, I cried because I was able to go where I would like to go, within reason, if it's legal. I cried because of all the tremendous bountifulness that was in the grocery store and of course we had to pay for it but you could pick out almost anything to your heart's desire and you had the freedom to pick that and of course pay for it.'

At one stage, while making inquiries about what happened, he received a call from the US State Department. It was a warning – stop asking questions, this is a matter of national security.

*

Stewardess Jacqui Hunter, who went on the run with Captain Brunyate's group, managed to draw strength from her ordeal:

> What followed was the process of being reunited with our families and trying to get in touch with our own emotions and realising that it didn't happen to somebody else, that it was our story. And for a long time I was able to tell everybody all about it, because it wasn't me. It was like it was somebody else. And the British Airways doctor said, 'That's not the way. I'm afraid it was you, and unless you accept that... you won't be able to move on. This will never be properly resolved.' So I read my diary and I think I broke down and realised the peril I'd been in, and that helped me... I will turn it to its advantage now and draw strength from it and appreciate life and the world and being free and being able to make the most of all the opportunities I have. So, I don't look on it as a negative thing in my life.
>
> When I was in Kuwait, I was there for a month, and I was in the kitchen with Maxine drying up, and I said, 'Maxine, when I get home, that will be the last day Saddam Hussein has of my life. I'm here, he's got me now, but I promise you, that'll be it. He'll have had his turn. He will not be allowed to destroy me, to hurt me. It'll be over.' And that – fortunately for me, very fortunately, it's not the same for everybody – is what happened. And I just praise the Lord that I got through it and I've got friends and family to nurture me and help me get the best out of it.

*

Daphne and Henry Halkyard, the New Zealanders who ended up as human shields because of their last-minute decision to travel on their British passports, were compensated for their lost baggage, but what they really wanted was an explanation, and an apology. The couple felt they were left high and dry by both the British government and British Airways. Their anger still burned when they were interviewed for a New Zealand television documentary. They had not been able to put the ordeal behind them. As Daphne said, 'It still haunts one. It's there every day. You get flashbacks and these moments of absolute terror and horror and you wake up in the night thinking you are still there.'

Henry Halkyard died in July 2003, age seventy-three. His daughter Rowan believes to this day that he never got over the ordeal. Daphne died in July 2019, age eighty-six.

*

Charles Kristiansson is still living in Luxembourg. He is now Charel Kristiansson, and he has painstakingly rebuilt his life and learned to confront his demons. Recently, he was finally able to talk to me about his brutal treatment while in captivity, and he has written a book about his time as a human shield, *Looking for Professor Dousouqui*, a reference to the absent man whose house he lived in during some of his captivity.

*

The journey of British Airways Flight 149 into a war zone and what followed has claimed many casualties and the list grows year by year. All three men in the cockpit – Richard Brunyate, Gordon Gault, and Brian Wildman – died at younger-than-average ages. So did Carole Miles, who checked the Inc team in at Heathrow. So did the BA operations manager at Heathrow that day, Mike Longden.

Few people emerged unscathed from their time as human shields. Whether they were taken hostage after landing on Flight 149, or picked up while working in Kuwait, the experience was harrowing for everyone. But at least some of the suffering of the passengers and crew on Flight 149 could be alleviated if they were finally told the truth. They need to hear the truth, even if it comes in the form of a justification rather than apology.

But the truth has proved elusive.

CHAPTER 21

THE SEARCH FOR THE TRUTH

For many of the passengers of Flight 149, the search for truth began with lawyers in the UK, France, and the United States. In the UK, the solicitors of the firm Pannone Napier began investigating the case in 1991 on behalf of some of the passengers who were seeking compensation from British Airways.

At the same time, in France, Nantes lawyer Dominique Menard was preparing a civil claim on behalf of French passengers. He claimed that the flight was forced to put down against the wishes of the crew. 'We believe the reason was that the British government wanted to pick up intelligence agents from the embassy.' In the United States, lawyer Leon Van Gelderen and others were preparing a class action for negligence against British Airways.

The search for the truth in the United States was spearheaded by Texan William Neumann, an expert in compensation cases with a winning track record, along with other lawyers in support. Neumann was hired by Jan Bhatt, who had walked into his office with an apparently incredible story about soldiers and spies travelling on

Flight 149. Bhatt had heard the rumours; now he wanted the truth, and some justice. Several other American compensation cases were in progress; George Saloom was one of the plaintiffs.

In the course of their investigations, the US lawyers discovered that British military personnel in Kuwait had been briefed about a possible invasion days before 2 August and provided with escape kits.

William Neumann took meticulous depositions – several hundred pages of them – from British Airways employees involved in the Flight 149 affair. As well as Laurie O'Toole and Richard Brunyate, he also interrogated: Amanda Ball from BA's Kuwait office; Ikram Minah, their Kuwait airport manager; Peter Clark, the pilot who was due to take 149 on to Madras; Richard Wyatt, BA general operations delivery manager; and Ronald Lindsay, BA Operations Contingencies and Control.

These depositions reflected badly on British Airways. The picture that emerged showed what seemed to be a confused response to monitoring a very dangerous and volatile situation, including a lack of communication between departments and minimal efforts to obtain regular up-to-date information.

It was also clear that British Airways had relied heavily on information given to them that day in two crucial meetings with British Embassy staff. At 1800 KLT (Kuwait Local Time) on 1 August 1990, at the British Embassy, Laurie O'Toole, BA area manager for Iraq and Kuwait, met Tony Paice, first secretary at the embassy and as such responsible for aviation security, and MI6's station chief in Kuwait for an update on the Iraq situation.

Paice allegedly told O'Toole that the invasion would not happen. Thirty minutes later O'Toole met Tony Milson, head of chancery at the embassy, and Bruce Duncan, commanding officer of the British Liaison Team, who gave him the same verdict. They said, according to O'Toole, that satellite photos showed the Iraqis were not moving towards the border.

US attorney Neumann questioned Laurie O'Toole closely about the fact that despite the supposed conversations indicating that there was no imminent invasion, his wife and children had left Kuwait on what turned out to be the last flight out before the invasion. There was a memorable exchange:

Neumann: Mr O'Toole, there are a few points I would like to clear for the record. As I understand it, you had been on holiday with your wife and your children in July 1990. Is that correct?

O'Toole: That's correct.

Neumann: And where did you go? Were you outside of Kuwait?

O'Toole: To Geneva.

Neumann: And you have a home in Geneva?

O'Toole: Yes.

Neumann: And when was it that you returned with your wife and children to Kuwait, do you remember the exact date?

O'Toole: Yes, it was a Sunday before the invasion, which is 30 July.

Neumann: And then, two days later, on 1 August, if I understand it correctly, you went back to the airport on the evening of the first with your wife and your children and they left on a Swissair flight back to Geneva, is that correct?

O'Toole: That's right.

Neumann: Now this videotape is going to be shown to a jury and a judge in Houston, Texas, sometime in the future. And I would like you to explain the circumstances in which your wife and children were to return to Geneva on the evening of 1 August after having only arrived from Geneva to Kuwait two days earlier. Could you tell us why?

O'Toole: Well, my youngest son, Oliver, who was born in Kuwait, is two at this time and was born with a collapsed lung and we subsequently found out that he had another cyst. He went into Intensive Care for the first few weeks of his life and he survived okay after an operation with the collapsed lung. But we subsequently found out that he had another cyst in his lung and it was a cyst that had caused this collapsed lung but he was not... we were told by experts that he wouldn't be able to have an operation to cure that problem until he was two. So at this time we were obviously rather concerned about the state of his health.

The risk was that if he caught a cold or a flu or pleurisy or something like that he could have a collapsed lung again. He was... when we got back to Kuwait after holiday, as we mentioned earlier, I was due back there because Amanda Ball, who was my deputy, needed to go to a wedding. So, the arrangement was I would go back to Kuwait and return... go back on leave myself on 20 August when she got back. Susie, my wife, and the boys were due to go back before 8 August because we were having carpet re-laid in our apartment in Geneva, but when we got back Susie found out that the specialist, the chest specialist that was looking after Oliver, Dr Louise Auger, a Canadian, had actually left and gone back to Canada for holidays. We had known that there was a chance that she was going on holiday but she wasn't sure when we originally left Kuwait. But Susie found out that she had.

Additionally, we found out that a Dr Davrajan, who was the head of paediatrics at the Al Sabah Hospital, which is the hospital Oliver went to after his birth with the collapsed lung, and who treated him, he had also left the country. So, Susie was extremely concerned that the two people who we felt knew the case and were in a position to help if there was a problem were both out of the country.

Neumann: Was that, as you have just explained it, the reason that your wife and children left Kuwait on the evening of 1 August or the early morning of 2 August 1990. Was that the reason as you just…

O'Toole: That's right, it was the first available flight back to Geneva.

Neumann: And what time did that Swissair flight depart on the morning of 2 August, as best you remember.

O'Toole: 1:45.

Neumann: Were there any other arrivals or departures of civilian aircraft at the airport after the Swissair flight departed at about 1:45 and before the Flight 149 landed?

O'Toole: Sorry?

[Question read back.]

O'Toole: Not to my knowledge.

*

O'Toole's explanation for his family's swift turnaround – arriving from and retuning to Geneva in just forty-eight hours – was bizarre.

Rather than permit such potentially embarrassing depositions to be heard before a Texas jury and made public in Europe, British Airways settled in secret and paid substantial sums in excess of six figures to William Neumann's clients.

In 1995, a French court ordered British Airways to pay at least £3million in damages to the sixty-one French Flight 149 passengers, stating that the airline was 'entirely responsible' for the landing in Kuwait. The court case named Anthony Paice as the MI6 station chief in Kuwait and clearly pointed the finger at a British government secret mission as the reason the plane landed in a war zone. The court noted the British denials about the mission but pointedly added in its judgment: 'The reality of this assertion cannot be legally established.' BA appealed twice but lost both times.

The British passengers were far less fortunate. The House of Lords in 1996 dismissed two appeals by Flight 149 passengers against British Airways, upholding previous British court judgments that the airline did not have a case to answer in the courts under the terms of the Warsaw Convention, which covers airline passengers. The convention, signed by most countries, was designed to ensure all passengers on a plane are treated equally in the event of death or injury after an airline accident, regardless of their nationality. It also limits the liability of airlines and specifies where and when a passenger can sue – in what country – and that depends on where they live, where the ticket was bought, and the final destination.

In reality, though, the court in the country that hears the case determines what law is to be applied. What is allowable to victims varies greatly from country to country. It is easier to sue in the United States than in the UK, as was clearly demonstrated by the 1996 House of Lords ruling. They decided that appeals by Flight 149 passengers seeking compensation for physical and psychological injuries could only be pursued under the Convention. But they then concluded that Section 17 of the Convention, which says liability is for damages suffered while on board the aircraft or when embarking or disembarking, meant they could not sue under the Convention, after all. It was a victory for BA on technical grounds and it meant that evidence against BA (and the British government) could not be presented in British courts. The merits of the case were never tested.

The scales of justice were thus unevenly balanced as far as compensation was concerned. The court cases showed how passengers on the same commercial flight who had suffered the same fate could end up treated differently according to their nationality, a state of affairs that still exists. The French and the Americans won financial compensation whereas the British got nothing.

Other restrictions were applied to limit the coverage of Flight 149 in the UK. Richard Brunyate, the captain, tried to write a book about his ordeal, based on his diaries. He found a publisher, HarperCollins, but the publication was blocked by his employer, British Airways.

When I interviewed him, a few years before he died of cancer, I asked him how he had managed so quickly to find a Kuwaiti resistance group in a city living in terror – where the Iraqis were hunting down and killing those in the resistance. The explanation he had given to his fellow crew members and some of the passengers at the time – that he had just knocked on doors until he found them – was not believable. But he stuck to his story. It was only much later that I found out about his connection to MI6.

Another avenue that might have brought some clarity on the full story of Flight 149 was also quietly shut down. Jerry Blears, REME soldier, left the army in 1993 – he was officially discharged a year later – and then brought a class action against the Ministry of Defence because they had, he alleged, failed in their duty of care to the families of the soldiers. After two years, his efforts collapsed because he was refused legal aid for his lawsuit. The case was not considered 'viable'.

*

I had commissioned an investigation by the *Independent on Sunday* to examine what was known about the flight, which revealed major holes in the government's version of events, particularly the version given by then Prime Minister Margaret Thatcher to the House of Commons in September 1990. The government consistently denied any complicity in the affair and so the investigation was stalemated. But in 1997, while making a programme on the SAS for New Zealand Television, I was introduced to an SAS contact in Hereford, the regiment's home base.

His name was Pete Warne, known in the Special Forces community as Snapper. He also went by the name Peter Winner. Snapper Warne had fought at the famous battle of Mirbat in Oman in 1972, one of nine SAS soldiers who took on hundreds of local guerrillas in one of the most famous battles in regimental history. As a staff sergeant he had served in B Squadron at Hereford, then in the Counter Revolutionary Warfare Wing. He had trained some of the best counterterrorism teams around the world, such as GSG9 of Germany and the US Delta Force, and was part of the team that trained both Chris Ryan (real name Colin Armstrong) and Andy McNab (real name Steven Mitchell) from the Bravo Two Zero mission.

Snapper was also part of the team that helped end the siege at the Iranian Embassy in London in 1980, and liberate the hostages. Later, he became known as Soldier 'I' and consulted on three TV series in the UK – *SAS Soldiers* for ITV, *The Real SAS* for Channel 4, and *Special Forces Heroes* for Channel 5. He was the ultimate authoritative source about the regiment.

Snapper confirmed to my colleague Rod Vaughan and me that there was indeed a secret military team on the plane and that they worked for the ultra-secret group called the Inc, run by MI6. He said he could not talk about the group, it was too dangerous. One of his friends had been on the mission, selected for the job because of his ability to pass as an Arab. When we confronted the Ministry of Defence with this story they refused to discuss the allegations with us.

When we asked British Airways to comment on the news, the airline agreed to an interview only to then pull out. British Airways responses to queries about Flight 149 over the years have been consistent. They were told by the British government that it was safe to fly to Kuwait and they did so. They say they have never been aware that any military personnel were on the flight. If they had known invasion was imminent, they would not have landed the plane.

I also talked to William Neumann in Houston, Texas, about his efforts to obtain a list of passengers – a passenger manifest – from British Airways. He, too, wanted to know the identities of the mystery men on the flight. Neumann had always felt that BA claims that the passenger list was missing was surprising and 'gives some fuel or support for the notion that perhaps there was someone on board that they didn't want the people to know about.'

Later, British Airways told me that there was a passenger list but they could not release it on privacy grounds. This contradicted what they had told Neumann and if the list did in fact exist, Neumann said they should have handed it over during legal discovery.

The next source arrived a few months later, in 1998, while I was making a programme about the Bravo Two Zero mission and interviewing the New Zealander who took part in it. Through him I was introduced to other contacts and eventually to another man who took part in the Flight 149 mission. He provided various details but on the understanding that none of it be broadcast or published in the United Kingdom until after he retired.

I also interviewed Richard Tomlinson. Tomlinson is a former MI6 agent who became disenchanted with British secret intelligence and was briefly a semi-public critic of it, much to the agency's discomfiture. When he tried to give a book synopsis about his intelligence work to an Australian publisher he was arrested and imprisoned under the Official Secrets Act. Tomlinson had tried to set up a website to disclose the existence of the Inc. He was stopped. Tomlinson also said that he had heard about the mission and later confirmed this to British Liberal Democrat MP Norman Baker, who was campaigning for an inquiry into the fate of Flight 149.

From Richard Tomlinson's statement to Norman Baker:

> Yes, I do remember that incident, we were told a little about it on our IONEC [Intelligence Officer's New Entry Course] training. It is quite common to use BA (known as Bucks Fizz in the service) to drop off Increment members. The operation was sanctioned with a submission to the Foreign Secretary at the time (Hurd, if I recall correctly), but an operation of that sort of potential risk would probably also have been signed off by the PM.
>
> The Bucks Fizz captains are informed about the operation

(a legal requirement), also obviously the top people in BA would be in the know.

Tomlinson's revelation that 'Bucks Fizz' captains would be part of the operation was further confirmation that Brunyate was an MI6 asset, which would explain his particular concern that he not be captured by the Iraqis.

I tracked down and interviewed Captain Lawrence 'Larry' Eddingfield. As captain of the US Navy warship USS *Antietam*, he had been involved in the rescue of the two Inc operatives from southern Kuwait in August 1990. Eddingfield subsequently held a senior role at the Pentagon, though when I met him he had retired and was the vicar of a church in San Diego, California.

He is an unimpeachable source and he gave a detailed account of a rescue mission that the British government still claims never happened.

The *Antietam* received a radio dispatch, he said, 'to proceed at best speed, to meet with a combat rescue helicopter, CH-53, to take up a couple of people who'd been rescued out of Kuwait…

'The helicopter landed on the ship with the men… one of whom was very ill. And they needed medical care from dehydration and… and basically, they'd been on the run for about twenty-four hours, until they were picked up by the combat rescue helicopter.

'We provided medical care, until they were stabilised enough to where they could be moved on to another facility.'

The men were in a bad way and were given saline solutions.

'They were very tired… one of was very delirious, could hardly walk and basically had to be carried down… But once there, and once they got rehydrated, they enjoyed the fellowship and camaraderie of their US allies and it was fun to have them on board…

'Actually, one of them had food poisoning very, very badly

and basically almost died from that... they travelled at night and became more and more delirious, and you know it's, it's amazing what two people can do together when they have a will to live and the necessity to get home to family... one of them fortunately had the will to live and the other one was fortunate enough to have him as a buddy and who took care of him and wasn't gonna leave him and made sure that they walked together and came out alive.'

Further confirmation of the Inc team came when I spoke to Ed Ciriello, a former CIA asset, who told me that he had been in Saudi Arabia in August 1990 and had been told about the Flight 149 intelligence mission by MI6 staff in Saudi Arabia.

Nathaniel Howell, the US ambassador in Kuwait, also confirmed he had been told that Flight BA149 had landed with a secret intelligence/Special Forces team.

Additionally, I interviewed another one of the Inc team, who looked back on the mission with pride. He is sorry that the passengers and crew got caught up in the mess but he is adamant that the intelligence sent back by the teams helped saved lives, as he made clear in one of our interviews: 'I feel strongly for the passengers as they were the innocents of this operation; but then wasn't the whole of Kuwait the same? I believe history will eventually show that it was an operation that had to be done and it was executed in the only manner it could have been done within the time scale and rapidly shifting decisions Saddam was making.'

But despite all this, the UK government in official statements continued to play fast and loose with the truth – usually falling back on the discredited convention that they do not discuss matters concerning Special Forces or the intelligence services (although they often do when it suits them).

At one stage, when asked about my investigation in parliament by Norman Baker MP, Geoff Hoon, then a Labour government minister, issued a bizarre statement. It seemed to me to fit the old Watergate template of a 'nondenial denial'. Rather than simply state that there had been no intelligence or military mission on Flight 149, Hoon said that he 'had been told' the government had not 'exploited' the flight in the way that had been alleged: 'What I can say… is that I have looked at the evidence to date and I have personally asked both the relevant departments with responsibilities in this area whether the outline allegations are in any way justified. I am going to read out some words very carefully, which go beyond what has been said before, and should not be capable of misinterpretation. I want to make it clear that I have been told that the government at the time did not attempt in any way to exploit the flight by any means whatever.'

This statement hinged on the odd use of the word 'exploit' – one meaning of which is to use unfairly. The government could just about claim that as 149 was merely the means of transport – and that the mission as planned envisaged it landing, unloading, and departing for Madras long before Iraqi troops arrived – they did not exploit the flight.

Of course, the whole point about deniable operations is their deniability, and the Inc is set up to be completely deniable, and it's worth noting that this statement came from a government, and a minister, responsible for publishing the totally deceptive weapons of mass destruction dossier before the Iraq invasion of 2003.

*

All the tools in a government's arsenal have been used to suppress the truth about Flight 149 – from the carefully worded official statements that amount to nondenial denials, to a refusal to release documents that outline what happened, to the obscuring of dates and timelines, to attempts to smear journalists investigating the story. At one stage, I was targeted with classic disinformation, documents that purported to be confirmation of the mission but which, on closer examination, were doctored. They had descriptions of the mission that I was able to confirm from other sources but dates and other information had been altered. The incident inspired me to study the techniques of misinformation and disinformation – after years of research, I developed a course in it at the University of Otago in my native New Zealand.

Governments of all stripes have not even been willing to admit the truth about what happened to the Flight 149 passengers and the other human shields *after* they fell into Iraqi hands. They have kept a secret dossier of the horrors suffered by the human shields, allegedly because of confidentiality pledges given by the 1,868 people interviewed for the dossier. Yet, all the hostages I have talked to for this book – without exception – want the full truth to come out. The £364,000 report by the special investigation branch of the Royal Military Police (RMP) traced people who were either in hiding or used as human shields, including the people on 149. About 725 were interviewed by a police team and another 1,056 were sent questionnaires. The secret report, known as Operation Sandcastle, was commissioned in 1991 by the then Secretary of Defence, Tom King.

The report is a dossier of human rights abuses in one of the largest hostage-takings in history. The report contains eyewitness accounts of one murder (Douglas Croskery), eight attributable deaths, up to seventy mock executions and serious physical assaults, seventeen rapes, and twenty-three sexual assaults, as well as details of eighty murders of Iraqi citizens witnessed by the hostages. Three of the people held by the Iraqis who provided information have since committed suicide.

According to a note placed in the House of Commons library,

the report concluded: 'There was considerable evidence for systematic and grave breaches of the fourth Geneva Convention by the Iraqi authorities, members of the Iraqi armed forces, and their collaborators against the personal and property rights of British subjects.'

Ann Clwyd, Labour MP for the Cynon Valley and chair of the all-party human rights group, reported the then Secretary of Defence Geoff Hoon to Ann Abraham, the parliamentary ombudsman, for breaching the 'open government' code by not publishing the report. She wanted the ombudsman to order the minister to publish the findings without naming the individuals, but nothing happened. In December 2021, part of the report was quietly released into the National Archives and it was even more damming than expected, listing over 3500 war crimes against UK citizens and those of other countries.

A government statement said: 'The report contains the confidential statements of individuals who witnessed or were subject to alleged acts of Iraqi brutality during the Gulf War, and the Ministry of Defence has a duty to protect the confidentiality of those who cooperated with the Royal Military Police.'

One might think that the government had other motives for not wishing the report to be released, such as reminding the public of the terrors suffered by the passengers of Flight 149 and the other human shields. Perhaps also more people would be prompted to wonder: why was the BA flight ever allowed to land?

Whatever the reason, British Airways received a huge insurance settlement after the destruction of the 747. It is an irony not lost on the British passengers and crew that BA received compensation for its lost plane – blown up by the allies – while they were denied compensation by the courts.

EPILOGUE

For three decades, British Airways has avoided accountability for what happened – settling with French and American passengers but sticking with their official story that they had been told it was safe to fly on 1 August 1990.

But the cover-up by London and Washington and by British Airways has always rested on shaky foundations.

One by one, the planks have been knocked down. But, in August 2020, the rest of the flimsy foundations were demolished when Anthony Paice, the MI6 officer who was based at the British Embassy in Kuwait in August 1990, broke cover with an extra-ordinary story, one that raised yet more questions about the misuse of intelligence in the lead-up to the Gulf War.

Anthony Paice had retired after a long and successful career. He read history and war studies at King's College London before working for the Liberal Party and on a BBC series, then joining the Foreign and Commonwealth Office (his position cover for MI6).

Through a mutual acquaintance, Paice reached out to Clive Earthy, the Flight 149 chief purser who had become a long-term friend and contact of mine. A meeting was arranged at a pub near Clive's home in Winchester, Hampshire.

Paice, who was about to get married, told Earthy he was writing his memoirs – despite the Official Secrets Act prohibiting British intelligence officers talking about their work – and that 'the shit was about to hit the fan'.

Paice said his role in the affair had been misrepresented and that in particular what I had previously reported – that he had advised British Airways that it was safe to fly to Kuwait – was wrong.

He was angry about the way he had been blamed and he intended to get the truth out. Then he stunned Earthy by talking about the secret mission that the British government had denied for three decades.

Paice said he thought the mission had indeed been an Increment operation, personally ordered by Margaret Thatcher and with the approval of her friend Lord King, then BA chairman, who had given permission for the Inc team to travel on Flight 149.

But Paice claimed he and the others at the British Embassy in Kuwait were kept out of the loop. In the conversation, Paice said he knew who organised the mission, and who was behind it. He had written about in it his book, which he had submitted for vetting, and was travelling to London for a key meeting with his former employers. He was anticipating trouble but he was determined to proceed.

At the end of the meeting, Paice agreed to Clive's request that he talk to me. He later wrote to me, complaining about some aspects of the story I had reported.

Dear Stephen Davis,

From the little I know, it would appear to be a little wide
of the mark, certainly as far as my role/action and my
embassy's part in the matter were concerned. I have had to
put up with repeated inaccurate allegations, lies and half-
truths for over thirty years now and firmly believe that it is
high time that history was owed the facts.

As Clive Earthy may have told you, I have a completed
book ready for publication which not only vindicates
me and my embassy colleagues, but points the finger
away from my old employers and shows that there were
assessment failures in London and Washington, but no
intelligence failure on the ground. I make it clear why
Flight 149 flew that night and that the Kuwait embassy—
– not least myself – were totally unaware of the so-called
deniable special operation involved.

My book is now being vetted and I have an important
meeting on 25 August to discuss the way forward. There
are circles in London that will be found with egg on their
faces when my account comes out. I am happy to talk after
the meeting, but am not interested in a further half-baked
rendition of what happened on 1/2 August 1990. On the
contrary, I will have some tough questions.

I wrote back:

Thanks for your prompt and frank reply. I have no problem
with tough questions… in my reporting of your role in
other print accounts, I relied on depositions under oath
from O'Toole and other interviews with BA senior staff.

297

I now understand through your conversation with Clive [Earthy] that O'Toole and BA senior staff may have been deceptive and that your advice was that Flight 149 NOT fly. In which case, I owe you an apology and a correction.

I am clear from my other sources that the special operation was, as you said to Clive, a Mrs Thatcher/MOD project.

I know it also involved the DSF [Director Special Forces] at the time and a little assistance from Lord King.

I too believe the full truth should come out. I guess you are anticipating there may be legal or other resistance to your manuscript but good luck at your meeting.

I look forward to talking to you after that.

Kind regards,

Stephen

Paice responded:

Many thanks. For your information, my exact words to O'Toole early evening on 1 August 1990 were: '*If you have a plane going through at midnight, that will probably get through. But any Iraqi invasion will be in the early hours, so don't bank on anything same time tomorrow.*' I don't think anyone could have given a closer steer. My ambassador said something similar. What O'Toole[7] did with our advice, I am unable to say, but he went home; I did not. Apologies accepted!

Kind regards,

Anthony Paice

---

7   O'Toole's career took off after the Kuwait fiasco: he left British Airways and landed a senior position at IATA, the International Air Transport Association, in Geneva. But other than in court depositions, he has never talked about the events of August 1990.

So Paice said he warned against landing a flight in the precise time period that Flight BA149 was due to arrive. BA should not have taken any risk at all with its passengers and crew. A warning like that should have led to the flight being cancelled or rerouted were it not for other, more powerful forces at play.

As our correspondence continued, Paice became more circumspect, understandable since he worked for an organisation whose existence the UK government long refused to admit, an organisation that had previously pursued former MI6 officer Richard Tomlinson around the world (and got him locked up in prison) for trying to write a book.

But, despite his caution, Paice – having emphasised his startling claim that he had warned BA of the dangers of flying – continued the correspondence.

When I said to him, 'The passengers on Flight 149, many of whom have suffered greatly in the last three decades (emotionally, financially, physically), deserve to have an explanation as to why the Inc team were put on the plane and to see an end to the out-of-date pretence that nothing happened,' he replied: 'Totally agree, Stephen, and I am trying to convince my erstwhile employers that they can help achieve this, not least by approving my account.'

He said the men on the plane used tickets from a military account in Hereford (home of the SAS) and that the physical presence of the military men on the plane could not be denied.

Paice was adamant on one point – that the embassy in Kuwait had been left out of the planning.

I am well-versed in the clearance of all operations, however sensitive, and know how the Flight 149 operation should have been signed off. It was certainly a last-minute operation, so planned hastily. After all, a well-planned and timely operation would not have had the lads board at the last moment. The tickets should have been bought at a nondescript bucket shop, so that there was no pointer back to the military. The lads would then have boarded as individuals, not as a group, along with everyone else. [The tickets] were clearly purchased shortly before the flight when it was too late to do so deniably. If I had been running the show, each man would have had to buy his ticket under his alias and at different shops. Clearly, there was no time for this sort of operational perfection!

Of course, it could be said, it's convenient for Paice – and the intelligence services – to absolve MI6 of responsibility and point the finger at other parts of the government just as this book was about to be published. When I asked him who provided logistical support for the team on the ground, he suggested a combination of Kuwaiti military intelligence and the CIA.[8]

But, crucially, what Paice said matched the findings of my investigation: that the Flight 149 mission had been hastily put together by the Ministry of Defence, under the orders of Thatcher, so it was entirely possible that the Kuwait station had been bypassed.

Paice had stayed behind after the invasion; he and the ambassador, Michael Weston, had shown great courage in holding the fort. Paice did not leave until he had helped get a large convoy of Westerners out of Kuwait and into Jordan via Iraq.

He was clearly a man who felt, with some justification, that his actions had been misrepresented by history. Paice also confirmed that he had sent a number of warnings to London about Iraqi intentions in the lead-up to the invasion. He also said the planners

---

8   This is not out of the question, given the operation was principally for the benefit of Washington. Curiously, when as part of my initial investigation I talked to Hunter Downs, the CIA station chief in Kuwait at the time, he said he could not help but pointed me in the direction of the British for answers. The US and UK are allies, but that does not mean the CIA and MI6 are always friends.

of the mission had completely overestimated the capabilities of the Kuwait military to hold out against an Iraqi invasion.

This, too, was significant. The mission as planned relied on the Kuwaitis holding out for several days. Instead, of course, Iraqi tanks reached the airport in three hours.

In August 2021, Paice appeared alongside me and some of the human shields at a press conference in London, again emphasising he had not told British Airways it was safe to fly that fateful night. Weeks later, the government was forced to admit they knew the invasion had started before 149 landed, thus owning up to another major deception. The government also officially confirmed Paice's account, making a nonsense of previous statements by British Airways absolving themselves of responsibility.

The government continued to stick to its non denial denial that there was a special operations team on the flight – nonsensical in view of the fact that the group were seen by most of the people on the flight.

Even then, they did let slip, in a partially redacted memo, that there had been 'defence section staff' on board.

After the press conference, further compelling evidence came from the accounts of two British Airways crew who had found themselves in captivity with five UK military personnel after the 1990 invasion. Diary notes taken at the time reveal that these military personnel knew a secret team was arriving on 149, knew the officer who escorted the men off the aircraft and extraordinarily, they said there was a British military presence in the control tower to ensure that the flight landed.

*

After three decades of lies and a cover-up by both London and Washington, what do the passengers and crew want, even now?

For the government to admit the truth.

Most of those I have interviewed over the years hold Saddam Hussein principally responsible for their ordeal. But they also believe believe that 149 should never have landed in Kuwait.

Saddam is now long dead, and he was never tried for the invasion of Kuwait or the taking of Western hostages and their use as human shields. Iraq and Kuwait have moved on. There have been other wars and other victims, and it is clear that London and Washington no longer have any interest in re-examining the events of August 1990 to February 1991, nor any interest in an inquiry into the misuse of intelligence in one of the most consequential decisions in modern history.

The operation as planned would have meant Flight 149 flying on to Madras and Kuala Lumpur rather than being trapped on the ground in Kuwait City. The mission planners were caught by surprise by the speed of the Iraqi army's advance. It certainly would have been better if another means could have been found to get the Inc team into Kuwait, and it is outrageous that the truth has been suppressed for so long and that so many lies have been told to the victims and to the public at large.

Most of all, it is unforgivable that the story of the human shields – victims of a mass hostage-taking who endured months of terror and decades of suffering – has been ignored.

And then there is perhaps the biggest lie of all – that Saddam was going to invade Saudi Arabia and that the threat justified putting American troops on Saudi soil, foreshadowing the death and destruction of the Middle East during the following three decades.

One can easily imagine a different, more peaceful world if the intelligence had been used in a different way.

STEPHEN DAVIS

APRIL 2022

ACKNOWLEDGEMENTS/
A NOTE ABOUT SOURCES

When I started investigating the Flight 149 story in August 1990, I was thinking of a few weeks' work and a feature article. Three decades later, I found myself writing about a neglected but vital – and misunderstood – part of modern history.

Most of the hundreds of interviews for this book were conducted over the last fifteen years, with all of the key characters interviewed at least twice, often three or four times.

I am grateful to all the human shields who took the time to talk about the terrors of their captivity and the pain and depression of the years since.

My intelligence and Special Forces sources would have faced legal and career issues in talking about state secrets. It is a depressing feature of governments of all political stripes that they will behave vindictively towards military and intelligence whistle blowers, even when no actual secrets are disclosed. Some of these attempts have backfired spectacularly: when the UK government went to court in the 1980s to stop the publication of *Spycatcher*, the memoirs of former MI5 officer Peter Wright (a story that I covered), they only succeeded in turning what was a rather dull book into an international bestseller.

Later, they refined their techniques, mixing legal threats with character assassination, often planting stories with friendly journalists.

The former MI6 agent Richard Tomlinson, whose story I reported on and who I eventually got to interview on camera despite various court injunctions, had his reputation destroyed by made-up stories as he was pursued around the world. Later he got an apology and a retraction of some of the claims made against him but it was too late by then.

Many ex-Special Forces soldiers – including some in this book – find work in the private sector in security after they leave the military, but those companies rely on government contracts, so speaking out can literally cost you your livelihood, or the company itself can be punished through loss of contracts.

Some of my sources are now retired but wish to protect their privacy and pensions. One still works for MI6.

To that group who trusted me with their stories, at risk to themselves, I owe a particular debt of gratitude.

Tony Paice deserves special thanks for his courage in speaking out when it would have been easier to stay silent. I am now glad to count him as a friend.

The human shields have also faced threats and intimidation while seeking the truth. British Airways staff were banned from speaking and threatened with the loss of their pensions if they gave interviews or wrote books. When George Saloom returned from captivity and began making inquiries, he received a call from the US State Department warning him to stop. Despite that, he has been very supportive of my investigation and gave me permission to use his remarkable diary.

Among the many others who have assisted my investigations, I need to single out Peter Wilby, former editor of the *Independent on Sunday* and the *New Statesman,* a great editor, friend, and fearless seeker after truth.

A number of fine journalism students assisted with research on the Flight 149 story over the years: Rachel Slack, Rebecca Magill, Alice Bhandhukravi and Madeleine Lindh while at the University of the Arts London (UAL), and Bene Earl at Macleay College in Sydney. London solicitor Akhtar Raja – a man interested in justice above all – has been a great help throughout the human-shields story, as was lawyer Bill Neumann in Texas.

John Levins's book *Days of Fear* proved to be an excellent primer to events on the ground during the invasion, written by a man who was there.

I would like to thank my wonderful agent, Emma Parry, and publishers Clive Priddle and Anu Roy-Chaudhury at Public Affairs, and James Hodgkinson at Bonnier.

To my darling daughters – Shannon, Katya, and Iona – who have lived with my pursuit of this story for many years, at last you have a book to show for it.

Finally, this book could not have been written without the encouragement, emotional support and excellent advice of my wife, confidante and researcher, Penny, who changed my life for the better.

My podcast series The Secret History of Flight 149 (produced by Crowd Network) is now available on Spotify and Apple.

INDEX

ABOUT THE AUTHOR

STEPHEN DAVIS is a TV commentator, documentary filmmaker, newspaper editor, foreign editor, US correspondent, war correspondent, and award-winning TV news and current-affairs producer. He has been on the front lines of journalism for three decades as a leading journalism educator, trying to uphold the ideals of the fourth estate and to inspire others to do the same.

Davis has worked for the *Sunday Times* in both London and Los Angeles and was news editor and foreign editor of the *Independent on Sunday*. He has been a producer for *60 Minutes* and *20/20*, a documentary filmmaker for the BBC and Discovery, and has taught journalism to thousands of students from all over the world. He has won multiple awards for his investigative reporting, including a silver medal at the New York film and television awards, and has designed and run journalism degree programmes in London, Sydney and Melbourne.

Now an author and educator, he developed a course on combatting fake news, disinformation and misinformation at the prestigious University of Otago in his native New Zealand.

His website is **stephendaviswriter.com**